THE ENNEAGRAM

THE ENNEAGRAM

Understanding Yourself and the Others in Your Life

Helen Palmer

1817

Harper & Row, Publishers, San Francisco

Cambridge, Hagerstown, New York, Philadelphia, Washington
London, Mexico City, São Paulo, Singapore, Sydney

Grateful acknowledgment is made for use of the following. For diagrams from *Transpersonal Psychologies*, edited by Charles Tart, Harper & Row, 1975. Reprinted by Psychological Processes, Inc., 1983. Reprinted by permission of Charles Tart. For a diagram from *Gurdjieff: An Approach to His Ideas*, by Michael Waldberg, Routledge & Kegan Paul, Ltd., 1973. Reprinted by permission.

FIRST EDITION

Library of Congress Cataloging-in-Publication Data

Palmer, Helen.
    The enneagram: understanding yourself and the others in your life.

    1. Personality.   2. Typology (Psychology).
3. Personality assessment.   4. Self-evaluation.
I. Title.
BF698.3.P35   1988   155.2'64   87-45716
ISBN 0-06-250673-0

88 89 90 91 92 RRD 10 9 8 7 6 5 4 3 2 1

To the hundreds of people who have observed their own internal dilemma and given us their stories.
And to Sir John Pentland
for his counsel and friendship.

Contents

Preface

I've never met anyone who wasn't interested in personality, particularly in finding out more about their own personality or type. I can recall that when I was in graduate school, specializing in the study of personality, I took every psychological test I could get my hands on, wondering what each would tell me about myself. Most other students did this too.

Why are we so interested in knowing about ourselves?

One motive is simple curiosity: the way minds and feelings function is interesting. Why do I see this situation the way I do? Why do I have this emotion when some people have another? Why does my friend, with the same knowledge about this situation, get angry about it when I get depressed? It's interesting to think about these things and interesting to talk with others about them.

A second motive is practical: there is a lot of suffering in our lives. Physical pain, unmet expectations, multitudes of petty annoyances and delays, people who don't treat us right, and so on, cause us suffering. A common reaction to suffering is to blame the external circumstances. If my back didn't hurt, if the contractor had come through on time, if commuting didn't take so long, if people really recognized my brilliance and charm, then I would be really happy. As we gain some self-knowledge, though, we recognize that, while there are external events that are annoying, we also create a great deal of our suffering in unnecessary ways. If I didn't pick up heavy objects with my back bent, if I hadn't unnecessarily set up such tight deadlines, if I left for work ten minutes earlier so I wasn't really under time pressure, if I didn't crave others' approval so much, a lot of suffering would disappear from my life. What is there about my personality that makes me impatient and so frequently causes suffering in a world that has a timetable of its own? Why does my type make me overvalue others' approval, even though I intellectually know it's not all that important?

Conventional psychological theories of personality can often be helpful in giving us insights into why we act and feel as we do. Less frequently, they actually allow us to change some parts of our selves that are causing us unnecessary suffering. Practical results are less frequent than insights because of several factors. Some of our insights, after reading about a theory of personality, for example, may be erroneous; we misunderstood the ideas. Further, all theories about personality are only partially true, so something that seems insightful and makes sense in the system may not apply in reality, or may actually be an obstacle to self-change. Too, aspects of our personality that aren't interested in real self-understanding (an inflated image of ourselves, for example) may block really effective application of any system of personality. And sometimes intellectual insight isn't enough: we need the emotional insight that usually only comes with the help of a skilled counselor or therapist or the shock of an intense life event.

There is another important reason most of us find personality theories intellectually interesting, but tend to be disappointed with their practical results. *Almost all the widely known and generally accepted personality systems do not go beyond ordinary life.*

Most people see counselors or therapists because they are unhappy about not being "normal." They have difficulty relating to others or feel bad about themselves or have self-defeating habits that cause great suffering. They want to be like *normal* people, who presumably relate to others easily, feel good about themselves, and don't sabotage their own lives. Normal life certainly has its ups and downs, but psychological counseling and therapy can sometimes (but far from always) help people live better, "normal," ordinary lives.

In the 1950s psychotherapists began seeing a new type of client, a type I have described in my *Waking Up* (Shambhala, 1986) as the "successful malcontent." This type of person is normally successful by contemporary social standards, has a decent job, reasonable income, reasonable family life, reasonable acceptance and respect in the community: all the rewards that are supposed to bring happiness in our society. Success doesn't mean there is no suffering or difficulty: some suffering and difficulty are part of normal life and are accepted as such. The successful malcontent knows that he or she is "happy" by ordinary standards but seeks therapy because he or she finds that life is nevertheless "empty." Isn't there more to life than money, career, consumer goods, social life? Where is the *meaning*?

Conventional therapy, based on conventional theories about the nature of humans and personality, was (and still is) of little value to these people. Loose ends in the personality structure might be straightened out, interesting insights about the origins of personality attained, but the central question of deeper meaning in life is largely untouched. As noted above, almost all of the widely known and generally accepted personality systems do not go beyond ordinary life, but the successful malcontent *must* go deeper than that.

The arrival of the successful malcontents helped trigger the development of humanistic psychology and transpersonal psychology, schools that recognize the usefulness of our psychological knowledge of ordinary life and the personalities necessary for it, but that also recognize that there is a vital existential and spiritual dimension to humanity. Once there is reasonable success in developing the skills needed for ordinary level living, a person *must* grow in the existential and spiritual dimensions if he or she is to continue to be healthy and happy. The personality theories dealing with ordinary level living are fine up to a point, but when we need to grow beyond that point, their lack of breadth shows and we become disappointed in them, perhaps without quite knowing why.

As a graduate student studying personality, I already had strong interests in the spiritual, transpersonal dimensions of life, and so found conventional psychological understandings of man useful, but constricted. The major exception was Jung: his idea of the *collective unconscious* was an opening into the spiritual dimensions of our existence. Jung was not well accepted in the psychological or psychiatric establishment, however, and so his ideas were not generally available as a working system. I later found personality theories and psychologies imbedded in various spiritual systems around the world (see my *Transpersonal Psychologies*, Psychological Processes, 1983) that also offer great possibilities for growth beyond the ordinary. One in particular, the Enneagram of personality types, offered high hope for practical application, but only the bare outline of it could be presented when *Transpersonal Psychologies* was first published in 1975.

The term *Enneagram* was introduced by G. I. Gurdjieff, a pioneer in adapting Eastern spiritual teachings for use by modern Westerners. A general form of the Enneagram was used in his teachings and given wider currency by *In Search of the Miraculous: Fragments of an Unknown Teaching* (Harcourt, Brace & World, 1949) written by his best-known student, P. D. Ouspensky. Gurdjieff, well aware of the useless suffering created by flaws in our personalities, taught that each of us had a *chief feature* that was the central axis around which the delusional aspects of our personalities revolved. If we could know that chief feature, the work of understanding and transcending the delusional aspects of personality (or *false personality*, as Gurdjieff called it, since much of it was forced on us as children rather than being freely chosen by us) would become much more efficient. Gurdjieff clearly used the Enneagram of personality in his work with his students, but, to my knowledge, did not pass the system on in any detail to his students.

I first became acquainted with the Enneagram of personality types during a graduate seminar on altered states of consciousness that I was teaching in 1972. One of my students, Jon Cowan, told me a little about it, including the fact that he had "typed me." In several luncheons that followed, Cowan outlined the system for me, drawing diagrams on the backs of napkins (there is a long tradition in science of exciting ideas being communicated on the backs of napkins!). Since my desire for growth was very strong at that time, I joined the Berkeley group, led by Chilean psychiatrist Claudio Naranjo, that my student was learning the system from. Naranjo had integrated the basic Enneagram system of personality with modern psychological knowledge in many brilliant ways.

I learned that Naranjo had been taught the basics of the Enneagram of personality during a period of study in Chile with Oscar Ichazo, who, in turn, claimed to have learned it from a secret mystery school, the Sarmouni Brotherhood, who had also taught it to Gurdjieff. This was pretty heady and romantic stuff that didn't sit too well with a young scientist like myself, passionately concerned with separating the sense from the nonsense if science was to deal with the spiritual. Secret brotherhoods may or may not exist, but talking about them in science is like waving a red flag in front of a bull! Since I was already investigating several areas that were suspect to the establishment at that time, such as meditation, altered states, and parapsychology, it seemed practically unwise to get involved with an obviously mystical system that went beyond ordinary life. Yet the fact that the Enneagram of personality went beyond ordinary life, that it discussed the existential and spiritual virtues that could be developed if we recaptured the essential life energy that was going into pathological defenses against our real nature, was one of its primary attractions.

So I was tempted to back away from the Enneagram system, but I had the sense to try to evaluate it on its own merits as a conceptual system, not on its "mythological" origins or what conventional psychology would think of it. Looking at it as a psychologist knowledgeable about personality theory, as a conceptual system, a theory of personality, the Enneagram system looked very good. It was clearly the most complex and sophisticated personality system I had ever run across, but it was a sensible, intelligent complexity, not confusion. Most conventional personality systems seemed like oversimplifications by comparison.

Although scientists make a big point about being *objective,* my own and others' studies had long convinced me that we are actually rather biased and personal much of the time in our work. It is the commitment to keep *trying* for objectivity that rescues science from becoming a kind of sterile scholasticism. My positive view of the Enneagram system expressed above is my attempt to evaluate it as best I can in the light of contemporary psychological knowledge. My personal reaction was just as important, of course. When the nature of my type was explained to me, it was one of the most insightful moments of my life. All sorts of puzzling events and reactions in my life now made excellent retrospective sense to me. Even more important, I could see the central way in which my approach to life was defective *and I had a general outline of the ways to work on changing it.* I understood the behavior of many of my friends once I could type them and was able to interact more effectively with them and be a better friend. Years of personal growth work following that initial set of insights identifying my Enneagram type continued to validate the usefulness of the system to me.

For some years the Enneagram of personality was generally available only to students of Claudio Naranjo or Oscar Ichazo and was taught as part of intense, small group psychological growth work. This is probably the best way to present the material, as it greatly increases the chances that the student will apply it. Today so many people, especially successful malcontents, are trying to understand themselves and transcend, that the limits of small group transmission are apparent. Thus it is a great gift that Helen Palmer has written this book, sharing her own understandings of the Enneagram of personality, adding her special understandings from her extensive work on the development and application of intuition to the basic system. Her work in seeing each Enneagram type as centering around styles of (mis)perception is extremely useful.

I believe the material presented in this book will be of great help to many people in not only knowing their types, but in transcending them. It is not the only method of personal growth, but it is a very useful one. It is far from perfect as a system and, as Palmer points out, a great deal of empirical, scientific research is needed to develop it even further—but it is already a practical, useful system.

Although the initial excitement of discovering the system has faded for me, after fifteen years of experience I still find the Enneagram of personality helpful in understanding, empathizing with, and relating to others. Nevertheless we should remember that a book, classes, or personal instruction about the Enneagram of personality can only communicate *ideas* about reality, not reality itself. As the old Zen saying reminds us, the finger pointing at the moon is not the moon.

The cognitive/emotional structure of the Enneagram of personality can be a useful guide for understanding and transforming our personalities, but it is not *The Truth*, it is not the actual reality of the moment-to-moment manifestation of our beings. It is a *theory* of personality. The Enneagram system of personality goes well beyond conventional approaches in reminding us that we live too often in an illusory world because of defenses that are no longer needed, that we mistake ideas and feelings *about* reality for reality itself. Used with this in mind, the system can be a splendid tool for each of us. Used as *The Truth*, used as a substitute for actual observation of ourselves and others, the Enneagram system, like any conceptual system, can degenerate into one more way of stereotyping ourselves and others, of continuing the life of illusion in our waking dream. This book presents a powerful tool: I wish you luck in using it to wake up to the reality of our deeper nature.

Charles T. Tart, Ph.D.
Professor of Psychology
University of California at Davis

THE ENNEAGRAM

I. ORIENTATION TO THE ENNEAGRAM

1. Background of the System and an Introduction to Type

The Enneagram is an ancient Sufi teaching that describes nine different personality types and their interrelationships. The teaching can help us to recognize our own type and how to cope with our issues; understand our work associates, lovers, family, and friends; and to appreciate the predisposition that each type has for higher human capacities such as empathy, omniscience, and love. This book can further your own self-understanding, help you work out your relationships with other people, and acquaint you with the higher abilities that are particular to your type of mind.

The Enneagram is part of a teaching tradition that views personality preoccupations as teachers, or indicators of latent abilities that unfold during the development of higher consciousness. The diagrams that appear in this book are a partial view of a more complete model that describes the levels of humanity's possible evolution from personality through a range of unusual human potentials, such as empathy, omniscience, and love. It is vital that this larger context not be overlooked by focusing attention on the nine character types, because the complete Enneagram is one of the very few models of consciousness that addresses the relationship between personality and other levels of human capability. The power of the system lies in the fact that ordinary patterns of personality, those very habits of heart and mind that we tend to dismiss as merely neurotic, are seen as potential access points into higher states of awareness.

We can easily recognize the value in the Enneagrams that describe personality because a great deal of our attention is focused on the thoughts and feelings that we identify as our self.[1] If, however, our own unique personality, or what each of us thinks of as "myself," is in fact only one aspect in a continuum of human development, then our own thoughts and feelings must in some way constitute a staging ground for understanding the next phase of our own unfolding. From this expanded psychological perspective, our neurotic trends can be seen as teachers and as good friends who lead us honorably forward to our next phase of development. And if, as the Enneagram suggests, our personality is a stepping-stone to a greater consciousness, then gaining a working understanding of our own preoccupations takes on a double purpose. First, it makes us more effective and happier as a person; and second, we learn how to set the personality aside in order to allow the next phase of consciousness to unfold.

The Oral Tradition

The Enneagram of types is part of an oral teaching tradition, and the material is still best transmitted by seeing and hearing groups of people of the same type speak about their lives. Seeing and hearing a group of articulate and willing people express a similar point of view transmits far more of the power of the system than can possibly be conveyed by a mere written record of their words. After about an hour a group of people who start out looking physically very different begin to seem the same. The viewer can sense the similarities in physical holding patterns, emotional tone, the tension points in the face, and the quality of personal emanation that are the more subtle signs of type. The auditorium fills with a definite presence as the character unfolds. There is a unique feel to each of the types, a distinguishing quality, a presence in the hall.

A group of the same type can initially appear to have nothing in common, because the viewer is paying attention to their differences in sex, age, race, profession, and personal style. Within an hour, however, they begin to look the same: their histories, their choices, their preferences, their goals. What they avoid and what they dream begin to seem the same. They even start to look alike, once your attention shifts from the surface features of apparel and a personable smile. When your attention shifts from surface cues, you can recognize type by falling into an appreciation of the aspirations and the difficulties that the members of a type will share.

The world looks very different to each of the nine, and by lending yourself to the way that others feel within themselves, you can shift out of your own point of view into a true understanding of who the people in your life really are, rather than what your ideas about them might lead you to believe. By lending yourself to the ways of others, a sense of compassion for their situations opens. When you see the world from the point of view of other types of mind, you are immediately made aware that each type is limited by a systematic bias.

I am always moved by the power of this teaching when I recognize the central patterns of my own life in the stories of a group of my similars. They are contemporary stories that take place in ad agencies and supermarkets and college classrooms and meditation halls. They are told by people who have my thought patterns and are living out their stories in the way that I live mine. I know that I can count on them for information, for counsel, for the revelation of what they have found out about themselves.

What makes the the telling of personal history stunning is that the self-disclosure of profoundly intimate material is given with the intention of putting oneself aside. The intention behind telling your own story is, of course, to get some clarity about the patterns that drive your life, but in this case, the goal of self-understanding is to learn to observe these patterns internally, detach attention from them, and eventually set the personality aside. The "setting aside" implied by a system that encompasses several states of consciousness means more than simply working a problem through until the suffering is gone. Setting the personality aside means being able to detach attention from thoughts and feelings, so that other perceptions can come into awareness.

The statements in this book are taken from the tape-recorded voices of people who spoke on a panel for their own type. They were willing to appear and to self-disclose so that an audience could learn to recognize type in the oral way. When I interview panels, the focus of attention is always on what makes a type distinctive from the others, so the line of questioning that I have developed is biased toward what is unique about each of the nine points, rather than how they are the same.

It is important to stress the ways that people are different from each other, because so much of the suffering that we experience in our relationships with other people is caused by the fact that we are blind to their point of view. We do not apprehend the reality in which the people who are close to us live out their lives.

For example, it takes real work for a couple who are romantically involved to understand the premises of each partner's love. If one is a Nine (the Mediator) and the other an Eight (the Boss), how will the Nine know that the way to love and trust is through a series of toe-to-toe confrontations? And how will the Eight know that a Nine partner will tune out direct orders, and stubbornly refuse to be pushed into action, but can easily be drawn out by other people's needs?

The Limitations of Categorizing People

One of the Enneagram's problems is that it's very good. It is one of the few systems that concerns itself with normal and high-functioning behavior rather than pathology, and it condenses a great deal of psychological wisdom into a compact system that is relatively easy to understand. If you can type yourself and the people who are important in your life, a lot of information is immediately made available about the way that you and another are likely to get along. There is, therefore, a natural tendency to want to put each other in one of nine boxes, so that each can figure out what the other is thinking and predict the ways in which the other is likely to behave. We want each other in a box, because it lessens the tension of having to live with the mystery of the unknown, and because in the West we have an addiction to reducing information to fixed categories so that we can try to make cause-and-effect predictions.

The Enneagram, however, is not a fixed system. It is a model of interconnecting lines that indicate a dynamic movement, in which each of us has the potentials of all nine types, or points, although we identify most strongly with the issues of our own. The structure of a nine-pointed star with interconnecting lines also suggests that each type possesses a versatility of movement between points. The nine points correlate well with current psychological typology[2] and the interconnecting lines indicate specific relationships between the different types that are only now beginning to be examined in the current psychological literature.

The interconnecting lines also predict the ways in which each point or type is likely to alter its usual behavior when placed either under stress or in a secure life situation; so that each point is actually a composite of three major aspects—a dominant aspect, which identifies a type's world view, and two additional aspects that describe behavior in security or under stress.

Beside the fact that we alter radically under stress or when we are secure, each of us alters in the degree to which we identify with the issues that define our type. There are days when we become so involved with the preoccupations that underlie our particular "box" that we cannot focus our attention on anything else. When attention is glued to a particular set of preoccupations that define our type, we are definitely in a box. We are not free. When we cannot detach attention from a recurring preoccupation, when we lose the ability to observe our own behavior in a dispassionate way, then we are under the control of our own habits and have lost freedom of choice.

But we are not always under the thumb of our personality. We can often shift our attention to see the situation in a different way. In terms of the Enneagram model, we are moving

upward in the evolutionary spectrum when we can free ourselves from the habits that limit our point of view and expand
our awareness beyond the preoccupations that define our type.

Typing can set up an unfortunate self-fulfilling prophecy. We
may learn to type people and then begin to treat others as car-
icature composites of a list of type traits, which very effectively
reinforces type. We are all molded by the ways in which we are
treated, and all of us tend to believe what others read into us.
All too often we begin to see ourselves in the way that we are
seen by others and to take on the characteristics of what we
have been trained to be.

This is why I say that the Enneagram's problem is that it's
very good. It is relatively easy to type once you know what
you're looking for, especially if you can empathize with another
type's point of view. The system is so good that I have seen
people able to pretend that they were psychic because they
could type quickly and accurately and could consequently come
up with an enormous amount of detailed personal information
about someone whom they had barely met. With a good system
and a wrong attitude about typing, we can forget that the purpose of knowing personality type is to learn to set it aside in
order to get on with the real work of embodying higher consciousness. A small-minded approach to typing reduces the value and purpose of a system that suggests that type is merely a
stepping-stone to higher human abilities.

The good news is that typing doesn't work in the real world.
It does not work, for example, for an employer to draw up a
list of "do hires" and "don't hires" for particular jobs. "Do hire
a Four (the Tragic Romantic) for a job in an art gallery" makes
no sense if the Four has no eye for paintings, even if he or she
does have a profoundly artistic temperament. "Don't hire a Five
(the Observer) for a high-visibility job" would be a grand mistake if the Five were busy cultivating some outgoing qualities
and were going to go all out to do the job well. Labeling will
not serve the matchmaker who wants a formula that says a
Three's ideal mate is a Seven, or that Twos and Fours are incom-

patible lovers but make good friends. The Two and the Four may have developed a fragrant chemistry that does not fit the number formula, and that is more than what they, or the matchmaker, can hope to understand. Neither will it work to put together an "ideal work team" based on the fact that Fives make good strategists, Threes are terrific salespeople, and Eights are great in a business turnaround. Labeling and boxing does not work, because people are far more versatile and complex than anything that could possibly be described by a list of character traits.

Why, then, be so concerned about type? If an accurate set of labels won't eliminate the risks involved in hiring employees or choosing a mate, why bother to uncover type at all? The reason for discovering your own type is so you can build a working relationship with yourself. You can count on the experience of your similars to guide you, and you can discover the conditions that will make you thrive rather than continue to play out neurotic trends. The most important reason to study type isn't so you can learn to spot other people's character traits, it's so you can lessen your own human suffering.

The second reason to study type is so you can understand other people as they are to themselves, rather than as you see them from your own point of view. This understanding of others can help work teams be efficient, infuse romance with magic, and help families to reunite. Although we cannot designate certain types for certain categories of employment and expect them to perform in stereotyped ways, we can learn to see a project from a work associate's point of view.

In the same fashion, we cannot pick out partners from a list of desirable character traits and expect that they will not also show the less than desirable features of the type. We cannot even assume that either partner will not react, paradoxically, against intimacy by becoming stressed out and confused. What we can assume is that by paying close attention to the ways in which each type opens to love, we can understand that point of view and change our attitudes accordingly.

History

The word *Enneagram* stems from the Greek *ennea*, meaning "nine," and *grammos*, meaning "points." It is a nine-pointed star diagram that can be used to map the process of any event from its inception through all the stages of that event's progress in the material world. The Enneagram model is intrinsic to Sufi mysticism, where it is applied to mapping cosmological processes and the unfolding of human consciousness. In its entirety the system is a highly articulated teaching that parallels the Cabala's Tree of Life and, in fact, overlaps with the Tree in several ways.[3] The parallel is interesting because the Enneagram describes the same terrain as the ancient Cabalist teaching, yet appears to have no written history of its own. We had no translated commentary from Islamic mysticism, yet the system is a model of the mystical premise that humanity is in the process of evolving toward higher forms of consciousness.[4]

What the West knows of the Enneagram began with George Ivanovich Gurdjieff, a spiritual teacher of enormous personal magnetism, who alluded to the Enneagram as a Sufi oral teaching device that he used to recognize his students' aptitudes for particular kinds of inner life training. There is a large amount of literature concerning Gurdjieff's work, and it includes a great many references to the system, but without specifics about how he used the diagram to see the potentials in people, or what kinds of information it made available to him.

Gurdjieff's students worked with the Enneagram's mathematical properties, but most of what they learned was transmitted through nonverbal movement exercises that were designed to give a felt sense of the stages that different processes go through when they begin and as they are played out in the material world. The movements are an impressive series of dances that are done in large groups. They are designed to teach certain nonobvious features of process, namely, that the rhythm of a process can be sensed through the physical body, and that it is possible to recognize those moments at which adroit "shocks," or new input, is necessary in order to keep a process on course and alive.

Gurdjieff tried to inculcate a felt sense of the Enneagram as a model of perpetual motion in his students. He had a nine-pointed star marked on the floor of the hall at The Institute for the Harmonious Development of Man. Students were stationed at the points of the circle marked One through Nine and performed elaborate movement patterns that demonstrated the various relationships between the points and along the inner lines One–Four–Two–Eight–Five–Seven. There are reports from students who discuss their felt sense of the inner rhythms and the natural moments of pause and realignment of forces that are brought about by dancing out the relationships between the points and the lines. They describe a bodily recognition that develops when attention shifts from thinking, and one becomes fully immersed in the physical movements of the dance.

There was nothing written about the Enneagrams of personality during Gurdjieff's lifetime, and the schools that continued his teaching were inclined to view personality preoccupations as something to be set aside in the movement toward higher consciousness, rather than as a useful source of information about how to reach those states of mind. Taking the view that our unique personality represents a relatively unevolved aspect of the full range of human potential, the schools focused on nonverbal movement exercises and Gurdjieff's attention practices (called self-observation and self-remembering) as a correct approach to the inner life.[5] The schools were probably confirmed in this view by the insistence on the part of the original teachers that the Sufi system of personality could be successfully applied only by "one who knows."

The knowledge of the Enneagram has for a very long time been preserved in secret and if it now is, so to speak, made available at all, it is only in an incomplete and theoretical form of which nobody could make any practical use without instructions from a man who knows.[6]

It is, of course, possible that the schools did not have access to the exact fit of the nine personality types on the Enneagram diagram, or that the state of the art of psychological diagnosis was not at that time in sync with what the diagrams suggested. The ways in which Gurdjieff alluded to the system, however, and his responses to direct questions about the relationship of the Enneagram to character type, indicate that he held the information back because he believed that his students simply could not have accepted it.

Gurdjieff was apparently convinced that the people of his time were not prepared to correctly identify their own internal patterns. Although the students worked with self-observation practice, Freud's theory of the unconscious was barely taking hold in the Europe of Gurdjieff's time, and the students possessed none of the psychological sophistication that we take for granted today. The concept that we are generally "asleep" to our own motivations, and that our perceptions are distorted by psychological defenses, was an immense insight for the students. Although they worked diligently at the practices, they did so in blind faith that the teacher could introduce them to something, for they had little psychological understanding of their own.

The Inner Observer

Self-observation is a basic inner life practice that appears in several traditional disciplines. The practice consists of focusing your attention inwardly and learning to become aware of the thoughts and other "objects of attention"[7] that arise within yourself. There are several ways to approach this practice, but the initial experience is always that of recognizing your own mechanical, or habitual, patterns, and the tenacity with which certain preoccupations recur within your mind. The fact that you can observe and talk about your own habits of thinking and feeling from the point of view of a detached outsider helps to make these habits less compulsive and automatic. Thoughts begin to seem "separate from myself" rather than "who I really am."

If the practice of observing thoughts and feelings is continued, your own preoccupations begin to feel alien and slightly irritating. When attention shifts to the stance of the inner observer, thoughts start to seem like "what I think" rather than "my real self," because there is a part of your own awareness that remains detached enough to watch the flow of thoughts go by. When attention is organized into a separate observing self, you are in a position to be more objective about who you really are; and with practice the observer, rather than any particular thoughts or feelings that you might have, begins to seem like your real self. Of course, when your attention shifts back to thinking again, the sense of a separate, detached awareness will dissolve, and you are likely to lose all objectivity and go "on automatic" again.

In a way, all successful psychotherapy depends upon the ability to detach attention from habits and to describe them from the point of view of a neutral outsider. Accurate self-observation is vital to being able to recognize your own personality type, because you will need to know your own habits of heart and mind in order to recognize yourself from the stories of your similars.

Although Gurdjieff did not believe that his students were capable of grasping the significance of their Enneagram type, he did a great deal to evoke the recognition of character. Two of his most-reported methods were "stepping on people's favorite corns" and "the toasting of idiots." Gurdjieff was an Eight on the Enneagram, the point of the Boss, and, true to type, his teaching method was to attune himself to the most sensitive areas of a student's character and to push hard until he got a defensive response.

The principle of pressing the most sensitive corn turned out to be miracle working for me. It so affected everyone who met me, that he himself, without any effort on my part whatsoever, as if with great satisfaction and complete readiness, took off his mask presented to him with great solemnity by his papa and mama; and thanks to this I at once acquired an unprecedentedly easy possibility of unhurriedly and quietly feasting my eyes on what his inner world contained.[8]

The toasts were another way to introduce students to the concept of type. Those who dined with Gurdjieff were required to drink a good amount of alcohol in a series of toasts to various classifications of people. A new guest would be asked to select the category to which he or she seemed to most belong and would then be toasted as that sort of idiot.

He uses that word [idiot], but in its original and not in its acquired meaning. It really signifies another word for type. There are a number of toasts to be drunk in the course of the meal, and the usual rule is one glass of brandy or vodka for every three toasts. The women are let off with six toasts per glass; and there can be up to twenty-five toasts per night.

You see, he's a Russian and Russians always drink a lot of vodka. But there is another and far more important reason why all of G's guests have to drink. . . . A great many people are passing through his hands, and he is compelled to see them as quickly as possible. Well you know how alcohol opens up a man so that what he has previously managed to keep hidden is revealed. That is what the Arabs mean when they say "alcohol makes a man more so."[9]

During the toasts Gurdjieff would often indicate features of temperament that he saw within one of the idiots. Sometimes this feature was named, and sometimes demonstrated.

"You are a turkey cock," he said to someone on the first evening. "A turkey cock pretending to be a real peacock." A few masterly movements of G's head, a guttural sound or two, and there appeared at the table an arrogant gobbler parading itself before a hen. A little later a much larger animal materialized before our eyes. "Why do you look at me as one kind of bull looks at another kind of bull?" he asked of someone else. And with a slight change in the expression of his eyes, in the carriage of his head, and in the curve of his mouth a challenging bull was produced for our inspection.[10]

Even with a great deal of evocation, and blatant insult, the definition of character type remained obscure. Was it that Gurdjieff did not possess the psychological expertise to work successfully with personality issues? Or was he, like many of our contemporary inner life teachers, impatient about raking up personal history, preferring instead to get on with the task of setting the personality aside?

Psychological Buffers

The main obstacle to the self-recognition of type is the presence of what Gurdjieff called buffers. He believed that we hide our negative traits of character from ourselves through an elaborate system of internal buffers, or psychological defense mechanisms, that blind us to the forces that are at work within our own personality. Given the fact that Freud was pioneering the concept of unconscious defense mechanisms in roughly the same time frame in which Gurdjieff's students were learning the practices of self-observation, the attempt to teach people to observe their own buffers, rather than probing the unconscious through the agency of an analyst, was a radical approach to the inner life. Today we are more aware of the fact that we depend upon psychological defenses as a way of maintaining our sense of self. The major defense mechanisms that are related to Enneagram types One through Nine, respectively, are reaction formation, repression, identification, introjection, isolation, projection, rationalization, denial, and narcotization.

Gurdjieff's students were psychologically innocent, and unfamiliar with such terms, and yet they were asked to search inwardly for their own unconscious systems of defense.

We know what buffers on railway carriages are. They are the contrivances that lessen the shock when carriages or trucks strike one another. If there were no buffers, the shock of one carriage against another would be very unpleasant and dangerous. Buffers soften the results of these shocks and render them unnoticeable and imperceptible. Exactly the same appliances are to be found within man. They are created not by nature but by man himself, although involuntarily. The cause of their appearance is the existence in man of many contradictions; contradictions of opinions, feelings, sympathies, words and actions.

If a man were to feel all the contradictions that are within him he would have constant friction, constant unrest. If a man were to feel all these contradictions, he would feel that he is mad. A man cannot destroy contradictions, but if "buffers" are created in him he will not feel the impact from the clash of contradictory views, contradictory emotions, contradictory words.[11]

Gurdjieff goes on to say that although buffers make life easier, they also reduce the friction within the system that can cause people to grow. With the aid of buffers we are lulled into a kind of sleep in which we tend to behave mechanically. Because we are buffered and asleep, we cannot observe who we really are, and how our perceptions of the real world are distorted by the point of view of our type.

Ouspensky, a prolific writer on the subject of inner development from the Gurdjieff point of view, also spoke of buffers as a way to lessen the friction between inconsistent parts of the self. He suggested that his students be on the lookout for buffers, which could be recognized by focusing attention on the issues in their lives about which they could be made to feel defensive.

A man with really strong buffers does not see any need to justify himself, for he is quite unaware of any inconsistencies within him, and accepts himself as entirely satisfactory as he is.

However, when our work on ourselves begins to reveal some of our inconsistencies, we know that a buffer is placed between these, and with self-observation we slowly become aware of what lies on both sides of the buffer. So be on the look-out for inner contradictions, and these will lead you to the discovery of buffers. Pay particular attention to any subject on which you are touchy. You have perhaps attributed to yourself some good quality, and that is an idea that lies on one side of the buffer, but you have not as yet seen clearly the contradiction that lies on the other side of it. Nevertheless you are a little bit uncomfortable about this good quality, and that may mean that you are in the neighborhood of a buffer.[12]

The idea that we are blind to much of our own basic character is commonly accepted in our time. The unmasking of blind spots, defense mechanisms, and cognitive dissonance within our own character structure is a vital issue for anybody who wishes to lead a psychologically mature life. It is a doubly vital task for one seeking to become what Gurdjieff called a real human being. The reason that those who seek must be especially wary of buffers is that unconscious defense mechanisms are very specific shifts of attention that cause us to see reality in a distorted way.

There was another reason why personality had to be first seen and then rendered less arrogant and less active. It is through the distorting glasses of our personalities that we always see everything not as it is, but as it appears to us to be. Nothing is viewed clearly or objectively, but always through an intervening haze of likes and dislikes, partialities and prejudices, obsessions and idiosyncrasies. How can we ever hope to see things and persons as they are unless we can manage to get rid of this quotient of personal error? How indeed can we obtain any more knowledge and more especially that kind of knowledge that comes through intuition, or direct perception, rather than through the intellect, unless the personality can be first got out of the way. The so-called intuition of a man controlled by his personality is only a manifestation of his prejudices and biases, and nothing more than this.[13]

Acquired Personality

The word *personality* is equivalent to *self* in everyday usage. In spiritual parlance, personality is also called ego, or sometimes false personality, which are simply terms that make the distinction between what Gurdjieff called our essential nature and the personality that we acquire during the course of our lives.[14]

The idea that we each possess an essential nature that is qualitatively different from our acquired personality is basic to sacred psychology. Essence has been described as what is "one's own," the potentials with which we were born, rather than what we have acquired through our education, our ideas, or our beliefs. In essence we are like young children: there is no conflict between our thoughts, or our emotions, or our instincts. We act correctly and without hesitation to maintain well-being, stemming from an undefended trust in the environment and in other people. As adults we are aware that we possess some sort of benign unconscious potential, because we occasionally tap into a sense of at-one-ment with the environment, in which we intuitively know, or act in a highly effective way. At those moments we know without knowing how we know, our bodies act before we know what we intend to do, and we hear ourselves speak an unexpected truth before we know what we will say.

The assumption that our own capacity for an intuitive relationship with the world stems from an essential nature with which we are born remains inherently unprovable. Those traditions that have passed on a methodology for reaching the higher human potentials, however, tend to agree that this is so; and they generally hold personality as against essence in the spectrum of development.[15]

The legacy of methods indicates particular ways in which physical energy and inner attention can be stabilized, each of which can lead to experiencing an aspect of essential connection with the environment and with other people. Essential experiences are total, in the sense that they replace the awareness of "myself." There is no awareness of "my personal thoughts" or "my individual feelings" during an essential experience, so in that sense we do leave the adult personality behind and reenter the state of mind of the child, before a personality was acquired.

The Enneagram's nine-pointed star suggests that there are nine major aspects of essential being and that each may be approached in a slightly different way. The search for a particular aspect of essence is motivated by the fact that you suffer from its absence. For example, if you are chronically afraid, then you have suffered the loss of the child's essential trust, in the environment and in others; therefore the search for courage will be a motive in your life.

We sense that something essential is missing from our nature at those times when we complain to ourselves about being "on automatic," when life has become so mechanical that we are alienated from ourselves. "I am sick of my habits," "I want to begin life over again," are statements that indicate that our own mechanical behavior keeps us from what is potentially our own.

The realization that we are acting out of habit also indicates the presence of an inner observer. Consider the difference between the statements "Life is boring" and "I am bored with myself." The same difference in placement of attention is indicated in a statement such as "I was so angry I forgot what I was doing" and "I watched myself get furious with her." The former indicates that angry feelings have replaced the capacity to observe, whereas the latter indicates that there is an awareness that remains detached.

The alienation "that I feel from myself" is often accompanied by a wish to "find myself," to discover "my real self," which can mean a wish to awaken a connection to what is one's own. The quality of this search is different from the desire to regress to the safety of childhood, or even the desire to be cherished by a mate. The search is motivated by a hunger for more than ordinary life and is often expressed by naming particular aspects of the human essence. "I want to learn how to love other people," or "I want to lessen my attachments," or "I want to find the courage to act." It is as if a certain aspect of ourselves gets damaged in early life, and that loss then helps us to focus our search. The search for what is missing rallies us and reanimates our lives. We feel neurotic and so we go to therapy, we suffer and so we learn to meditate.

Personality develops because we must survive in the physical world. A contradiction develops between the child's essential trust of the environment and the family reality, which must be obeyed. From the point of view of a psychology that includes a concept of essence, personality develops in order to protect and defend essence from injury in the material world. What that means is that a particular aspect of the child's undefended connection with the environment is threatened, and so the child must protect itself from any further harm. Forming defenses to protect a threatened aspect of essence could be called the loss of essential connection, or the fall from grace.

From the perspective of developmental psychology, the essential connection could be described as the period of life during which young children relate to the mother and to the environment in a highly sensate but undifferentiated way. Young children cannot tell the difference between themselves and others, having no boundaries or defenses of their own. As children grow they must develop a separate self, which is adapted to the stress of early family life; Western psychology, however, does not attribute any special aspects of consciousness to the early undifferentiated connection, or stress the importance of reconnecting with these original perceptions.

From either point of view, we mature with an odd combination of talents, interests, and defenses that make each of us absolutely unique. Eventually our mobility of attention narrows to the preoccupations that we have acquired; and with that shift of attention, the essential connection with the environment and with others is forgotten and relegated to unconscious life.

What replaces the essential connection is what spiritual tradition would call a false personality, a set of ideas and beliefs derived from imitating our parents, cutting our losses and learning to pretend. As adults, however, we still retain some connection to the memory of our essence, which we remember as "when I was happy," "when I feared nothing," "when I was open to love." Furthermore, we know that the essential perceptions still exist within the unconscious, because as adults we occasionally tap into them in moments when we are "outside of ourselves," or in moments of extraordinary need.

When attention shifted from its internal connection to essence, we lost what was our own and were left staring out at the physical world, where satisfaction comes and goes, and where we rarely feel completely safe and at peace. Survival depends upon creating a successful set of boundaries and defenses, which is naturally incompatible with living out one's life in a highly sensate, unguarded attunement with the environment and others.

If the fears and desires of our acquired personality begin to weaken, however, and start to feel like "what I do" rather than "who I really am," then the wish "to find my real self" awakens, like a call to come back home. The relearning of our original connections with the environment and with other people can be thought of as a way back home, and the way implies an integration between a mature personality and the ability to experience the different aspects of essence at will. The hope is that the talents and skills of a mature adult can become the vehicle through which essential abilities can be used for the common good.

There is a Sufi saying that addresses the kinship between personality and essence. It says, "To become that which you were before you were, with the memory and understanding of what you had become."[16]

Chief Feature

The discovery of one's own type can be quite shocking, because simultaneous with the discovery comes the awareness of how type narrows our options and restricts us to a limited point of view. It can be astounding to realize that we perceive 360 degrees worth of reality in a very limited way and that most of our decisions and interests are based on highly sophisticated habits, rather than on real freedom of choice. Gurdjieff spoke of type as being organized around a Chief Feature of character.

Those around him see a man's Chief Feature, however hidden it may be. Of course they cannot always define it. But their definitions are often very good and very near. For instance "So-and-So" (G. named one of our party). "His feature is that he is never at home. . . ."

To another of our party he said on the question of feature that his feature was that he did not exist at all. "You understand, I do not see you," said G. "It does not mean that you are always like that. But when you are like that now, you do not exist at all."

He said to another that his Chief Feature was a tendency always to argue with everybody about everything. "But then I never argue," the man very heatedly at once replied. Nobody could help laughing.[17]

In esoteric schools the question of type was revealed slowly and with care. The idea was to introduce the concept that we are not free in as constructive a way as possible and in light of the fact that the preoccupations of type are potential allies in our efforts to regain our essence. For example, if you observe that you characteristically overburden yourself with things to do, and therefore cannot move on the task that is most essential in your life (point Nine—sloth), then paying attention to your priorities and the call to right action will be your natural allies. For Nines, sloth has been a good friend and protector against the pain of having to move on a personal position, because Nines have become convinced that their position will be discounted anyway.

If you are a Nine, then the fact that you get overwhelmed with secondary projects, and the fact that you have a terrible time saying No, will be constant and faithful reminders that you forget to pay attention to your own essential needs. If you can observe the moment in time when your habit starts to take over, then you will know exactly when to withdraw your attention from a secondary pursuit and return to your own priorities.

Likewise, if you find that you are a Seven on the Enneagram, and that your life is run by the wish to keep multiple options open so as not to miss out on any exciting adventures (point Seven—gluttony), then mastering the ability to focus on one thing at a time could be a big relief. If you are a Seven, the multioptional approach to life will lead you to believe that you are not limited and that you exercise daily freedom of choice. That illusion will continue until the time arrives when you try to make a permanent commitment, or try to meditate by collecting your attention into a single point.

Then your allies will come to you. A faithful flood of brilliant plans. The more you try to steady your attention, the more seductive your thoughts and plans will be. The concept of higher consciousness will be an appealing option to you until you discover that you can't control your mind. If you are a Seven, however, then monkey mind will be your personal inner teacher. When attention jumps from pole to pole, you are well reminded to bring it gently back to heel.

We in the West have particular difficulty with the concept that our personality is a limitation to our freedoms. In the West we are free to travel, free to learn, and free to climb the ladder of success. As long as our attention is commanded by the issues that preoccupy our type, however, we may be able to choose the job we take and the style of clothing that we wear, but our attention will be taken up with the issues that support a narrow point of view.

It is very important at a certain stage of self-study to find one's Chief Feature, which means chief weakness, like the axis round which everything turns. It can be shown, but the person will say: "Absurd, anything but not that!" Or sometimes it is so obvious that it is impossible to deny it, but with the help of buffers one can forget it again. I have known people who gave a name to their chief feature several times and for some time remembered. Then I met them again and they had forgotten. Or when they remembered they had one face, and when they had forgotten they had another face, and began to speak as if they had never spoken about it at all. You must come near to it yourself. When you feel it yourself, then you will know. If you are only told, you may always forget.[18]

We all experience difficulty in observing the nuances of our own personality at work. It is often easier for friends to see our traits of temperament than for us to see them for ourselves. Nicknames are often an indication of the feature, a kind of code name that is a key to a person's inner life.

Always the same motive moves Chief Feature. It tips the scales. It is like a bias in bowling, which prevents the ball going straight. Always Chief Feature makes us go off at a tangent. It arises from one or more of the seven deadly sins, but chiefly from self-love and vanity. One can discover it by becoming more conscious; and its discovery brings an increase of consciousness.[19]

The Passions

The Enneagram identifies nine chief features of the emotional life. They are parallel to Christianity's seven capital sins with the addition of deceit and fear at points Three and Six. These emotional habits developed during the fall from grace into the material world. They could also be called the passions of the emotional shadow that stem from the need to cope with early family life.

If a child develops well, then the passions are worn lightly, presenting themselves as mere tendencies. But if the psychological situation is severe, then one of the shadow issues becomes

THE PASSIONS

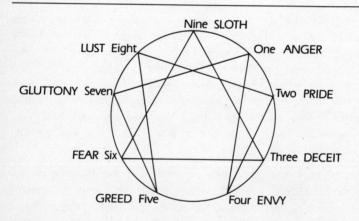

From chapter by John Lilly and Joseph Hart, The Arica Training; Transpersonal Psychologies, ed. Charles Tart, Harper & Row, 1975, reprinted by Psychological Processes, Inc. 1983.

an obsessional preoccupation; the capacity for self-observation weakens and we cannot make ourselves move on to other things.

The hope is that by naming our own Chief Feature we can learn to observe the many ways in which this habit has gained control of our lives. Then our neurotic skew of attention can be enlisted as an ally whose presence makes us suffer and causes us to remember what we have lost. Chief Feature is a neurotic habit that developed during childhood. It is also a personal teacher, a reminding factor that has a constant presence in the privacy of our inner life.

2. Attention, Intuition, and Type

Attention and Type

Once personality is formed, attention becomes immersed in the preoccupations that characterize our type. We lose the essential, childlike ability to respond to the world as it really is and begin to become selectively sensitive to the information that supports our type's worldview. We see what we need to see in order to survive and become oblivious to the rest.

For example, if you and I walked into a roomful of strangers, your habit might be to seek approval; whereas if my habit is to be fearful, I would look for reasons to leave. What is important to your sense of security would have to be pointed out to me, because I would be preoccupied with something else. But the fact is that neither of us would be in our essence. We would be full of the thoughts and emotions characteristic of our types, and we would not be in that place that is outside of ourselves or the place that we touch during the peak experiences of our lives. Neither would we be seeing events as they are objectively played out in that room, because our attention would have narrowed to pick out the information that is specific to our point of view.

To extend the example, if we go to a party together, you to seek attention and approval, and I having to overcome my fear, we might as well be going to parties on different planets. By the end of the evening we would have picked out different strangers to talk to, had radically different conversations, presented ourselves differently, and pocketed different sets of phone numbers before we left the room. If we decided to compare notes later on, we would find that we drew different conclusions from the same conversation and believed that we saw different intentions emanating from the same stranger's face.

I have exaggerated the picture to make the point that you and I are likely to focus our attention on different aspects of an identical scene and to restate the fact that neither of us sees the complete 360-degree scope of possibilities. We do not see the same reality because we are oblivious to what does not attract our attention and tend to focus on the information that is important to our type.

The preoccupations of a type are easy to name. This book is filled with self-descriptions by acute self-observers who have been generous enough to describe their habits of heart and preoccupations of mind. They name the issues that their attention is attracted to but, more important from the point of view of learning to extricate attention from our habits, they also tell us *how* they pay attention to the issues that drive their lives.

It is not surprising that practiced self-observers, many of whom have been serious meditators for many years, should be able to tell us how they focus their attention with respect to the issues that preoccupy their minds. Observation and attention are a meditator's language: What are you aware of? Are you present or spaced out? Note the object that you're attending to. Watch where your attention goes.[1] Once a stable inner observer develops, it is easy to recognize the differences between the mental and emotional objects that flow through the inner space. It is, however, of great interest to me that we have become so preoccupied with naming *what* our attention is attracted to that we have neglected to look at *how* attention is organized when we perceive the information that interests our type.[2] We are alert to our issues, but not to the ways in which we gather information that supports those psychological concerns.

To extend our comparison of types, or points, the one who seeks affection and approval (point Two—pride) and the one who is afraid (point Six—fear), we could ask the Twos what happens to them when they want approval from someone, and we could ask the Sixes what happens when they become afraid. Inexperienced self-observers are likely to respond with something like, "I get attracted and want to flirt," or "I get shaky and want to run away." If Twos and Sixes cannot observe their own internal shifts of attention, then they will not be aware of the ways that they pick up cues, or be able to describe any subtle adjustments that they make within themselves. These Twos and Sixes may be genuine experts at recognizing minimal cues that promise affection or indicate potential harm, but they may not be able to describe their sensitivity or show us how to work with our attention so that we can enter into their world-view.

With experienced self-observers we get a better description of the typical placements of attention that determine the point of view of a type. Here is a classic Six self-observation. If you are not a fearful type, but have driven the California 101 coast highway, you'll be sympathetic to her state of mind.

I worked in L.A. while my husband took his degree at Cal Poly and was driving Highway 101 a couple of times a week. I had it down and had no problems unless I was upset about something, and then I had to really concentrate on the road. It was actually better for me to be the driver, because if I'd had a bad week and my husband was driving, I just couldn't look out the window on the slope side. These images would come in on me of the tires slipping or us not making the turn that were so strong they'd make me sick.

So one Sunday I really didn't want to go back to L.A., and I found myself having to turn off and pull myself together, because my mind kept putting me over the cliff and onto the rocks below. The end of the story is that I wound up in the hospital, not because I went over the cliff, but because I saw myself going over, and just before I hit the rocks, I reflexively swerved the wheel, crossed the oncoming traffic lane, and plowed into the mountainside.

This Six was clearly in the grip of a mental projection when she tried to save herself from a fall that was happening in her mind. She went on to say that the fall seemed very real: she felt herself going over, she saw the rocks, and she believed, when she turned the wheel, that it was useless to try to save herself. She was also quite aware that the whole incident happened in a few seconds, and once she recovered, she courageously got behind the wheel again, keeping her attention safely away from her imagination, while driving Highway 101 for the remainder of her husband's time at school. The same woman had this to say about her childhood.

I used to be terrified of my mother. She was a drinker and could change within fifteen minutes from her usual personality into an incredibly nasty person who did not wish me well. The question was always on my mind when she started to drink. Would she go over that line, and how bad was it going to be?

I used to watch her all the time to see if she had hidden a bottle; and when she drank I would watch her face and imagine what she was going to be like later that night. I would look at her and try to imagine, Does the face look steady? Is it going to scream at me? Does it start to look grotesque? Does it fall asleep? I would imagine her other faces when I first saw her begin to drink, and I would plan to stay or to escape based on whatever it looked like her face was going to do.

This Six is both blessed and burdened by an imagination that has been strengthened by a lifetime's worth of daily practice. She is blessed in the sense that she has potential access to a rich and detailed world of inner experience and burdened in the sense that her imagery is strong enough to momentarily replace objective reality. She was clearly projecting when she swerved the wheel. In that instance there is no question that her inner imagery projected outward and caused her to misread her situation. She would agree that projection was also at work when she tried to get a reading on her mother's drinking habits. A large percentage of her observations were doubtless based on Mom's familiar physical cues and the fact that she was terrified of being humiliated or abused.

But it is also true that she resorted to her visions at a time when, in the life of a child, circumstances were desperate; and her images were strong enough to replace her thoughts. She had learned to ask questions of her visualizations, she used the "other faces" as a source of information to support herself emotionally, and she acted upon what she saw.

Intuition and Type

The same Six also reported a definite psychic experience, apparently in the same state of mind where the car "fell" and her mother's "other faces" appeared.

A dear friend of mine finally got pregnant after a couple of years of trying. When she called, she sounded great, and we planned to get together to celebrate. When I saw her, she was radiant; so when her other face started to come out, it wasn't because I had the wish to have it show me something.

It was bizarre. We were eating a Mexican dinner, and she was really happy, but overlaid on her face as she was talking, I could see tears and lines of sadness from loss. I think it was great that I couldn't tell her, because I knew she was going to lose that child. Her real face went right on talking, but I saw her other face go grim. The whole other face hardened and I knew it was determined, and then it went peaceful, and then it went away. I had the whole story in just a few seconds. She was going to miscarry, try again, symbolically with a very hard jaw, and the second time would be O.K.

This Six went on to describe her emotional reactions to having seen a future event played out and also said that the episode seemed quite natural and somehow familiar at the time. She added that the sequence indicated by her friend's other face was completed in a little over a year's time.

Attention Practices

Intuition can best be understood as the emerging side effect of the withdrawal of attention from habitual thoughts and feelings. Without a basic attention practice, we tend to overly focus in the thinking state, so that equally present impressions are not accessible in a reliable way. The Six woman would benefit greatly by learning to recognize when her mental habit of imagining the worst begins to take over and how to shift her attention elsewhere before her imagery becomes too real. She was, in fact, performing a shift when she was able to stay present to herself, in the car, on the road, rather than allowing her imagination to become overpowering.

But could this Six learn to make a clean discrimination between fantasy images and accurate intuitive visions when the two kinds of impressions are so closely intertwined? Could she learn to produce accurate intuitive imagery at will?

To make some practical use of her mental habit, she would have to learn to tell the difference between thoughts, fantasies projected from personal thinking, and the kind of accurate intuitive impressions that she saw in the face of her friend. These advanced discrimination practices do exist within the sacred technology; and, as always, the preliminary work depends upon strengthening the inner observer.

It is not within the scope of this book to discuss even basic internal practices. Practices are best learned with an experienced teacher, in a supportive setting, rather than out of a book, where even the most precise language is sure to fall short of what is necessary to gain access to an altered state of mind. This book is about the preoccupations that are characteristic of different types of people, so for our purposes, it is important only to point out that the way in which each type pays attention to its preoccupations can be both a burden and a blessing in disguise.

The burden is that our habit of attention serves to keep us unconsciously in touch with the very information that supports our neurotic concerns. This Six's habit is to imagine the worst, and she does not know that she forgets to imagine the best. She follows the habit that was suited to her childhood security needs and, oddly enough, imagining the best would seem to her like make-believe. Imagining worst case possibilities have become her touchstone of reality; imagining the best would be dismissed as childish fantasy.

The blessing of imagining the worst is that this Six has become so good at it that if she can learn to voluntarily replicate the shifts of attention that underlie her defensive strategy, she may discover that she is a specialist in a certain kind of intuitive style.

My particular interest in the Enneagram is in the stories of people who have had intuitive and essential experiences. From their stories we get a working hypothesis of the ways in which our neurotic concerns can lead us honorably forward into other states of mind. It has been a wonderful opportunity for me as a teacher. I have gotten to hear very detailed descriptions of my students' inner processes as they learned to modify their attention. I have seen the ways in which intuition both burdened and supported their lives. And I have been able to chart some highly ingenious attentional shifts that students have inadvertently resorted to as a way to stay intuitively connected to their preoccupying concerns.

I hear a familiar story over and over again. It goes something like, "My parents gave mixed messages, and I had to know the truth." Or, "I could feel myself adjusting to become what other people wanted me to be." There are repeating childhood memories of having to get a reading on adults in order to survive the stress of family life.

As adults, my students are convinced that they have an edge of intuitive insight into the areas that were problematic in childhood. To continue our comparison of types, the Sixes (fear) uniformly believe that they have finely tuned bullshit detectors that are organized to see the real intentions of other people that lie hidden beneath a surface facade. The Twos (pride) uniformly believe that they have the ability to intuitively alter their self-presentation in order to gain acceptance and love.

Allowing for the fact that Sixes (paranoid) would feel safer with an idea of themselves as able to predict, and therefore ward off, potential harm, and that Twos (histrionic) would feel more lovable by believing that they could assume the characteristics of an appealing person, I am still struck by the possibility that a type's preoccupations predispose it to develop intuitive ways of sensing the very information that would perpetuate neurotic concerns. The importance of attention practice to transcend neurosis is clear. The students win twice by learning basic practices. First, they are relieved of a biased worldview. Second, they have an opportunity to become consciously aware of an intuitive style that may already have been operating in unrecognized ways.

Experienced self-observers use revealing language when they talk about the ways in which they pay attention to loaded personal issues. There are many versions of "the other faces," many ways for attention to shift to an inner visualization. There are also statements such as "I merge," or "A part of me gets pulled forward," or "I take their feelings on," or "I become them," or "I detach and watch." Are these statements based purely upon the distortions of psychological projection? Do they stem solely from an inflated desire to believe that we can have access to special information about the loaded issues in our lives? Are they based upon minimal physical cues, or do these statements stem to some degree from a genuine sensitivity to the issues that underlie our type?

For example, in contrast to the Six who is afraid, the Two, who wants to please is likely to come up with an "I merge" impression of the way that he or she mobilizes attention. The Two might be quite capable of learning how to "see the other face," but the reports coming from Twos seem to be "I merge" stories, rather than stories about imagining the worst.

It is also possible to get an "I merge" story from a borderline psychiatric patient, who has never developed a clear set of personal boundaries. "I merge" is also the profound experience of a lover whose awareness shifts beyond the boundaries of a personal self. But when a practiced self-observer is asked to detail an "I merge" kind of statement, it starts to sound remarkably like a layperson's version of the attentional underpinning of specific meditation practices.

The description given by people who say "I merge" or "I become" sounds remarkably like my venerable martial arts teacher, who is a living demonstration of the ability to include other people within his own perceptions.

My teacher's verbal instructions are, "Drop to the *hara* [shift the attention to the belly], open the sense field, and blend."³ In the "open sensing" attentional stance, he can exactly mimic the random movements of a training partner who is standing many feet away and is hidden behind a screen. The classical Rondori, or multiple-person attack, is another impressive demonstration of the ability to sense at a distance.⁴ In Rondori, which can be performed blindfolded, you are simultaneously attacked from several directions, necessitating a continuous clear perception of the space surrounding your body, especially the space at your back.

Likewise, a statement such as "I see the inner face" sounds remarkably like the fruit of an inner eye visualization practice that develops the capacity to discriminate between fantasies that are projected from personal thinking and accurate intuitive visions that are not directed by the thinking/feeling self.⁵

Why are these perceptions likely to show up at the psychological damage points of our type? The fact is that a preoccupation to which attention habitually returns is the psyche's starting place for observing the different placements of attention that keep us unconsciously in contact with the environment and with others. We develop powers of attention when we become neurotically concerned. We want the goods, and so we stretch out with our senses and we pay attention very well.

For example, children who are desperate for love may learn to inwardly shift attention in such a way as to merge with a parent, or to unconsciously feel others' wishes within their own bodies and therefore alter themselves in order to please. Likewise, frightened children are likely to become unwittingly but accurately attuned to the potential for hostility in bigger, stronger people who have power over their lives. These abilities can continue on into adult life as real sensitivities, but as adults we can only name our preoccupations, rather than how we remain informed about our neurotic concerns.

The way that you pay attention to the key issues in your life can be well over the line of ordinary perception and into an intuitive zone without your being aware that anything unusual is going on. This is not a question of having learned to look for subtle physical cues, such as body language or facial signs. Intuition is a knowing that stems from a nonthinking state of mind. It is closely connected to ordinary thinking states and, if you are not too hesitant about altering your perceptions slightly, your intuition can be trained. If an intuitive connection supported your sense of security and well-being when you were young, then as an adult you probably use intuition as a source of information in many unrecognized ways. It can give an edge to decision making and lend special qualities of sensitivity to your personal life.

If intuition did not serve you well when you were young, if you would have had to become aware of things that were emotionally unbearable to see, then you have probably turned your attention away from your inner perceptions and may experience resistance to penetrating what mystics call the perceptual veils.[6]

Intuition and Essence

Intuition makes a great range of information available to us and is consequently a highly desirable human resource. But intuition is not essence. It is only a source of insight and a vehicle of creativity. In essence, there is no need to be doing a spiritual practice, or having an insight, or being guided by intuition, because in essence there is no sense of a personal self. There is nobody doing, or having, or being guided. Attention is stationed in an at-one connection with the environment and with other people; and in that state of mind, we act naturally and accurately without being aware of personal thoughts or feelings.

We are in our essence at those times when our body moves correctly before we know what we should do, and we speak the truth before we know what we are going to say. From time to time we quite naturally fall into one of the many qualities of essence, and in those peak moments we have a glimpse of what the human race could be.

3. Structure of the Enneagram Diagram

Structure of the Enneagram

The nine-pointed star maps the relationship between two primary laws of mysticism, the law of Three (trinity), which identifies the three forces that are present when an event begins, and the law of Seven (octaves), which governs the stages of implementation of that event as it is played out in the physical world.

The law of Three is represented by the Enneagram's inner triangle. The triangle conveys the idea that three forces are necessary for creation, rather than the visible two, cause and effect. This concept is preserved in the Christian trinity of Father, Son, and Holy Ghost; and in Hinduism's three divine forces of creation, called Brahma, Vishnu, and Siva. The trinity of forces could also be called creative, destructive, and preserving, or active, receptive, and reconciling. Gurdjieff, a primary source for the Enneagram system, called them simply force One, force Two, and force Three, and it was his observation that humanity is third-force blind.

A precise understanding of how the trinity of forces works together can help an event to survive through time, rather than falling helplessly apart, because the three forces change signs at different phases during the stages of an event's lifetime. For example, the reconciling force that is present when the event begins will inevitably become the active force during the next stage of that event's progress through time. A fuller understanding of the Enneagram symbol indicates that it is a model of perpetual motion. The diagram indicates certain nonobvious aspects of process, such as the moment when a new influx of energy is needed in order to perpetuate the lifetime of an event.

The central triangle of Three–Six–Nine can also be mathematically described as the attempt of the trinity of forces present in the original creation to be reconciled back into one. This is illustrated arithmetically by dividing 1, or unity, by 3, which results in a fraction, the last numeral of which repeats infinitely, that is, $1 \div 3 = 0.3333. \ldots$

Once an event is begun, the law of Seven, or the law of octaves, comes into play. The law of octaves is preserved in the musical scale as Seven notes with a repeating Do and governs the succession of stages by which an event is played out in the material world. The relationship of Seven to unity can be expressed by dividing 1 by 7, which yields the repeating series $0.142857142857, \ldots$ which contains no multiples of three. The full Enneagram is a circle divided into nine equal parts that represents the fusion of the law of Three and the law of Seven, which interact in specific ways along the diagram's inner lines.[1]

When the Enneagram model is applied to the human condition, the central triangle suggests that there are three core mental preoccupations: image (or glamour, point Three), fear (point Six), and self-forgetting (point Nine). The core mental issues have corresponding emotional passions. The diagram that follows indicates the mental and emotional preoccupations of the three core personality types.

The Nine Types

1. The Perfectionist

Critical of self and others. Convinced there is one correct way. Feel ethically superior. Procrastinate for fear of making a mistake. Use *should* and *must* a lot.

Evolved Ones can be critically astute, moral heroes.

THE ENNEAGRAM OF PERSONALITY TYPES

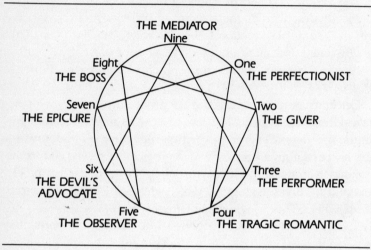

CORE MENTAL ISSUES   CORE EMOTIONAL ISSUES

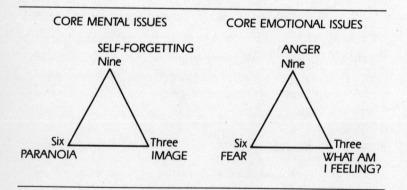

2. The Giver

Demand affection and approval. Seek to be loved and appreciated by becoming indispensable to another person. Devoted to meeting others' needs. Manipulative. Have many selves—show a different self to each good friend. Aggressively seductive.

Evolved Twos are genuinely caring and supportive.

3. The Performer

Seek to be loved for performance and achievement. Competitive. Obsessed with image as a winner and with comparative status. Masters at appearances. Type A personalities. Confuse real self and job identity. Can appear to be more productive than actually are.

Evolved Threes can be effective leaders, good packagers, competent promoters, captains of winning teams.

4. The Tragic Romantic

Attracted to the unavailable; ideal is never here and now. Tragic, sad, artistic, sensitive; focused on the absent lover, the loss of a friend.

Evolved Fours are creative in their way of life and able to help other people through their pain. They are committed to beauty and the passionate life: birth, sex, intensity, and death.

5. The Observer

Maintain emotional distance from others. Protect privacy, don't get involved. Doing without is a defense against involvement. Feel drained by commitment and by other people's needs. Compartmentalize obligations; detached from people, feelings, and things.

Evolved Fives can be excellent decision makers, ivory-tower intellectuals, and abstemious monks.

6. The Devil's Advocate

Fearful, dutiful, plagued by doubt. Procrastination—thinking replaces doing—afraid to take action because exposure leads to attack. Identify with underdog causes, antiauthoritarian, self-sacrificing, loyal to the cause. The phobic Sixes vacillate, feel persecuted, and cave in when cornered. The counterphobic Sixes feel perpetually cornered and therefore go out to confront the terror in an aggressive way.

Evolved Sixes can be great team players, loyal soldiers, and good friends. Will work for a cause in the way that others work for personal profit.

7. The Epicure

Peter Pan, the *puer aeternus*—the eternal youth. Dilettantish, dance-away lovers, superficial, adventurous, gourmet approach to life. Trouble with commitment, want to keep the options open, want to stay emotionally high. Generally happy, stimulating to be around, habit of starting things but not seeing them through.

Evolved Sevens are good synthesizers, theoreticians, Renaissance types.

8. The Boss

Extremely protective. Stick up for self and friends; combative, take charge, love a fight. Have to be in control. Open displays of anger and force; great respect for opponents who will stand and fight. Make contact through sex and toe-to-toe confrontations. Excessive way of life: too much, too late at night, too loud.

Evolved Eights are excellent leaders, especially in the adversarial role. Can be powerful supporters for other people; want to make the way safe for friends.

9. The Mediator

Obsessively ambivalent; see all points of view; readily replace own wishes with those of others and real goals with inessential activities. Tendency to narcotization through food, TV, and drink. Know other people's needs better than their own; tendency to space out, not sure whether want to be here, or not, whether want to be on the team or not. Agreeable; anger comes out in indirect ways.

Evolved Nines make excellent peacemakers, counselors, negotiators, achieve well when on track.

The Wings

The points that appear on either side of the Three–Six–Nine triangle are variations of the core personalities. That means that the two wing points of Three, which are Two and Four, share a common preoccupation with image and also live out variations of the question "What am I feeling?" The wings of Six (Five and Seven) share an underlying paranoia, as well as emotional habits of fear. The wings of Nine (Eight and One) share a core predisposition toward the sleep of self-forgetting, which is the forgetting of personal priorities, as well as a predisposition toward anger.

The wings of the Three–Six–Nine triangle represent an externalized and an internalized version of the core preoccupations, and in therapy the core predisposition is likely to emerge as healing takes place. That would mean that a Seven (externalized fear type), looking initially not at all afraid, would be likely to become more overtly furtive and paranoid (core of Six) as psychological defenses weaken.

Only the Three–Six–Nine triangle points show an external and internal version of themselves at the wings. For example, the wings of Eight, which are Seven and Nine, do not represent an externalized and internalized version of Eight. The wings of any point are influential, however, because they give a flavor to that personality type. For example, in the anger group at the top of the Enneagram, a Nine, who will prefer to express anger indirectly and passively, will lean either to the Eight side (the Boss), making for a blunt and stubborn "don't push me" kind of passive anger, or to the One side (the Perfectionist), making for a nitpicking criticality, which will still be acted out in indirect ways.

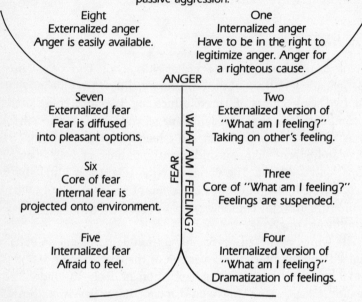

Nine
Core of anger
Anger that went to sleep;
passive aggression.

Eight
Externalized anger
Anger is easily available.

One
Internalized anger
Have to be in the right to
legitimize anger. Anger for
a righteous cause.

ANGER

Seven
Externalized fear
Fear is diffused
into pleasant options.

Two
Externalized version of
"What am I feeling?"
Taking on other's feeling.

Six
Core of fear
Internal fear is
projected onto environment.

Three
Core of "What am I feeling?"
Feelings are suspended.

FEAR

WHAT AM I FEELING?

Five
Internalized fear
Afraid to feel.

Four
Internalized version of
"What am I feeling?"
Dramatization of feelings.

Likewise, someone with a noncore point, such as Four (the Tragic Romantic), who expresses feelings in a dramatized way, will lean either toward Five (the Observer), in an internalized depressive stance, or toward Three (the Performer), in a more hyperactive effort to keep melancholia at bay. The flavors of the wings help to make each personality highly distinctive. No two people who belong to the same type are identical, although they share the same preoccupations and concerns. In Enneagram classes we have taken to distinguishing the differences in flavor between members of the same type by naming the flavors. For example, a fiveish Four would be a more withdrawn and private kind of Four, whereas a threeish Four would be a more flamboyant, dramatic Four, who maintains an active schedule, but still relates to the Four stance of melancholy, sadness, and loss. Each type is affected by both of its wings, and although the flavor of one of the wings will predominate in the personality, it would be improper to discount the fact that the other exists as a potential.

The Dynamics of the Types

The law of Three also applies to the fact that each personality type is composed of three aspects: the predominating aspect, which is operative under usual conditions, which is called your type; the aspect that operates when you go into action (or are placed under stress); and the aspect that comes into play in secure (nonstressful) situations. In the following diagram the action (stressful) point is in the direction of the arrow, and the nonstressful aspect is away from the arrow. Thus each type is really a union of three aspects, each of which is likely to be stimulated by particular life situations. For example, when an Observer (usually quiet and withdrawn) is under stress, she or he moves to the position of the Epicure (paradoxically more outgoing and friendly in an effort to reduce stress by making contact with people). When she or he is secure, the Observer tends to become a Boss (directive of others and controlling of personal space).

Working with Security and Stress

The fact that our mental and emotional preoccupations change when we move from a secure life situation into action, and therefore into some degree of stress, has created something of a cult of security among Enneagram enthusiasts. A security reaction sounds infinitely more appealing than an action/stress reaction, and the strategy of moving toward security suggests that the way to health lies in cultivating the better aspects of the security point. The Enneagram's security enthusiasts tend to see a move along the lines of the arrows, toward action and therefore toward stress, as furthering the compulsions of their

THE ARROWS

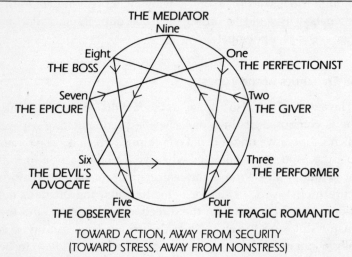

THE MEDIATOR
Nine

Eight
THE BOSS

One
THE PERFECTIONIST

Seven
THE EPICURE

Two
THE GIVER

Six
THE DEVIL'S
ADVOCATE

Three
THE PERFORMER

Five
THE OBSERVER

Four
THE TRAGIC ROMANTIC

TOWARD ACTION, AWAY FROM SECURITY
(TOWARD STRESS, AWAY FROM NONSTRESS)

type. The support for this view appears to be based on the simple logistical maneuver of naming the positive aspects of the security point and the negative aspects of the stress point.

My interviews with panelists do not at all suggest that a clear move-to-security opportunity, such as falling in love with an appropriate and willing partner, will necessarily bring out the better qualities of the security point. A good opportunity can paradoxically produce a stress reaction, because of inexperience or insecurities based on past experience. I have interviewed people who slide straight into the negative aspects of their security point when faced with a promising life situation; and I have also recorded many stories of those whose character has been formed by developing the best aspects of the action/stress point of their type.

Cultivating the healing possibilities in the so-called stress point is implicit in techniques such as Gestalt therapy and Tantric meditation practices, in which negative emotions are deliberately cultivated and engaged. The intention behind moving toward stress is to skillfully raise our passions to the overflow point and to release the compulsion of a negative habit by experiencing it fully and completely. A tantrum might be cultivated, rather than detachment, or a student might be placed in a living situation designed for maximum irritation. Pride types might find themselves scrubbing a lot of floors, and fear types might be sent to meditate at full moon in the local cemetery. Gurdjieff's method of stepping on people's favorite corns illustrates the idea that deliberately raising and working with the energies produced by stress can be as growth-producing as cultivating the ability to detach attention from the so-called negative emotions.[2]

The interdependency between a strategic cultivation of emotional passion while at the same time learning the practice of detachment was expressed in the Delphic mysteries by the worship of Apollo and Dionysus within the same temple. Dionysus represented the feminine world of "the life mystery of blood and of the powers of earth." He was worshiped alternately during the same calendar year with Apollo, who embodied the masculine qualities of clarity, distance, and detachment.[3] Dionysian worship demands the full surrendering of attention to sensation and feeling, which, if they are allowed into full expression, naturally turns to the desire for objectivity and detachment from feelings. Likewise, the Apollonian ideal of distance and clarity, the "rejecting of whatever is too near," depends upon the presence of passionately raised questions in order to develop clarity and on having developed a full emotional life before detachment makes any sense.[4]

Apollo, the God of light, of reason, of proportion, harmony, number— Apollo blinds those who press too close in worship. Don't look straight at the sun. Go into a dark bar for a bit and have a beer with Dionysios, every now and then.[5]

4. Contributors to the System

Contributors to the System

With a graph like the nine-pointed star, everything depends upon a correct placement of the types on the diagram, because they relate to one another in such specific ways. The correct placement of the emotional passions was produced by Oscar Ichazo, and with that deceptively simple arrangement of what Gurdjieff called Chief Feature, the Enneagram code became available to us.

Following the Sufi idea that personality preoccupations are indicators of the lost qualities of essence, Ichazo went on to name a higher quality of mental and emotional life to which each of the nine types is predisposed. The qualities of essence are simply the opposite of the most damaged aspect of each of the nine. For example, an evolved fear type is likely to act with courage, and an evolved pride type is likely to have developed genuine humility. Ichazo named the higher mental quality the Holy Idea and the higher emotional quality the Virtue.

There are very real problems attached to a correct understanding of the higher mental capacity and the emotional virtues. They have nothing to do with ordinary thoughts and feelings and, in fact, are not directed by the thinking/feeling self. The higher capacities are the lost qualities of essence, each one of which represents the successful resolution of a painful neurotic trend. The higher mental aspects are an automatic orientation toward particular qualities of knowing that are not mediated by thought, and the Virtues are automatic bodily responses that are not directed by personal likes or dislikes.

Because the higher intelligences are different from their coun-
terparts in the personality, it is easy to form an *idea* or a *concept*
that we are in our essence when we think humble thoughts or
force ourself to be brave. These ideas that we hold about ourself
are only tangentially related to an undefended, open attunement to the environment and to other people.

Ichazo's work was unknown until 1970, when he announced
a psychospiritual training in the desert near the town of Arica
in Chile. About fifty Americans attended, among them John
Lilly, Claudio Naranjo, and Joseph Hart, who brought back the
report that Ichazo was using the Sufi concepts familiar to many
through the Gurdjieff work. He was using exercises to develop
the "three brains," or the three kinds of human intelligence that
Gurdjieff had described as mental, emotional, and instinctual;
he was also using the teaching method of animal qualities, and
he had written a short précis of the nine personality types,
which was subsequently published in a chapter on the Arica
training in *Transpersonal Psychologies*.[1]

Most important, Ichazo had placed the types correctly on the
nine-pointed star, so that the relationships among the types
could be verified through interviews.

In a rare public statement, Ichazo indicated that he had been
taken on as an apprentice to a teacher when he was nineteen
and that through his teacher's group he had been exposed to
Zen and the esoteric basis of Sufism and the Cabala. The group
also used techniques that he later found in the Gurdjieff work.[2]
Ichazo eventually founded the Arica Institute, which is current-
ly based in New York City. About his place in the transmission
of the teachings he says, "Arica is not so much my invention as
it is a product of our times. The knowledge that I have contrib-
uted to the school came to me from many sources that I have
encountered in my peculiar quest."

The Enneagrams that follow are from a John Lilly and Joseph
Hart article on the Arica training that was included in *Transpersonal Psychologies*. The words that name each of the preoccupations of the nine points were used as fundamentals by the

THREE CENTERS OF INTELLIGENCE

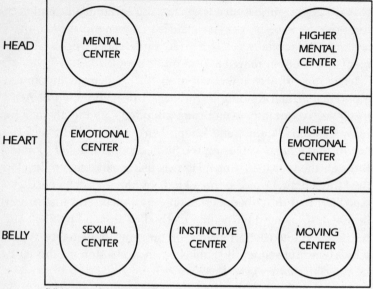

(Michael Waldberg, *Gurdjieff, An Approach to His Ideas,* (Routledge and Kegan Paul, 1973), 112.

Enneagram teachers, who have been interviewing panels of the types, and compiling their traits and behaviors, for many years. The diagram of the mental center includes the original names for the types, which I have chosen to change in the interest of moving the system away from the Gurdjieff ideal of "naming the devil in order to route him out." The original names and the original lines of questioning necessarily emphasized the negative preoccupations of a type, simply because negative habits are blatant enough that they make the task of identifying differences between the nine much easier. For example, without distinctions like "Under pressure I create conflict" (point Eight—the Boss) and "Under pressure I withdraw" (point Five—the Observer), we would have no way of telling the difference between these two types, and we would not be able to strategize ways in which to help either type to evolve. If we took statements only from Buddhas or unusually evolved people, we would be hearing statements originating from higher mental centers, such as, "I never seem to experience pressure, I simply know how a problem will conclude" (point Five—Omniscience), or "I follow the force that flows through my body" (point Eight—Innocence). In other words, we could not tell the types apart.

Although the negative differences among types makes the work of identifying them easier, I think that an overpreoccupation with the peculiarities of types diminishes their importance as teachers and guides to the higher states of consciousness.

The Subtypes

The operation of the belly center is largely unconscious, but can be recognized by the fact that we each have pressing concerns about issues that affect our physical survival (self-preservation), sexuality, and social life.

There is a teaching that relates to the subtypes. A cowherd sat on a three-legged stool to milk. The milk may refer to the nourishment of teachings or the nourishment of life. One leg of the stool was damaged, and so as he milked, his field of perception was slanted toward the damaged leg of his base. What the story suggests is that we have three primary areas of relationship and that one of these areas is more afflicted than the other two. As a result of one area of relationship being damaged, a mental preoccupation develops that lessens the anxiety that surrounds that area of our life. The three kinds of relationship are sexual (intimate and other one-to-one relationships), social (group), and self-preservation (our relationship to personal survival). As adults, we are sensitive to all three psychological preoccupations that apply to our type, but one will predominate as a more deeply felt concern. For example, all Threes will focus a lot of attention on security, prestige, and

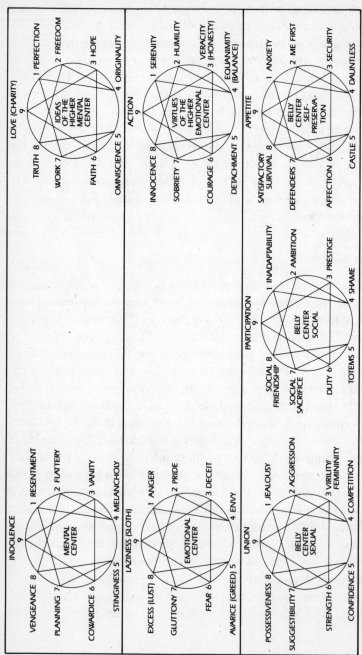

LOVE (CHARITY) 9
1 PERFECTION
2 FREEDOM
3 HOPE
4 ORIGINALITY
OMNISCIENCE 5
FAITH 6
WORK 7
TRUTH 8
IDEAS OF THE HIGHER MENTAL CENTER

ACTION 9
1 SERENITY
2 HUMILITY
3 (HONESTY) VERACITY
4 EQUANIMITY (BALANCE)
DETACHMENT 5
COURAGE 6
SOBRIETY 7
INNOCENCE 8
VIRTUES OF THE HIGHER EMOTIONAL CENTER

APPETITE 9
1 ANXIETY
2 ME FIRST
3 SECURITY
4 DAUNTLESS
CASTLE 5
AFFECTION 6
DEFENDERS 7
SATISFACTORY SURVIVAL 8
BELLY CENTER SELF-PRESERVA-TION

PARTICIPATION 9
1 INADAPTABILITY
2 AMBITION
3 PRESTIGE
4 SHAME
TOTEMS 5
DUTY 6
SOCIAL SACRIFICE 7
SOCIAL FRIENDSHIP 8
BELLY CENTER SOCIAL

INDOLENCE 9
1 RESENTMENT
2 FLATTERY
3 VANITY
4 MELANCHOLY
STINGINESS 5
COWARDICE 6
PLANNING 7
VENGEANCE 8
MENTAL CENTER

LAZINESS (SLOTH) 9
1 ANGER
2 PRIDE
3 DECEIT
4 ENVY
AVARICE (GREED) 5
FEAR 6
GLUTTONY 7
EXCESS (LUST) 8
EMOTIONAL CENTER

UNION 9
1 JEALOUSY
2 AGGRESSION
3 VIRILITY/FEMININITY
4 COMPETITION
CONFIDENCE 5
STRENGTH 6
SUGGESTIBILITY 7
POSSESSIVENESS 8
BELLY CENTER SEXUAL

Adapted from *Transpersonal Psychologies*, Edit. Charles Tart, Harper & Row, 1975. reprinted by Psychological Processes, Inc. 1983, Charles Tart.

masculine/feminine image, but one of those words will be the focal point of more concern than the other two. If the Three has been most damaged in the area of self-preservation, then we could also hypothesize that the primary area of concern, which would be security, would also be affected by the chief feature of vanity and the passion of deceit.

The Bridge to Contemporary Psychology

The difficulty with Ichazo's Enneagram was that his précis was built on only one of the many dominant issues characteristic of a type, and his descriptive language did not readily translate into psychological terminology. The missing piece in the transmission was supplied by Claudio Naranjo, a Chilean psychiatrist, who attended a part of the Arica training and was able to place the Enneagram into the context of psychological ideas. Naranjo had already developed a reputation as a synthesizer of Eastern and Western approaches to consciousness with *The One Quest*.[3] His contribution to the Enneagram successfully joined the insight and methods of a mystical path of transformation with the intellectual power of a Western psychological model. It also brought the question of typing out of the domain of "those who know," and made it possible to develop lines of questioning so that people could identify their own type by seeing and hearing the stories of their similars.

Naranjo gained his insight by interviewing individuals who were psychologically sophisticated, and who could describe their preoccupations of heart and mind. One of his Enneagrams is a mapping of the major defense mechanism that supports each of the nine. To me it is a completion of what was implied through Gurdjieff and developed through Ichazo. Without this kind of exact placement into Western typology, the Enneagram would still be in the realm of the mysterious.

I learned the Enneagram from Naranjo, who taught the material in the oral way. He was interviewing groups of high-functioning people who were involved in spiritual disciplines. It is

FOCAL POINTS OF ATTENTION

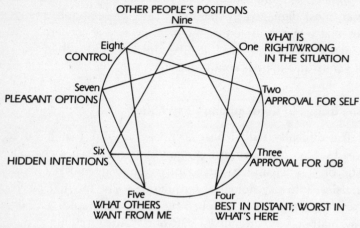

From the Work of Helen Palmer

always inspiring to hear people describe their reasons for seeking higher consciousness and to listen to the stories of how they have gone forward in their search for something that is beyond the personal self.

The system was being developed as an esoteric psychological tool. My own interests were in the areas of spiritual practice and intuition training, rather than psychology, but I wanted to see if people of the same type were attracted to similar meditation practices, and I wanted to uncover typical practice problems that each type was likely to encounter. My moment of truth came on Five night (the Observer). Naranjo was interviewing a group of Fives about their early family life, and one highly contracted Observer type, who sat for the entire night perched high up on the arm of a sofa, watching the action from a safe distance, said something like, "I knew what my family wanted to get from me before they knew it themselves."

I remember feeling suddenly relieved and grateful. The Five's casual remark had fallen on an awareness that had been developing in me for a long time, and his physical presence, coupled with what he said, was the trigger that drew me to the Enneagram. I knew immediately that he was intuitive in that one area, that his sensitivity had developed as a part of his childhood survival strategy, that he was probably astute enough to describe how he altered his perceptions to "know other people's expectations," and that if he could clarify to himself what he was already doing in that one small, defensive area of his life, he would have a good chance of gaining voluntary access to an intuitive state of mind.

There were others in that original class who would eventually contribute to the Enneagram system in very different ways. One of my good friends, Bob Ochs, a Jesuit priest and Enneagram enthusiast, wrote out some thoughts about the different points and the ways in which they related to Catholic thought. Those few pages of Ochs's took off in the Jesuit community in an extraordinary way. The religious communities that live and work together, often under taxing conditions, have taken the system to heart, precisely because they must understand the inner point of view of the people with whom they live and work. Another original student of Naranjo's, Dr. Kathleen Speeth, has added her capable psychological understanding to the system and kept the material alive during a period of Naranjo's illness and semiretirement.

I began to interview panels of my own students in 1976 as part of a larger program in intuition training. What started out as a group of forty in my living room has, over time, expanded to several thousand people who have recognized their types by seeing and hearing panelists talk about their lives. The statements that are excerpted in this book are taken from the tapes of those classes. I was immediately drawn to developing a line of questioning that would highlight intuitive and essential experiences; and the material on attention and intuitive style that appears in this book is my own contribution to the Enneagram's continuing transmission. I have made it a policy to verify an issue by presenting it to panels over and over again before including it within the characteristics of a type.

Ichazo has continued to develop his insights into the system through the Arica Institute. He is the major modern source for the material and continues the task of exploring the Enneagram as a model of the transformation of human consciousness.

Focal Points of Attention

1. Evaluates what is correct or incorrect in the situation.
2. Desires approving attention from other people.
3. Wants positive attention relative to tasks and performance.
4. Awareness shifts relative to the availability or unavailability of objects and other people. Selective focus on the best in the absent and the worst of the present.
5. Wishes to maintain privacy. Sensitive to others' expectations.
6. Scans environment for clues that indicate the hidden intentions of others.

THE ENNEAGRAM OF DEFENSE MECHANISMS,
OR GURDJIEFF'S BUFFERS

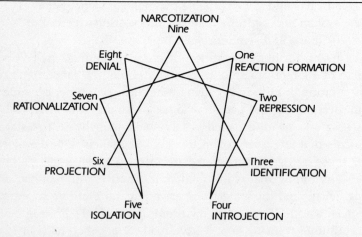

NARCOTIZATION
Nine

Eight
DENIAL

One
REACTION FORMATION

Seven
RATIONALIZATION

Two
REPRESSION

Six
PROJECTION

Three
IDENTIFICATION

Five
ISOLATION

Four
INTROJECTION

From the Work of Claudio Naranjo.

7. Attention shifts to pleasant mental associations and optimistic future plans.
8. Looks for any indication of potential loss of control.
9. Attempts to determine other people's agendas and points of view.

The concept that we possess three kinds of intelligence—mental, emotional, and belly-based—also suggests that there are actually three different forms of intuitive connection—through the mind, through the feelings, and through a gut-based intelligence that is centered in the physical body. The top of the Enneagram, points Eight, Nine, and One, tend to be naturally belly-based. They most easily receive intuitive impressions through the physical body. The feeling types are at the right-hand side of the diagram, Two, Three, and Four, and they receive impressions largely through emotional reactions. The mental types are clustered at the left, Five, Six, and Seven, and they perceive intuitive impressions primarily in a mental way.

It is important to remember that we can develop a range of intuitive abilities and that we are not limited to the particular way in which our type characteristically perceives intuitive information. But because each type does focus on a particular dimension of the 360-degree total reality, the types are likely to have developed a way of paying attention that is appropriate to their own concerns. The Nine cluster tends to perceive through the physical body, as if in answer to the inner question What is my position relative to the environment? The feeling-centered Three cluster tends to perceive through the emotional body, as if in answer to Who am I with? and the head-centered Six cluster tends to perceive mental impressions as if in answer to the question What is this situation about? Thus people of each cluster tend to habitually place attention in either the head, heart, or belly centers, and although those of each type can learn the placement of attention that those of other types use, it is more likely that they will recognize the intuitive style that is particular to their own.

THE ENNEAGRAM OF INTUITIVE STYLE

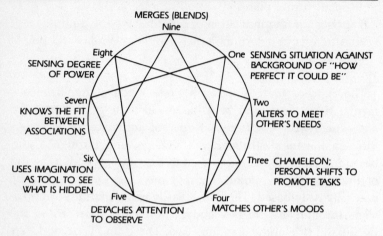

From the Work of Helen Palmer

Each of the intuitive styles is based on specific shifts of attention that operate automatically as part of a type's ordinary perceptions. When brought under close self-observation, these same shifts appear to resemble the underpinning of basic meditation practices that train our ability to detach and attach (focus) attention in specific ways.

Body-based Intuition: Points One–Nine–Eight

One—Sensing the possibility of perfection in ordinary events. What is incorrect stands out because it is sensed as a foreground error that mars the ongoing perception of "how perfect things could be."

Nine—Taking others within oneself. Like a mirror that absorbs the impression of whoever stands before it, reflecting a replica back to the beholder. At the time of connection the Nine feels merged with the other's point of view. See "Points Two and Nine Look Alike," which follows.

Eight—Sense of physically enlarging oneself "to fill the space." Sensing the qualities of presence and power in people and in situations. With training, can sense a large range of qualities.

Feeling-based Intuition: Points Two–Three—Four

Two—Empathically altering to meet the needs of others. The feeling of becoming what other people want. Emotions alter before the mind can intervene. See "Points Two and Nine Look Alike," which follows.

Three—Chameleonlike shift of persona and personal presentation to embody the qualities necessary to get the job done. Focus of attention is on the task, or on the reaction of others to the task. Persona can shift automatically and appropriately before the Three has mentally decided what to do.

Four—Matching the emotions of others. Taking on their pain. Emotional resonance. Fours say that they can tap into the emotional state of absent family, lovers, and friends.

Mentally Based Intuition: Points Five–Six—Seven

Five—Detaching attention from thoughts and feelings in order to impartially observe. Mentally witnessing without interference from personal thoughts and feelings.

Six—Seeing the unspoken intentions that lie beneath a surface facade. Using the imagination as a tool for unmasking hidden points of view.

Seven—Knowing the fit between remote associations. A problem goes on the back burner of the mind while other activities continue. Something in a secondary task sparks an association that solves the original problem.

Points Two and Nine Look Alike

Both Two and Nine will say "I merge" when describing their intuitive connection with other people. Twos first alter emotionally, and then merge that emotional aspect while other aspects fade into the background; at the time of merger a Two can feel completely caught up in the excitement of being what others want. It is somewhat related to the phenomenon of multiple personality: a Two's many aspects may each feel quite genuine, but do not exist at the same point in time.

Nines do not alter their self-presentation. They take on the worldview of others as a whole, rather than altering into becoming what is desirable to others. Nor do Nines say that they shift between multiple aspects of character. When Nines merge they say that they cease to exist to themselves and, having forgotten their own position, they merge with the feelings and the point of view of other people, which are felt more strongly than their own.

Focus of Attention in Relationship

One of the great advantages of knowing your type, and the types of those who are close to you, is that you can see at what points on the diagram you and another are likely to meet and the points at which you will have to work to understand each other. In general, if two people are of the same type, there is a good chance that they will collude in their point of view. I have, for example, seen several double-One couples (Perfectionist), who tend to collude in their notions of the perfect way of life in matters of taste and correctness. They also tend to get annoyed at the constant reflection of their own internal criticality.

In a *folie a deux* relationship, the worldview of a type is confirmed by the type's partner. A double-Three couple (Performer) would agree that life is a series of challenging projects, and a double-Four partnership would agree that life centers on intensity of feeling and fear of abandonment.

When you and your partner meet at a point, there is a natural understanding about the issues that belong to that point. When you shift to a position on the Enneagram that your partner is not naturally inclined to understand, however, you may find that you tend to misread each other's intentions. For example: a Six–Eight couple will meet at Seven, Five, and Nine. They will not meet when the Six moves to stress at Three, or the Eight moves to security at Two (Two and Three are adjacent to each other, but they are not schematic wings). We could hazard some predictions based on the issues that pertain to these points.

Meet at Seven

Pleasant gossiping about the day, sharing of positive future plans, trips, gatherings of friends, things to do. Planning mutual projects. Supportive of each other's goals. Sexually playful, not uptight.

Meet at Five

Hiding out in the home; either together in the same room, reading, or wanting a private place to which to withdraw. Nice to have the partner around, but not too close. Probably not sexual in this position (wing of Six as minor aspect, stress of Eight). The Eight wants privacy in stress, and it is to be hoped that the Six has enough sense to not project that the partner's withdrawal means that the relationship is finished. Eight will come out when she or he wants to.

Meet at Nine

Actively merged. Six will have put performance anxiety aside, but may be caught up in trivia and loose ends (the low side of Nine). Puttering around the home, watching the soup pot, doing chores. Lust (wing of Eight and security for Six). If Six can be sexual without becoming afraid and shutting down, Eight will match Six all the way. Possibility for Six to feel relaxed enough to sense real feelings of love. Paradoxically, for Six, the realization that the partner matters a lot can lead to anger. Anger will probably be expressed first through a projection that the mate is up to something. If the Six moves to the high side of the security point, she or he will allow herself or himself to be affected by love for the Eight.

Eight moves to Two, its security point

Eight's behavior changes from heavy control to expansiveness. A kind of giddy generosity and the desire for lots of the good things in life. All is forgiven. Eight wants to be taken care of, rather than be in control. Little gestures matter a lot. Eights are body-based sensualists, so good food, entertainment, toasts, and flattering camaraderie are appreciated at Two. If the Six is wise, she or he will join the party.

Six moves to its stress point at Three

In this position Six is probably focused enough on a task to be wobbling in and out of the paranoia zone. When identified with a task, Six's attention vacillates between excitement and a paranoid frenzy concerning the success or failure of the project. If Eight tries to assume control or pressure Six into action, or launch into a lecture about Six's problems in taking action, Six may cut and run from both the project and the Eight.

Eight, however, can support the partner by taking charge of certain mechanics of the project about which Six may procrastinate and delay. If the project stays in motion, then what seemed like insurmountable obstacles to the frightened Six are seen in their proper perspective, and Eight is the heroine or hero of the day. Eight will have to be respectful of the difference between a heavy-handed takeover and appropriate support. Six will have to tread a fine line between caving in and delegating responsibility.

The Enneagram of Diagnostic Categories

The following Enneagram is an array of major diagnostic categories that appear in the *Diagnostic and Statistical Manual III, Revised*. The DSM IIIR is used nationally in the United States for health insurance purposes. A summary of research findings that support this placement of the types is included in the Appendix.

Only the most careful research will allow the Enneagram to take its proper place in the psychological thinking of the West. I have, for example, seen several "matches" of the system with current tests and measures claimed without any basis whatsoever in either research findings or in the phenomenological approach of questioning panels of types. These so-called matches look promising and appealing, but they do the Enneagram no service, because they are not grounded in research findings. A summary of on-going work toward formulating an empirical framework for the Enneagram, and in developing a paper-and-pencil assessment inventory, is described in the Appendix.

Based on Naranjo's insight into the major defense mechanisms and the many stories that I have heard on panels over the years, the Enneagram that follows is the array that fits most closely with current psychological understanding. One test of this array lies in the fact that it is self-verifying. This means that good self-observers should be able to place themselves from a description of the issues of their type and respond correctly with regard to their change in behavior when they move to stress point and security point.

The DSM categories describe severe pathologies. From the point of view of attention practice, this means that the ability to stand back and observe has been lost. Without the ability to shift attention to the neutral vantage point of the internal observer, our traits become "what I am" rather than "what I do." In pathology, attention becomes immersed in the thoughts and feelings that are characteristic of our type, and we are unable to adopt another point of view.

The inner lines of the diagram position the types in relationship to one another in ways that are just now surfacing in the psychological literature. For example, the inner triangle alone indicates some fascinating correlations. It suggests that obsessive compulsive (Nine), paranoid (Six), and workaholic (Three) tendencies coexist within the same individual and predicts the particular life situations (normal, stressed, or secure) in which each behavior is likely to occur.

THE ENNEAGRAM OF PATHOLOGY

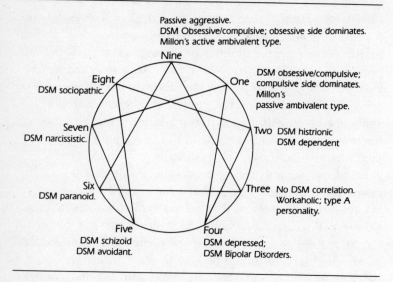

Passive aggressive.
DSM Obsessive/compulsive; obsessive side dominates.
Millon's active ambivalent type.

Nine

Eight
DSM sociopathic.

One DSM obsessive/compulsive;
compulsive side dominates.
Millon's
passive ambivalent type.

Seven
DSM narcissistic.

Two DSM histrionic
DSM dependent

Six
DSM paranoid.

Three No DSM correlation.
Workaholic; type A
personality.

Five
DSM schizoid
DSM avoidant.

Four
DSM depressed;
DSM Bipolar Disorders.

Diagnostic Clarifications

Body-centered Types: Core of Nine, Wings of Eight and One

Point Nine

DSM obsessive compulsive; obsessive side dominates. Millon's active ambivalent type. Ambivalence in decision making, caught between the desire to rebel and the desire to obey. In Enneagram terms, Nine is caught between being good (One) and being disobedient (Eight).

Nine tends to stay in the conflict rather than taking a position that will create change. The internal question is more "Do I want to be here?," rather than a One's preoccupation about Am I doing the right thing?" An uncommitted stance. The defense against having to act on the obedience/defiance issue is to spread attention to inessential and secondary tasks. Narcotization and spacing out as major defenses. Ambivalence may be actively stated, but anger is passively and indirectly expressed.

Some Nines report passive aggressive traits. These are the more stubborn, complaining individuals who, in Enneagram terminology, lean to the Eight (actively defiant) wing. The paradox for the passive aggressive Nines is that although they share the same ambivalence about personal position as the more obsessively inclined Nines, they will not go along with others' agendas. Here the stance is to merge with the wishes of others and appear to go along, but with the addition of a lot of blaming, footdragging, and other oppositional tendencies.

Point One

The compulsive side of the DSM obsessive/compulsive stance. Can be internally as ambivalent as a Nine, but this is not expressed. Millon's passive ambivalent type. Polarized to the "good" side of the obedience/defiance conflict. Reaction formation prevents anger and real wishes from surfacing into awareness. Rigid adherence to codes of right and wrong. Compulsion to do the right thing. There is one right way.

Point Eight

DSM sociopathic type. My way is the right way.

Feeling-centered types: Core of Three, Wings of Two and Four

Point Three

No corresponding DSM category. Recently recognized type in Western psychological thought. Feelings are suspended in the interest of doing. Attention is on task, not on self. Although Threes report some narcissistic traits, such as believing in their own superiority in areas of achievement and merit, this merit is earned by hard work, rather than assumed as an automatic entitlement. Threes sacrifice themselves to maintain a winning image, rather than adopting the more narcissistic stance of substituting ideas about future success for hard work in the present.

Points Three and Seven Look Alike

Both are high-energy extroverts. Both are optimistic, self-promotional, and want approval. Both project the image of a winner. Threes, however, will work until they drop, and Sevens will work only as long as the project stays interesting. Threes want to get into power over others, to be recognized leaders, to make a commitment to do the best, most responsible job. They are conformists, they look to others for approval, and they work hard for an immediate return.

Sevens want a taste of everything good. Want adventure more than power. They need not conform for approval, because they see themselves as above social conventions. They are exempt from responsibility, look to themselves for approval, and are entranced with a positive vision of the future, rather than working for immediate goals.

Point Two

DSM histrionic and dependent types. Both need constant affirmation and approval. Sense of self is contained within a partner relationship. Both adapt to other's needs as an assurance of love. "I become what my lover wants." Dependent type adapts by docile compliance, usually clinging to a single relationship. Histrionic type takes aggressive and manipulative posture to achieve control of the mate.

Point Four

DSM depression and bipolar functioning. In Enneagram language, an agitated presentation can occur at the stress of Two (histrionic depressive), or from leaning toward the wing of Three into overdrive activity to fight depression.

Mentally Centered Types: Core of Six, Wings of Five and Seven

Point Six

DSM paranoid.

Point Five

DSM schizoid and avoidant types. Panelists of each type report the same presenting traits centering on social detachment. Some say that they are self-sufficient and not concerned about closer personal contact with others (schizoid, passively detached), and others report feelings of frustration at social isolation (avoidant, actively detached).

Point Seven

DSM Narcissist. Entitlement based on sense of superior endowment. Entitlement is assumed rather than earned. See the preceding "Points Three and Seven Look Alike." Attention is projected into an imaginative and optimistic future that forestalls the need for immediate commitment or work. "Above all I must be true to myself."

II. THE NINE POINTS OF THE ENNEAGRAM

5. Introduction to the Points

The best way to understand how the types interact with one another is to first read the three core points of the inner triangle Six–Three–Nine and then proceed along the variations of the core points in the sequence One–Four–Two–Eight–Five–Seven. In classes we seat the panels in that order of presentation, because by following the lines the viewer can more easily see the ways in which each type changes when it moves toward action/ stress. I have placed the chapters in numerical order One through Nine simply for ease of reference.

Each chapter begins with a statement of the psychological dilemma, a typical family history and a discussion of the basic issues that preoccupy the type. I have also included a précis of how the type tends to behave in intimate relationships and with authorities.

The sections on the way in which each type pays attention and the intuitive styles that are common within each of the types are of particular interest to me. Attention practices seem to me to be a bridge between intellect and intuition and a powerful way in which we in the West can begin to regain a connection with what sacred tradition describes as the qualities of essence. I have interviewed many individuals who have had either intuitive or essential experiences and have relied upon my own intuition as a tool with which to penetrate into the workings of this intimate area of the human psyche. I see the small sections on attention and intuition that are included in this book as preliminary work toward a fuller understanding of these attributes of our nature.

Although each type does have a particular predisposition toward an intuitive capacity, it is important to remember that every one of us has the opportunity to embody all of the intuitive styles. You might find, for example, that you have resorted to the style that is most common to your own security point, or to the style that is typical of people who identify with your point of action (stress). Each of us is unique in the way that we have learned to cope with our lives, but by examining the way in which we pay attention and by cultivating the inner observer, we can recognize that we are often in touch with intuitive information that influences our decisions and our relationships in unrecognized ways.

The more evolved aspects of each type are described in a section on the higher mental ability and the emotional Virtue. The difficulty with describing aspects of essential human nature is that they can easily be confused with ideas about what it would be like to embody such attributes, as if essence were merely an extension of the personal self. The actuality is that essential qualities become available when we are in an altered state of awareness that is not directed by the thinking/feeling self. These qualities have little to do with our ordinary consciousness and, unfortunately, they can be easily trivialized into a concept of how evolved people would be likely to behave.

The first step toward actually embodying an essential quality is to cultivate the inner observer; second, to master many levels of meditation, movement, and energy practices; and third, to integrate the essential qualities into a mature personality.

I have also included material on what helps those of each type to thrive, special issues to be aware of, and the subtype variations for each type.

All of this material has been developed during class hours over the past twelve years of interviewing panels, so the book is really a synthesis of the stories of thousands of students who have participated in the work.

Each Chapter Includes

Précis of the dilemma
Typical family history

The type's major issues
Intimate relating patterns
An example of a couple relationship between two types
The type's relationship to authority
An example of an authority interaction between two types
Attention style
Intuitive style
Attractive environments for the type
Unattractive environments for the type
Famous representatives of the type
The higher quality of mind
The virtue
Assets
The subtypes
What helps a type thrive
What a type should be aware of

6. Point One: The Perfectionist

	ACQUIRED PERSONALITY		ESSENCE	
HEAD	Chief Feature:	RESENTMENT	Higher Mind:	PERFECTION
HEART	Passion:	ANGER	Virtue:	SERENITY
	SUBTYPE WAYS OF BEING			
	Sexual:	JEALOUS		
	Social:	NONADAPTABLE		
	Self-preservation:	ANXIOUS (WORRIED)		

The Dilemma

Ones were good little girls and boys. They learned to behave properly, to take on responsibility, and, most of all, to be correct in the eyes of others. They remember being painfully criticized, and as a result they learned to monitor themselves severely in order to avoid making mistakes that would come to other people's attention. They quite naturally assume that everyone shares their desire for self-betterment and are often disappointed by what they see as a lapse of moral character in others.

The Perfectionist outlook is encapsulated in the image of our Puritan ancestors. They were hard working, righteous, fiercely independent, and convinced that plain thinking and goodness would prevail over the shadow side of human nature. Ones are convinced that life is hard and ease must be earned, that virtue is its own reward, and that pleasure should be postponed until everything else gets done.

Perfectionists are usually not aware that they deny themselves pleasure. They are so preoccupied with what they "should" do and "what must be done" that they rarely ask themselves what they want to get out of life. Their natural wishes were forbidden when they were young, and so they learned to block out their desires by focusing attention on the correct thing to do.

There is always room for improvement, and severely compulsive Ones can spend much of their relaxation time working to make themselves better people. Sitting on the bus going to work means practicing a set of posture exercises, eating lunch means ten chews per bite, and free time means doing something constructive and educational.

Ones say that they live with the kind of severe internal critic that most of us would experience only if we had committed a serious crime. They commonly experience a judging voice as part of their own thinking, and although they know that the voice originates within themselves, it can be as invasive as if it had an external source. The internal critic most commonly judges whatever a One is thinking or doing. For example, if a One is giving a lecture, the internal critic might offer a running commentary on the performance. "You could have given that opinion more precisely, your voice is nasal, stick to the point." The childhood fear of criticism has caused Ones to develop an internal surveillance system that automatically monitors thought, word, and deed.

Ones associate their exacting inner critic with a part of themselves that is higher, or better than, their ordinary thoughts, and even though they realize that the inner critic originates within their own thinking, there is a tendency to listen to the righteous internal commentary as if it had its origin in some higher plane of existence.

Ones often say that their own thoughts judge them for being angry or feeling sexual, and that when their inner voice becomes severely critical, they develop a deep resentment toward those who appear to be breaking the rules without any evidence of remorse. To the extent that Perfectionists try to measure up to the pressure of the internal critic's demands for excellence, they will feel driven to be good while internally judging those who disobey the rules.

The internal critic is so integrated into the way that Perfectionists think that they can only assume that everyone else also lives with a stream of judging thoughts. When others opt for pleasure over correctness, a One can only believe that they are deliberately cheating.

A Perfectionist's attention is so focused on the question of what should be done or what must be done that there is no mental space left for their own real wishes to emerge into awareness. They are therefore resentful, a word that describes a chronic feeling of irritation. Resentment could be defined as the degree of difference between forgotten real desires and the compulsion to work hard in order to satisfy the mental critic's demands.

There is a sense of correctness about deferring pleasure. Relaxation and fun will be considered after life is set straight and obligations fully settled. Time is scheduled and blocked out with all the necessary ingredients for a perfectly balanced life: the music hour, the exercise period, the visit to a sick friend, the block of study time. Time is controlled by the slots of an appointment book, a cell-block schedule of excellent shoulds that effectively eliminates free time when real needs could emerge. A young Perfectionist described her desire to go to art school as

wanting it so badly that I got stuck on the preliminaries for two years. Every step of the decision had to be so perfect that I couldn't get myself enrolled. First I had to square my desire to paint with my political beliefs, because from a political standpoint I saw my own expressionist leanings as socially self-indulgent. Then I had to measure my love of nature and the outdoors against the choice of art as a sedentary occupation, and review my spiritual convictions, which made me lean toward focusing on particular artistic themes. My entire world picture had to be reformed before I could fill out the admissions packet.

The art student had to account to her inner critic before she could focus on her excitement, her expectations, and the fact that painting gave her pleasure. In our Puritan past, dancing and games were forbidden because they were opportunities for pleasure and passion to rise past the censorship of the inner critic.

The Perfectionist worldview stems from an assumption that there is one ultimately correct solution for every situation. Ones are dedicated to the one right way as a statement of character, regardless of how attractive other ways might be. The notion that there can be multiple right ways, or that what is right for one person may be an incorrect approach for another, feels like opening the door to chaos. If people were allowed to do as they pleased, what would prevent evil from destroying all that was good?

A One's judgments usually center upon anger and sexuality, because those impulses were punished in childhood. They do not usually know when they are angry. Even with a noticeable tightening of the jaw and a pursing of the lips, as if to hold critical words in check, they do not perceive that they are annoyed, because their perception of a "bad" emotion is blocked out of awareness. A red-faced and actively critical One can be unaware that his or her anger is radiating throughout a discussion and may leave the interaction believing only that a few important points were made.

Because anger is seen as a bad emotion, Ones cannot acknowledge their own resentment until they are absolutely certain that they are in the right. When Perfectionists are sure of a position, however, great waves of physical energy become available. The mental critic recedes when a One is assured about being right, and the ventilation of withheld anger feels liberating. With mature Ones, this energy can be used for highly constructive purposes. They are often in the forefront of humanitarian causes, which they serve selflessly in the same way that others work for salary or personal fame. With immature Ones, the same attraction to a worthy cause serves the purpose of creating a righteous platform from which others can be denounced for wrongdoing.

A One lives in a divided house. A critic lives in the upper story, and this critic is largely unaware of the tides of feeling that periodically flood the cellars of the house. If the tide of passion rises sharply, a One is likely to leak off unacceptable feelings by focusing on someone else's wrongdoing, or by getting drunk or drugged enough to put the internal critic to sleep. Binge drinking, episodal rages, or periods of intense sexual activity are ways in which a One can release the pressure that periodically builds from unacknowledged needs.

The image of the divided house also applies to Perfectionists who develop a "trapdoor" relationship between the mental critic and the flood of feelings that get trapped in the basement of the unconscious. Trapdoor Ones are people who develop a double-life solution to the problem of living in a divided house. They develop two distinct temperaments, one for "where I'm known" and one for "far away." They are responsible and well respected where they are known, but become more relaxed and sexy in an environment away from family and friends. The trapdoor solution can be acted out in as innocent a way as going on a vacation to a place where there is anonymity and no responsibility, or it can be acted out in bizarre combinations, such as librarian/prostitute or missionary/thief.

Another way to relieve the tension of living in a divided house is through forgiveness. If error can be admitted, then the internal critic recedes, and Ones are able to see their own small sins in a more forgiving light. The pivotal point in forgiveness is the admission of error without the attached humiliation and punishment that Ones are conditioned to expect. They are the most patient and constructive people on the Enneagram when it comes to mending a mistake once they can admit that a mistake has been made. They are also able to experience the pleasure of a job well done with a gratitude that soars in their bodies like a flight of angels. The sense of perfection can be stimulated by simple things: a clean house, a well-constructed sentence, or a moment in a conversation when everything is perfectly in place.

The preoccupations of Point One include

- Internal standards of correctness that can become puritanically demanding. Stream of self-criticizing thoughts.
- A compulsive need to act on what seems to be correct.
- Doing the right thing.
- A belief in their own ethical and moral superiority. The better people. The top 10 percent, who do things right.
- Difficulty in recognizing real needs that do not conform to standards of correctness.
- Mentally comparing oneself to others, "Am I better or worse than they are?" Concern about criticism from others, "Are they judging me?"
- Procrastination in decision making, stemming from the fear of making a mistake.
- Do-gooder. Displacement of the anger generated by unmet needs toward what appear to be legitimate outside targets.
- The emergence of two selves: the worried self, who lives at home, and the playful self, who comes out away from home.
- A way of paying attention that is based on correcting error, which can lead to
    - Superb powers of criticism, and
    - A background awareness of the potential for perfection in any given situation, against which, by comparison, error stands out as the foreground perception. "Think how perfect it could be."

Family History

Ones commonly report that they were heavily criticized or punished when they were young and that they eventually became obsessed with trying to be good as a way of staying out of trouble. This seems to be a family situation that produces obedient children, but which forces the children to control their behavior by internalizing the parents' critical voice.

Many were expected to take on adult responsibility prematurely and often became like parents themselves in order to stabilize immature adults in the family.

My father wanted to be a writer, but had a family instead, and essentially hated his life. I felt that he took it out on us, because he hadn't followed his own dream, and felt trapped by what he had settled for. Our mother was ill a great deal of the time, and I was expected to care for the younger children. It was an uptight household, with everyone walking on tiptoes so as not to irritate the parents, and always feeling like you had too much to do.

I remember one summer, I was assigned to wash walls for the whole house and found myself staring out the window at the kids playing, with the shredded living room drape in my hand. I had been so furious at having to take care of everybody that I had ripped a heavy drape off the hooks without ever realizing how much anger I was carrying inside.

The atmosphere was one of high expectation without rewards. Virtue was supposed to be its own reward, and so Perfectionists were scolded for wrongdoing, without being made special for the sacrifice of being good. Being a perfect person requires a great deal of self-deprivation and demands tight internal control. Eventually the pleasure of rewards can be submerged in favor of the pleasure of self-control. This highly successful but chronically anxious accountant describes the way in which he controls his own pleasure.

All through school I would get myself motivated to study by promising myself that if I worked faithfully for the week that I'd go shoot baskets on Saturday morning. So Saturday would come, and I would have finished everything, but instead of going to play, I'd think, Okay, I got the job done, and that was the purpose of promising myself, so instead I'll trade off basketball for two chores that I've been avoiding. If I do the chores I get to go, otherwise I don't. I made myself earn my fun and often wouldn't give in to myself even if I'd earned it.

When Ones deprive themselves, a critical level of pressure develops that causes them to ventilate their resentment in such a way that their own anger still remains hidden from themselves. This architect describes the way in which he released his pent-up aggression.

I was a good boy at home and could find no real reason for my anger at my parents or at school. I had a retarded brother, who embarrassed me, but whom I tried to protect, and my mother was also thought to be fragile and did eventually have a breakdown. The truth was that I was big, healthy, and made to feel guilty about any fun that I allowed myself.

My anger came out in vandalism, but I never knew that I was angry. The feeling would just start to build in me that I wanted to wreck something, and I'd eventually start imagining myself smashing windows and would wind up going after some abandoned building late at night with a sledgehammer. It felt absolutely wonderful.

A Passion for Righteous Anger

Many Ones are unaware that they are angry. Their minds may be needle sharp with judging thoughts, which broadcast through tense body language and the fact that the Ones are busy correcting everyone else's behavior, yet unless they get to the breaking point, Ones may believe themselves to be "feeling energetic," or "having a small peeve," or "getting a lot done today."

There is a great attraction to expressing anger through the vehicle of a righteous cause. Anger can be expressed without self-recrimination for harboring bad feelings if the point of view is correct. It is for this reason that Ones are attracted to purist points of view, which provide a safe launching pad for righteous anger in the name of a worthy cause.

The fact is that it feels dreadful to force yourself to be good while others remain oblivious to your sacrifice and efforts. It feels unfair to Ones that there are few rewards in life that are given for honesty and effort. Because their own desires were punished in childhood, Ones are out of touch with what they really want, but are acutely sensitive to what they believe should be done. Ones can therefore become very angry at people who bend the rules, but they will not speak out unless they feel completely convinced that they are in the right. This kind of unacknowledged anger will be held internally, so that when a legitimate grievance finally appears, it will draw out a great deal of pent-up fury. This apparently mild-mannered beautician reports her traffic peeve.

Traffic is an incredible annoyance to me. If everybody would just obey the rules, I could live with it, but there have been times when I've become so incensed that I have taken action. My feeling is that we're all stuck in traffic and if one person takes advantage of the situation, then we all have to suffer for it. My breaking point is when a driver sidles along the line on the exit ramp, wanting to be let through before it's his or her turn. My response is to break out of line myself and publicly crowd the car off onto the shoulder.

Trapdoor Release

The anger and pain of Perfectionists stem from the fact that personal needs are not being met. Authentic wishes have been repressed and replaced with a list of shoulds. The resulting deprivation causes a chronic irritation that constantly reheats just under the surface of polite behavior. Ones are particularly annoyed by those who act out the shadow side of human nature, because those are desires that Ones cannot admit as existing within themselves.

Remember that Ones live in a divided house. Their attention is dominated by a mental critic that blocks awareness of unacceptable feelings. If a One's real wishes threaten to flood up from the unconscious, the critic will become punitive in an attempt to block out the rising tide of reaction. Any small mistake suddenly takes on overwhelming importance. Attention is obsessively attracted to error that needs to be set straight. "You must do this, he should do that." Every beautiful face is blemished, every room has a corner full of dustballs, and every beautiful sunset misses the mark.

Occasionally Ones find a way to equalize the pressure between their own needs and the mental critic by living two lives. There will be a proper public life, in which the One follows rules and procedures, and a private life in which forbidden fantasies are acted out.

When I was a kid in New York City, I used to like to go to the different neighborhoods and see if I could pass myself off as Italian, or Yiddish, or—in Greenwich Village—as an artist. I liked being somebody else, because I didn't worry about what people thought of me and could afford to say things that I wouldn't have let myself even think at home.

The first time I went to Europe was pure liberation. Nobody knew me, my parents were far away, the buildings were little stone palaces, and the currency looked like Monopoly money.

While I was traveling I started to play at being different characters in the same way that I had back in New York. I'd get on the train without a destination and let one of my characters take hold of me until I felt like I was ready to play. Then I'd get off at a town and spend days being someone else. The strongest identities were a jet-setter and a whore. As the jet-setter I had a great time meeting people, speaking three languages and talking about all the places I had seen. As the whore I cruised for money, wore stiletto heels and the sleaziest clothes I could find. The turn-on was in being invisible, in being right out there sitting at the bar, letting the whore take hold of me without anybody knowing my name.

Perfectionism

Ones say that it is very painful to be criticized by others, because they are already burdened by self-judgment. It is almost equally hard for Ones to give out compliments, because it makes them feel smaller by comparison. The preoccupation with correctness developed during a time when the child felt obliged to conform to adult standards of behavior and comes out in a concern for appropriate dress and conversation, an attention to details, an inquiry that researches an issue down to its basic elements, and a tendency to find fault in what others would accept as a job well done. From a One's point of view, compliments are earned through intense self-scrutiny and the perfect execution of every step toward every goal.

I put myself through college as a housepainter. The day was completely blocked out into slots for what was necessary. There was always me pressuring myself to get it all done, and all done right. I couldn't leave before the day's work was perfectly done. At the same time that I was redoing a wall for the third time, I was hating a mistake on the ceiling of another room, and the mistake of not being at home in time for the family, and the fact that I was losing study time. Everything seemed necessary. If the wall got done right, the lost family time and the study slot stuck out by comparison.

How can Ones find themselves right when their own minds measure their best effort against unattainable standards of perfection? The young housepainter compares a job well done to all the jobs that he had to leave out. Even if he had managed to finish them all, and perfectly, he probably would have demanded more of himself.

Ones will occasionally report that the internal critic has become so established in their thinking process that they monitor their own thoughts for unacceptable content and error.

For a couple of years I had a relationship with a woman who wanted to become a Christian Science practitioner. The system had a peculiar appeal for me. I thought that I had found a way to spiritualize our love by controlling the content of my thinking. I was driven to think purely and got heavily involved in watching my thoughts for hidden motivations. It got to be like a teacher giving out gold stars—"That's a good thought, that's a bad thought." I couldn't make a move until I examined the thoughts, and the motives behind the thoughts. All of my reactions to the woman had to be honorable and had to occur at the correct time and place, and all the while that I was relating to her I'd be monitoring my thoughts to keep my intentions pure.

A preoccupation with goodness implies an obsession with avoiding badness. The young suitor's habit of replacing his thoughts with "better" thoughts effectively blocked out any opportunity for him to discover what he really wanted from his relationship. In trying to find a correct approach to relating, he did not allow himself enough mental space for his real feelings to emerge.

One Right Way

Allowing real wishes to come into awareness can be frightening to those whose childhood security depended upon rigid self-control. Perfectionism rests on the assumption that there has to be one correct solution for any given situation, and that once the one right way is discovered, then people with other opinions will naturally see the light of reason and want to agree. It is shocking for Ones to realize that others do not subscribe to the one-right-way approach to life, because to a Perfectionist the idea of multiple correct approaches looks like an invitation to anarchy. It is a fundamental insight when a One realizes that people manage to behave in a reasonably moral way without having their behavior supervised by an internal critic; and that opening the trapdoor to emotional and sexual feelings does not necessarily mean that people become obsessed with desire or depraved through overindulgence.

For years I held my criticality back for fear of alienating someone who was important to me. It felt completely unconstructive to be pointing out the errors in everybody's ways; and I wanted to protect them from the kind of criticism that I gave myself. It finally dawned on me that there was no such thing as an absolute right or wrong that applied to everyone. Once I got the idea of relative right, I could see how everyone was struggling to do the best that they could based on their separate views of the situation; and it relieved a lot my judgment against them.

Once I could describe the situation from another person's point of view, I could be as critical as I liked, because people realized that I could see things from their side and that what I had to say was critical but was also constructive.

Procrastination and Worry

The conflict between unrecognized desires and the need to be correct comes into sharp focus in decision making. Decisions are a Catch 22 where choosing for correctness can make Ones angry because they don't get what they want, and choosing what they want makes them worry about making a mistake.

A One's anxiety mounts as pleasurable goals become possible. There is concern about being compromised in the eyes of other people, about losing the virtue of the work ethic, and about lowering standards to the level of the riff-raff, which to Ones are people who take what they do not deserve and have not earned. The crosscurrents of worry become most powerful when a One has to take responsibility for acting on a desire that may not be approved of by others.

When anxiety mounts, Ones are vulnerable to hearing implied criticism where none is really present. Innocuous conversations seem laced with negative overtones, and they suffer from the false belief that others are secretly judging them. At those times when Ones are most convinced that they are being looked down upon, it is enormously helpful for them to get a reality check on other people's real opinions.

Intimate Relationships

A Perfectionist's deepest need is to feel loved even though imperfect. Love has been equated with good behavior in the past, which makes Ones feel unlovable if they find imperfection within themselves, and makes it hard for them to believe that a partner could love them as they are, accepting both good and bad aspects of character.

Small sins get blown out of proportion as intimacy deepens. What if I get angry? What if she doesn't like my taste in art? Perfectionists live with an operating assumption that something about their mannerisms or habits is sure to repel the partner. They therefore approach intimacy with a tension that stems from monitoring themselves severely in an attempt to keep the shadow hidden. This inner state of tension is compounded by the belief that pleasure and happiness have to be deserved and earned, and that if badness is revealed, the partner will be driven away.

When the tension level becomes critical, Ones start to feel so vulnerable to rejection that they are likely to start judging the partner in self-defense. Fights will happen, fueled by the conviction that the partner will be driven off eventually, "so why not have it over with now before we get any further involved?" Ones are usually unaware of the intensity of their own anger, of how their unspoken judgment broadcasts to others in nonverbal ways, and of the fact that the intensity with which they deliver criticism is often as hurtful as the bad news itself.

Ones are searching for the perfect relationship, which makes it hard for them to accept that good and bad qualities must coexist within the same person. They want to devote themselves to the excellence that a partner brings to the relationship, and as a consequence, they tend to place the partner on a pedestal, forgive any weaknesses of character, and render themselves unable to see the intermingling of positive and negative traits. Once they have seen the good in someone, Perfectionists can hang in forever with the hope of reforming the other's less-than-desirable side. Perfectionists report that the defensive wall of judging thoughts vanishes for long periods of time when they are in love.

If Ones lose touch with what they want from the relationship, or begin to feel threatened or jealous, an intense criticality about the partner's lapses of character will return. Needing an outlet for pent-up frustrations, Perfectionists will begin to monitor their partner's actions, making angry attempts to pin them down and force them to behave.

On the low side of intimate relationships, if Ones perceive their partner as embarrassing, or clearly breaking a rule of behavior, they will become actively angry and unable to recapture the view of the partner as good. Old grievances will be brought back to life and argued again and again and will remain alive as long as a vent is still needed for the relief of current irritation.

On the high side of intimate relationships, Ones are very responsive to people who are able to admit to their mistakes. A One's mental habit of judging others goes away if error can be admitted, and they are particularly loyal if they are able to sense struggle, effort, and good intentions in their partners.

My biggest concern is about what other people are thinking of me. When I first meet someone, their outstanding qualities really come across to me. I can see them as infinitely witty, or well informed, or gracious or whatever. So long as I like them, then it's fine with me that they look that way. It's when I feel that I have to defend myself, or when I get uncomfortable with how great I've made them in comparison to me, that I start checking out the caps on their teeth in order to even the score.

An Example of a Couple Relationship: The Double-One Relationship, The Perfectionist Couple

Two Ones are often a couple because they collude with each other over the perfect way of life. They love each other's ethics and capacity for work; they are in touch with the difference between mere cleverness and basic human qualities of honesty and effort. The couple can enjoy the satisfactions of living a practical and independent life that centers on respect for physical health, correct livelihood, and the value of earned achievement. Their ability to appreciate these basic qualities of survival gives them a touchstone of stability.

If either partner becomes unsure about real wishes, unrecognized feelings of frustration will start to build. Ones do not easily fathom their own psychological needs, particularly if those needs are not in sync with their own incredibly high standards of ethical behavior. In an intimate relationship this can come out as repressing anger as a bad emotion, being unable to talk about feelings of jealousy, because they are wrong, or simply holding back on talking about things that need to be changed. If these feelings are not dealt with, even self-observant Ones will know that they are mad enough to want to throw dishes—but the actual incident that makes them angry may not come to mind.

An unobservant One may be visibly angry but unaware that remarks have become sharp and accusative. It is enormously helpful if either partner is able to recognize the signs of anger building in the other and can intervene to locate the source of frustration. It is a sign of intimacy if a One accepts another's help in recognizing buried needs. Just listening to a recital of what a One wants, rather than what should be done, is felt as a vote of confidence by those with a childhood history of being punished for giving in to personal needs.

If unrecognized anger is allowed to build, the partners will either withdraw from each other in an uneasy, silent agreement to not open up discussion, or one of the partners is likely to conclude that some longstanding bad habit of the other is to blame, and go after him or her. A One's anger can be frightening, because it is volcanic and is usually out of proportion to the real situation. The anger also reheats just under the surface even after an argument, as if an old grudge never quite goes away with time. The reason for this is that a legitimate grievance provides the necessary release valve for the ventilation of other frustrated needs. Until those needs are met, there will always be a sense of irritation about the sins of the world, and in relationship, there will be a small case building against the other until each partner is assured that he or she will not be abandoned for wanting something that the partner finds objectionable.

The direct expression of anger is a sign of security in the relationship, because anger is seen as a bad emotion and is usually bitten back. Ones say that they feel defeated if they become angry, because it means losing control to a negative emotion. They also say that if the partner will hear out an angry attack, and not withdraw, that they feel loved. Once anger becomes acceptable, other forbidden impulses can come to expression, such as creativity and an appetite for sex. For Perfectionists, the opening of sexual feelings can herald a parallel opening of creative expression. When the prohibition against one forbidden area of emotional life is lifted, the mental critic recedes, and the entire power of the unconscious becomes more available to them.

At the point where anger becomes acceptable, Ones often report that they can observe themselves becoming angry and starting to build a mental case. Because self-aware Ones know that a case often forms because they have neglected their own needs, they are in a position to use their anger as a reminder to trace down and satisfy real wishes. When these are satisfied, the case often recedes to its actual level of significance rather than obsessively dominating their attention.

Authority Relationships

Perfectionists are looking for the ultimately correct authority, and if competent authority were to be found, would happily hand over the decision making to someone else. Their preoccupation with correctness, however, makes them sensitive to errors or unfairness on the part of those in charge. Ones will want authority to establish guidelines, so that they know precisely what is expected, and will feel safer with a clear designation of responsibility. If the leader is perceived to be capable and fair, Ones will take on responsibility. If not, there will be a tendency to play it safe and to shift blame rather than be found wrong. Ones will build trust in an organization through a series of critiques, especially about detail and procedure. These small critical points are intended to shape up the situation and to establish clear areas of responsibility, but will come off as disagreeable detail control. Compliments and full commitment are withheld until the last trace of error has vanished from the scene.

It is vital that the rules not be changed arbitrarily. Ones function by the rule book, and if procedures are changed they may feel that they are being set up for criticism. They must respect the performance level of others in order to function well. They will stand back if they feel compromised or if they have to go first in a risky decision. They will work extremely hard if they feel that others are also going all out, or if they can be inspired by the right cause.

There may be a buildup of unrecognized frustration that will be obvious to fellow workers but not to the One. If good performance is not recognized by someone in charge, then Ones are likely to focus on some legitimate but irrelevant area of error in order to let off steam.

On the high side, Ones have fine organizational abilities and are capable of taking real pleasure in developing their work skills. They can hold a loner's stand against all opposition if they are firmly convinced that their point of view is correct. Once convinced that they are right, Ones become invincible because their internal critic recedes, and they cease to be concerned about making a mistake or what other people think. Firmly established in the one right way, Perfectionists will work tirelessly until the job gets done.

On the low side, Ones are afraid to oppose authority openly because of the fear of retaliation and the possibility of having made an error in judgment. They are predisposed to mistrust authority, but are hoping that those in charge will notice good performance and offer deserved rewards. They will criticize points in a program, but have difficulty proposing a solution because of the risk of error. They are not comfortable in interactions that require a high tolerance for differences of opinion. They prefer a predictable structure and rules.

An Example of an Authority Relationship: One and Five, the Perfectionist and the Observer

If the Five is boss, she or he is likely to supervise from behind closed doors, acting as a decision maker who leaves the follow-through to others. Fives are capable of making high-risk decisions because they do not become emotionally involved, but have difficulty with the meetings and confrontations required to carry out those decisions. Fives value connections with people who can make things work in the world, and the Five will make policy if the One can carry it out.

Both types have a tendency to inner criticality, and this trait can be turned to good advantage in refining an organization. They share an abhorrence of being dominated by unfair hierarchical relationships and will maximize the organization's freedom from unfair control.

If the One is boss, important decisions will tend to get delayed, particularly if the risks are high. Attention will spread to secondary tasks, time will get filled with overly complicated procedures, and tension will mount as deadlines approach. The Five employee will see through any unnecessary complications, feel drained by detail overload, and resist any attempt on the part of the One to supervise or control. Fives are especially shy of those who use anger as a way of trying to move a situation ahead. A crisis can develop if the anxious One pushes forward to gain control of the situation. The One wants rules and progress reports, and the Five will draw inward, say very little, and become as unavailable as possible. Each will attempt to control the situation by setting limits, the Five by minimizing contact and production, the One by tightening controls and assigning blame.

The situation could be greatly eased if the One could relinquish control and ask for help. If put in an advisory role but not pressed for production, a Five will open up. A One could be helped by having an outsider recognize and legitimize unrecognized anxiety buildups. If worry can be acknowledged without the One being made to feel wrong, then anger will disappear, the overly complex nature of procedures will lessen, and priorities will suddenly become clear.

How Ones Pay Attention

Perfectionism is supported by the habit of making mental comparisons. It is a way of paying attention in which thoughts and actions are automatically judged against an ideal standard of how perfect the situation could be. The internal terrain of a One's decision-making process carries the image of a courtroom scene. An opinion is mentally brought into court, where it is then attacked, defended, and finally judged for correctness.

I am sitting in meditation, and become immediately aware of the loudness of the critic in my head. A small space of deep quiet, and I hear, "Not deep enough" or "Was better last time you sat." Then the argument starts: "Sit up straighter." "You're not trying." "Yes I am."

My mind gets caught between attack and defense, as if I have no say in the situation and can only listen to the voices in my head until one side or the other wins out. Each quiet space in the meditation is interrupted by mental comments, until, happily, I can disengage from my thoughts.

Ones also suffer from the habit of comparing their own levels of achievement against each other. Was this meditation productive? Am I improving or am I slipping back? There is a painful need to check out progress in order to feel assured of a continuous march toward self-improvement, which can also produce the feeling of never measuring up to the mark.

In meditation practice this way of paying attention is called judging mind. To some extent we all judge our progress against standards of excellence, but Ones live with an internal measuring rod that also extends to chronically comparing themselves to other people. It is like an internal seesaw in a children's park: one child goes up, the other goes down. She goes up because she makes more money, but she goes down because I have status. I'm up on this point, but I'm down on that point. His face is handsome, but my body's better. The making of mental comparisons by Ones is often an automatic and unrecognized factor in their perception of daily life events and is a major cause of suffering. Ones automatically notice what is right and what is wrong in any given situation, and because they are attached to a one-right-way point of view, another person's win makes the One feel like a loser.

When Ones begin a self-observation practice, they realize, perhaps for the first time, how pervasive the mental habit of making comparisons can be. Because judging mind is clearly a source of suffering, Ones can become highly motivated to learn to meditate so that judging thoughts recede.

Ones can begin to change the Perfectionistic style of attention by noticing when the mental chalkboard goes up. Each time attention shifts into a detailed account of someone else's pluses and minuses, and the feeling that when that person is one up that the Perfectionist is one down, there is an opportunity for learning to shift attention to a neutral ground.

Intuitive Style

The intuition of Perfectionists stems from the characteristic way in which they pay attention. They habitually notice error and what is wrong in any given situation, which implies that they are also aware of a background perception of how perfect that situation could be.

They recognize the perfected possibility in any given situation because judging thoughts vanish and their bodies "feel right." There is a physical sensation of letting go and being bodily at ease when in the presence of an ultimately correct solution. If words were put to that feeling, the sentence would read, "How perfect this will be!" The sense of letting go is noticeable to those who by habit are physically tense and mentally critical. The bodily sense of rightness is so certain that by comparison, the errors of the situation stand out in glaring contrast. Ones say that when they sense how perfect a situation could be that they can become desperately eager to clear up mistakes. They say that when they lose contact with the background sense of rightness and become anxiously preoccupied with clearing up the foreground of error that they are perceived as being overly critical.

I have moments of wonder during the course of the day, I call them my brief epiphanies, those times when everything "comes together," and the judge goes away.

They can be as simple as an exact balance on a tally sheet, or the precise fit of a definition of terms, or a sudden glimpse of nature that stops my thoughts and makes me glad. There is no error, everything is in its proper place, and there is a release of good feeling that can last for hours. I can also feel the corrections of a decision in my body. I can be troubled for weeks trying to make up my mind, and finally I'll know what to do because my body feels right about it although my mind may stay confused.

Attractive Environments

Attractive environments include jobs that require organization and meticulous detail. Teaching, accountancy, structural organization and long-range planning. Ones like situations that rest upon etiquette, protocol, and formal social procedures. They are researchers, grammarians, and preachers. They are found in religions and belief systems that require strict adherence to the rules. Religious fundamentalists, party-line leftists, moral majority extremists. They gravitate to jobs where procedures need to be enacted. Ethics committees, umpires, the Legion of Decency.

Unattractive Environments

Unattractive environments include jobs requiring risk of error in decision making or high levels of personal accountability for controversial decisions. Interactions that require the acceptance of multiple points of view, or that require a high toleration for differences of opinion. Interactions where decisions must be made on the basis of fluctuating or partial information, rather than on the basis of clearly stated guidelines.

Famous Ones

Famous Ones include *Emily Post*, the chronicler of etiquette and appropriate behavior. Her audience is made up of those who cultivate attractive habits and are able to put their turmoil aside in order to mind their manners and present a happy face at dinner.

Ralph Waldo Emerson □ Mary Poppins
George Bernard Shaw □ Charles Dickens □ Jerry Falwell
Martin Luther

Perfection as a Higher Quality of Mind

Ones suffer because they habitually compare the way things are against "how perfect they could be." There is a constant awareness of the discrepancy between the way something really is and the way that it should be. They live with a kind of desperate drive to realign ordinary reality with perfection. The world looks either black or white. It is either perfect or it has a fatal flaw. Ones suffer because they want a fixed and permanent perfection; as if lovely children suddenly became unspeakable because they ran out to play in the mud.

Real perfection is composed of the balance of positive and negative elements that blend together at every moment. The fact that the conditions of perfection change from moment to moment is a radical insight to Perfectionists, who operate from a one-right-way approach to life. Any perfect product has had to go through stages of what appear to be bad risks and bad timing, it can therefore be of enormous benefit for Ones to see that what can look like terrible mistakes are connected to an ultimately correct outcome and that they are responsible only for doing the best job that they can at any given time.

The idea that experimentation and mistakes are a necessary part of the path to perfection undercuts the foundation of the Perfectionist worldview. Allowing room for error or, worse yet, room for multiple points of view, seems like an invitation to madness. From childhood onward Ones have labored under an unrecognized assumption that correct thinking and hard work will lead to a just reward and that evil will be recognized and punished. The fact that hard work leads to more hard work not only seems unfair, but also points out the fact that other people labor in the service of pleasurable life goals rather than in meeting the repressive demands of a severe internal critic. For a One to be able to say "What is right for you may not be right for me" involves a quantum leap in personal growth.

Ones commonly report shock at having to see that virtue and good behavior do not necessarily lead to rewards and recognition. Yet giving up the the one-right-way approach to life is as frightening as losing a last defense against the unconscious forces of desire and hate.

The Virtue of Serenity

Ones describe themselves as being filled with energy that can't get out. They say that resentment feels like waves of fire moving through their body that gets stuck in the throat. They use images such as "a bottle that's been shaken and wants to pop its cork" or "being filled with a scream that I can't let out." The more the internal critic judges real feelings, the more energy builds in the body, seeking an avenue of escape. Corked, bottled anger is one way to describe the dilemma, because Ones can get physically rigid with energy while clamping down at the throat and jaw, unable to speak, to ask for help, or to let the angry scream come out.

The obvious direction for meditation and therapy is for Ones to learn that when the so-called negative emotions are accepted that their exaggerated importance vanishes. Ones report that judging thoughts are an excellent indication that some truthful impulse is being blocked out of awareness. Another indication is when a wave of resentment floods through the body, but nothing comes to mind as to what might be causing the tension.

Serenity is really the automatic side effect of allowing all feeling impulses into awareness, without deflecting the unacceptable ones. Each moment is in balance in the sense that the interplay of all the positive and the negative feelings is allowed to move through the body without inhibition from the thinking self.

When Ones allow themselves to get angry, they have enormous energy available to them that is usually bottled up in the body. The discharge of tension leaves them feeling temporarily energized and free to experience whatever comes to mind, without judgment. Anger has been expressed and has been survived, and for a time there is the serenity of allowing unimpeded feelings to rise and pass away again without blocking anything out.

Assets

Ones are dedicated to worthwhile causes. Once convinced of the correctness of a cause, or the good intentions of the people involved, they will work for the reward of satisfaction in a job well done in the way that other people work for the rewards of security and power. The neurotic need to do good, which can come out as an annoying "I am better than you are" do-goodism, can also be put to use in a sustained effort toward improvement.

Because they are committed to making the world a better place, Ones make dedicated teachers. They are devoted to excellence and want to teach others to appreciate the very best. There is an eagerness to clarify, to research and to transmit precise information, and a certainty that people can radically change their lives through correct information.

They will not cooperate if standards are to be compromised and, depending on which set of standards they have adopted as the one perfect way, will figure prominently in the programs of either the radical left or extreme right.

The criticality of Perfectionists can be easily disarmed if the other people involved are able to admit error, or are clearly disadvantaged. There is real patience with those who show effort but are handicapped through no fault of their own. They can show enormous patience toward those who struggle against the odds. There is also an immediate extension of good-will toward people who are able to admit an error, and who make an effort to help themselves.

Subtypes

Like its core point Nine, One has fallen into the sleep of self-forgetting. Nine has forgotten real wishes by developing an obsessive concern about whether to comply with the opinions of others. A One's way to self-forgetting is through the replacement of real wishes with an obsessive concern about the right thing to do. The severe self-scrutiny necessary to maintain correctness creates a schism between disowned personal wishes and the need to do the right thing as a statement of personal worth.

Jealousy, unadaptability, and worry develop from the tension between forgotten desires and the need to act correctly. The words describe painful preoccupations that, because they are uncomfortable, can act as an easily readable focusing device. When these uncomfortable feelings arise, Ones can use them to recognize the fact that their real wishes may be in conflict with their ideas about correctness.

Jealousy (Heat) in One-to-One Relationships

Jealousy takes the form of monitoring the mate's actions and of critically judging whatever comes between the self and the mate.

It's an explosion in the body and an insane need to get it straight with my partner. What's she going to do? Who's she going to choose? It's where my mind goes out of control. What's he got that's missing in me? It goes on and on—he gets a point, I'm down; I get a point, I'm up. I'm murderously angry and at the same time judging myself for being mad. It would be wrong to act out on him and I can't not act out because I'm dying inside.

Inadaptability in Social Relationships

Inadaptability comes about through the confusion between personal desires and the need to rigidly align with a correct social position. For example:

I'm an apostate in a religious order. After five years I'm still uncomfortable about a full commitment to final vows. I have no trouble with my order's view of religion, but am critical about the internal hierarchy, and certain views on world politics. Other men seem able to go along with these discrepancies without questioning their relationship to the order, but to me it feels like I'm living a lie even when I disagree with small issues of procedure.

Anxiety (Worry) about Self-preservation

Ones worry about not being perfect, about not deserving to survive, and particularly about making a mistake that would jeopardize survival.

It's a nagging voice that constantly wrings its hands about what might go wrong, or what other people might be thinking of me. It can be just as loud about the details of life as when there's really something to worry about. There's a lot of concern about money and survival; I've worked as a contractor for over twenty years, sometimes with a lot of money behind me, and sometimes on pure speculation. The nagging worry about finances is just as loud when there's plenty of capital to get the project through.

What Helps Ones Thrive

Ones often have difficulty going to therapy because of the admission that something is wrong and sometimes avoid meditation practice because of the fear of losing control to an altered state of awareness. The typical reasons for seeking help are anxiety attacks, bouts of substance abuse (to escape the internal critic), or a physical disorder that has its roots in psychological tension. The presenting problem is usually a mask for real feelings. Ones can help themselves by

- Not falling into compulsive doing; not having back-to-back responsibilities so as not to have to think about real priorities.
- Needing to modify the severity of internal standards. Needing to question the rules.
- Not turning insight into self-attack. "How could I have been blind to my own errors?"
- Getting a reality check. When the belief that others are judging arises, check this out with the people involved. When worry arises, get factual information to eliminate unnecessary anxiety.
- Seeing when a one-right-way solution begins to limit the chance for compromise or other options.
- Paying attention to the worth and consistency of other people's value systems.
- Learning to ask for and receive pleasure.
- Learning to question the difference between what "should" be done and what is really desirable.
- Using awareness of anger at others who "are getting away with it" as a clue to the fact that what they get away with is desirable.
- Sensing unrecognized anger: "putting on a happy face" while being angry inside; polite words with a critical sharpness in the voice; a smile and a rigid body.
- Learning to fantasize shadow side emotions.
- Using the imagination to ventilate anger. Imagine the worst to an enemy until the anger goes away.

What Ones Should Be Aware of

Anger and judgments about the self or others stem from the fact that personal needs are not being met. Ones should make efforts to recognize and act on real needs and be aware that the following issues may arise during change:

- A sense of two selves, one playful and the other punitive.
- Blanking out on personal wishes.
- Anxiety about developing awareness of own anger. "I try to protect others from my anger."
- Tying up time so that there is none left for pleasure.
- Procrastination. Overcomplicating simple procedures so as to delay a final commitment.
- An increase in pressure from unconscious wishes seeking expression, which leads to an increase in displaced irritation.
- Need to find fault with the environment.
- "Scorched earth policy." The need to redo a project from the very beginning because an error has been found. Inability to compromise. Tear the entire house down because the staircase is in the wrong place.
- An increase in the need to assign blame to others to balance the intense criticality already directed toward the self.
- Rigidity of attention. Focusing intensively on one sector of life that needs correcting and not paying attention to other sectors as they fall to pieces. A way of sectioning off and forgetting areas of conflict.
- Intolerance of multiple points of view. "I want things to be either right or wrong."

7. Point Two: The Giver

	ACQUIRED PERSONALITY		ESSENCE	
HEAD	Chief Feature:	FLATTERY	Higher Mind:	WILL (FREEDOM)
HEART	Passion:	PRIDE	Virtue:	HUMILITY
	SUBTYPE WAYS OF BEING			
	Sexual:	AGGRESSIVE/SEDUCTIVE		
	Social:	AMBITIOUS		
	Self-preservation:	ME-FIRST (PRIVILEGED)		

The Dilemma

Twos move toward people, as if seeking an answer to the inner question Will I be liked? They have a marked need for affection and approval; they want to be loved, to be protected, and to feel important in other people's lives. These were children who earned love and security by meeting other people's needs. As one outgrowth of their search for approval, Twos develop an exquisite personal radar for the detection of moods and preferences.

Givers say that they adapt their feelings to suit the concerns of others, and that by adapting, they are able to ensure their own popularity. They also report that if they are not getting the approval that they need that the adapting habit can become compulsive, to the point where they forget their own needs in a driven attempt to flatter others as a way of buying love.

Because Givers were raised with the understanding that survival depended upon the approval of others, relationship stands out as the most important area of existence. Twos report that they find themselves inadvertently altering themselves to meet other people's ideas of desirability. They say that they know how to present themselves so that they will be liked, and that this becomes burdensome, because it allows them to buffer possible rejection by giving people what they want. The habit of altering to please often produces a feeling of having fooled other people, by showing them only what they want to see.

Twos experience themselves as being many selves, of being able to change to suit the needs of the important people in their lives. A considerable degree of confusion can arise between the several selves, the sense of Which one is the real me? and Do you really know me, when I've shown you only one of my selves? They are particularly prone to giving themselves over to relationships with powerful people and often describe the sense of losing personal identity by altering themselves to become the personality that will be most pleasing to a mate. Whole sections of a Two's previous life and interests may drop away as attention shifts to the aspects of the self that are most compatible with what a mate desires.

The early phases of a relationship are dominated by a Two living out those aspects of herself or himself that will flatter the partner's needs. The later phases of a relationship are dominated by the feeling of being controlled by the partner's will, coupled with an overwhelming desire for freedom. As a relationship matures there are often hysterical outbursts of anger as the aspects of the self that were forgotten during courtship begin to surface. Twos experience a conflict between the habit of molding self-presentation so as to be ultimately irresistible to a partner and wanting the freedom to do whatever they please.

Because Givers have suppressed their own needs in the interest of pleasing others, they tend to become indispensable to the partner, or to people in power, as a way of getting those forgotten needs met. The liaison with power guarantees personal survival, while at the same time maintaining the posture of the giver. Twos meet their own desires by winning the love of people who can make those desires materialize. The successful control of a partnership is not achieved by force or overt coercion; control is achieved through helpfulness. If results fail to materialize, there is a good deal of complaining because the balance between giving and getting didn't even up. Complaining is also an attempt on the part of the helper to make others recognize just how much they owe.

Twos believe that others look to them for special qualities of understanding and that family and friends are dependent upon the help that they give. If their efforts are not recognized, or approval is withheld, Twos feel punctured, as if their worth depended on how they stood in other people's eyes. A pat of approval inflates self-importance: "They couldn't have pulled it off without me." A disdainful look from someone important produces painful feelings of deflation. "I've got to get that person to like me again."

This is the type of the "Jewish mother," the helper, and the advice giver. If special attention fails to materialize from having given such excellent support, what will emerge is the manipulator for privilege, the behind-the-scenes operator, the power behind the throne.

The preoccupations of Two include
- Gaining approval and avoiding rejection.
- Pride in the importance of oneself in relationships. "They'd never make it without me."
- Pride in meeting the needs of others. "I don't need anyone, but they all need me."
- Confusion between the many selves that develop in order to meet the needs of others. "Each of my friends brings out a different part of me." "Which me is my authentic self?"
- Confusion in identifying personal needs. "I can become what you want, but what do I really feel for you?"
- Sexual attention as a guarantee of approval. "I don't want to sleep with you, but I want to know you'd like to."
- Romantic attachment to "the great man," "the inspired woman."

- Fighting for personal freedom. Feeling controlled by other people's needs.
- Hysteria and anger when emerging real needs collide with the many selves that have developed in order to please others.
- An attentional style of altering oneself to meet the needs of others, which can lead to
  - Empathic connection with other people's feelings, or
  - A manipulative adaptation to the wishes of others as a way of assuring their love.

Family History

Twos were the children who were loved for being pleasing. They quickly recognized the qualities in themselves that were appealing to the different adults in their lives and learned to put on a performance that met those needs. They were loved children, who learned how to keep the flow of affection coming their way:

My father was remote and hard to get, which in a way made the game of getting his attention more exciting, because none of my brothers or sisters were any good at it. I felt like a barometer, always feeling out where he was at. I'd get home, and go to his study, and I remember hesitating at the door until I could feel out what his mood was like, so I would know how to be that evening.

It felt like figuring out which of my characters I should be for the night, and once I got into the character that seemed to fit, then I'd be that one to please him. I gave them all names years later in a therapy session, where I also remembered whole sets of feelings that they each had.

The one I liked best was Princess. She was very sweet, and when I was Princess I'd tell him all the things that I had done during the day while he was at work. I would also sometimes pretend that I was Princess during school when he wasn't there, and then I could speak out very bravely, because I felt like I was a king's daughter, and I was representing him.

Another common scenario is reported by Twos whose sensitivity to the needs of others developed because they had to support their parents emotionally.

I was a helpful child, who believed that my family was basically incompetent, and needed a lot of support. So by taking care of my parents I made them strong enough to take care of me. I got my parents to go to Sunday services because I thought that it strengthened them, all the while knowing that I was Jesus' favorite in the Sunday school for bringing them to the faith.

As an adult, there was a repeating pattern of giving myself over to a man and, by serving him, getting him to serve me. I would work and give him the money to support us, so that he could "pay my way." If I thought that I was actually taking care of myself, it felt like not being loved, because I wasn't being taken care of by him.

Another childhood prototype is described by Twos who recognized the manipulative possibilities of becoming indispensable and loved and used their seductive abilities to extract what they needed from other people.

I had a real triangle situation. My father was generous and a lot of fun, and my mom was in the way. So I just always put her first, and myself second, and by keeping the peace with her I could get anything I wanted out of him.

It was extremely seductive in a nonphysical kind of way. There was always this intense bond between us. He wanted control, so I would either flatter him by being pretty and playing up, or else I would outright disobey him. I disobeyed not because I really had to date the wrong fellow, or get home too late, but because I got an intense kind of possessive attention out of my father when I disobeyed, which made me feel like I really mattered.

Multiple Selves

Twos say that their sense of self develops from how other people react to them. They can be inspired to their best performance by other people's regard, but also sense that they adapt to other people's images of desirability in order to ensure themselves of a supply of love. Twos can feel as if they have a part of themselves parceled out to each of their friends, but nobody knows about the whole person.

The altering habit often makes a Two feel as if he or she is fooling friends, which as a defensive posture means that a Two does not have to risk being fully seen or potentially judged; but which also recreates the childhood belief that love is bought by hiding what is unacceptable. By shifting identity to correspond with the aspect of themselves that pleases a certain friend, Twos run the risk of losing touch with their authentic feelings. Their own feelings are forgotten as their focus of attention merges with the wishes of others.

Approval isn't something I think about, like what gift to give person X. It's more like a way of being, where I automatically go out to others and find myself searching them for clues about how they work or what they need. It feels unsafe unless I can predict how I can be useful to them.

All through high school it was like waking up and deciding who I was supposed to be that day. I had collected really different kinds of friends and had a repertoire of different ways to be for them that each felt very genuine and real to me.

However, having them all together in the same room could be very uncomfortable, because I didn't know which one of my selves to be, and if a new person joined the group, I'd feel myself having to adjust, hoping that the others wouldn't notice that I would start to behave slightly differently to the newcomer.

Last month I had my thirtieth birthday, which turned into a real trial because of all the different friends that I collected together who had absolutely nothing in common except knowing me. It ended up with a screaming fight in the kitchen between a nurse and a dope dealer who hated each other on sight. Yet I considered each person in that room to be a close personal friend.

There is a definite feeling that each of these selves has its own integrity, although they may be radically different from each other. Self-presentation may be quite different from one friend to the next, but each friend is truly met, and some of them deeply so. The fact that different people cause different aspects of the self to emerge does not necessarily imply that these selves are faked in order to seduce other people into a false friendship. There are, however, major problems that stem from a lifelong habit of finding security in the positive regard of other people.

One such problem is that Twos are generally far more aware about ways to accommodate other people than they are about their own motivations. A child whose security depends upon giving will develop a kind of pride in becoming necessary to others, as well as a reluctance to recognize personal needs. Needs bring up the possibility of disagreement with potential sources of affection. Consequently, attention is so trained to focus outwardly that personal needs are disregarded, in order to ensure lovability.

I work as a dental assistant, and it's absolutely vital to me that the patients like me. If it's somebody new, I'm totally insecure until I can develop a conversation that lets me know what they're like and what their interests are. It's like fishing, and finally I get a bite into a topic that they're interested in. Once I get that bite, I'll feel safe enough to figure out whether I like them or not; but it's almost impossible to know what I feel about them until I'm covered by agreement.

If it's an old patient, it can get to feel like a Rolodex. Person A means I'm card A in the Rolodex, and the matching personality molds right into the conversation. It's an exhausting procedure, always being extended for some sign that you're doing okay.

Umbrella Effect: Giving to Get

Twos often say that they have trouble with maintaining a sense of permanent identity in different relationships. The "real" self can get lost in the shuffle of alterations that go on in the course of an ordinary day. They say that it's easy to fall into being what somebody else wants, but that it is difficult to know what their own needs are.

Because Twos suppress their own needs in the interest of pleasing others, they tend to become indispensable to a partner, or to those in power, as a way of getting those forgotten needs met. This maneuver both guarantees personal survival and maintains the posture of the giver.

The first thing that I look for in a new place is who's the heavy; who's got the power in the room. I do it mainly by hanging back until I see how people are responding to each other, and it's clear to me who has respect. Once I know that, meeting them feels challenging. It's like everybody else went away. I get more animated and try for eye contact, but even if it's across a crowded room and I can't manage that, I feel that I am in a current of contact and I know if they're going to be available to me. It's the feeling that I am being drawn to them, and they seem to be coming across the room, although they haven't moved physically at all.

Givers get their own desires met through people who can make those desires materialize. The successful control of a partnership is not achieved by overt action, but by a Two metaphorically offering an umbrella to shield a partner from the rain and then being taken along on the other person's arm.

It is important for Twos to realize that what they give to others is what they will expect in return. If an umbrella is given, then a Two wants to be protected from the rain. If a birthday is remembered, then a Two wants to be remembered in return. When Twos offer support, it is probably with the expectation of being included in a successful enterprise; and at the time that they offer support, Twos are likely to be so identified with the aspect of themselves that will be most acceptable to the enterprise that it may be difficult for them to distinguish between a genuine desire to help and their habit of expecting help in return.

The habit of giving to get often operates at a deeply unconscious level of behavior and, like all fixated ways of being, needs to be brought to a conscious level of awareness in order to be released. Twos talk about several patterns of giving to get that they have observed within themselves.

It feels like I've got a web of life support systems extended out to all of my friends. The juice runs from me to them, and eventually I get fatigued with having to be enthusiastic about whatever they're up to. I do a lot of different activities with a lot of different people, and in the end I'm exhausted with doing for others and always putting up an enthusiastic front, until the point where I want to withdraw and not do anything for them anymore.

Because this woman's identity depends so heavily on the regard of others, she inserts herself into the lives of her friends, makes herself essential to them, and then complains about her exhaustion if returns fail to materialize. There is a good deal of complaining if the balance between giving and getting doesn't even up and an unconscious attempt on the part of the helper to force others to recognize how much they owe because she has cared for them.

The "Jewish mother" syndrome is only one unconscious tactic in which one person gives to another in order to get something back. Another tactic is to section off parts of the self to different people, as in the "madonna and whore" presentation, where the same woman offers radically different aspects of herself to different men; or, in the case of a man, he offers different aspects of himself to various women.

Another example of giving to get shows up in certain Givers' flagrantly sexual self-presentation. Many Twos report that they are unaware of the times when they have slipped into feelings of merging with another person and are not aware that their habit of emanating the qualities that are desirable to another is quite visible and obviously seductive.

If the seductive maneuver is unconscious, Twos are often confronted by those who resent the implications of a strong sexual presence. In such cases Givers wind up defending themselves. "I was not seductive, I said nothing out of line, it was innocent." And they may truly believe that story, because they are just not aware of how powerfully their inner alterations broadcast to other people. An unaware Two can appear in revealing clothing and turn a conversation to considerations of love, without realizing how explicitly he or she is giving out a sexual signal in order to get back the response that he or she is attractive and loved.

Seductive Self-presentation

All Twos are seductive in the sense that they are adept at maneuvering other people into liking them. They live with an ongoing assumption that almost anyone can be made available to them with the right approach and the proper dose of subtly applied special attention; and most Twos can, in fact, align themselves with other people's feelings so that just the right amount of personal contact is made.

The motivation behind a seductive presentation is to get attention. It feels safe to be wanted in any area of another's life, but especially safe to be physically desired. Because Twos know themselves through the reactions that other people have to them, they are extremely vulnerable to presenting themselves in a way that will flatter a partner's fantasies while at the same time suppressing their own sexual needs. Those Twos who report a history of having obtained approval through being a precocious Mommy's little man or a flirtatious Daddy's little girl may as adults exude a provocative self-presentation, but they often say that their appealing image is coupled with diminished sexual feelings.

My daydreams are about love and revenge. Being a secret lover to a great man, the one he tells everything to, and the one he comes to when he needs comfort. There's a lot of replaying of intimate moments: how a certain man's face looked when he wanted me, how I felt when he said I was the best lover of his life. And if the relationship goes bad, there's an equal amount of how to win him back, while looking like it's no big deal, or how to get even with him for humiliating me.

There's a lot of delight in being able to pull a man into an intimate conversation, or getting a man to stop what he's doing and pay attention to me. Those small seductions are such a turn-on that for years I thought that I was very sexy, but was holding back because of my scruples about married men. Now I see that it's not the sex that I want, but the attention that I get out of knowing that it could be there, and sealing that promise with a special hug, or hearing one of them ask for me by name.

Twos commonly report that although they want to present an appealing image, they are more interested in sexual attention than in being promiscuous. There is often a real fear of intimacy, because close contact exposes the fact that the self has been sold out to please others, and this exposure can be terrifying to someone whose personal security depends upon being seen as deeply and intimately connected to other people.

On a psychological level there is often a terror of deeply felt sexual urgings, because these feelings were originally directed toward one of the parents, or were sensed as originating in a parent and incestuously directed toward the developing child. The child had to suppress these early sexual responses in the interest of emotional survival, but at a deep level of being, the feelings between parent and child were never given up. In this sense Twos can be afraid of intimacy, but will use a sexy self-presentation as a way of checking out the unconscious sexual climate in a new situation. What they want to know is who is willing to give attention without making too many actual physical demands and who might be "dangerous" to them sexually.

For me, seduction and challenge seem synonymous. I'm great so long as there are obstacles in the way, and we haven't gotten together yet. I enjoy the subtleties of trying to make contact, the innuendos, and the thrill of sending out my signals until I get a smile or just the right kind of recognition. Once the chemistry gets going, I will follow that and drop everyone else in my life.

There's a special perception that I get around women. I'm not convinced that it's always accurate, but I have the idea that I can merge with them and become whatever kind of man that they want. I have a very clear memory of myself when I first tried this idea out: it was at a high school party, and I stood against a wall and changed into something different for every girl on the dance floor.

The Independence-Dependence Issue

Twos are likely to experience great confusion during the period of a relationship when the sense of a real self needs to emerge in order to make a truthful commitment. In a way the confusion between the altered self and surfacing real wishes is a hopeful sign. It indicates the desire to define the real self that was forgotten long ago in order to be pleasing to others. Less aware Twos can live out their entire lives either dependently merged with the wishes of a partner, or convinced that they are totally independent of a partner who can be controlled through flattery.

My need for freedom has been the dominant issue during an ultralong twenty-year mariage. We're both in the L.A. music scene. My wife is a performer, and I score and arrange for movie soundtracks.

When I first saw her on stage I was knocked out. She was a very powerful performer, and very inaccessible. Part of the hit was the impossibility of the attraction: she was beautiful, she was lesbian, she played an entirely different kind of music, and she had no real interest in what I was trying to do. For two years I was jumping over hurdles, and finally won out.

When I got her I started to get claustrophobic. I had given myself away to her—supported her career, scored her material, started to do her arranging—and I wanted to take myself back. I felt tied down and rebellious and wanted my freedom again. A part of me was totally devoted to her, and a part of me wasn't.

All the time that I was trying to reassert myself I felt confused. I remember once during that time, sitting in a drugstore over coffee, feeling pretty good actually. I looked up in the middle of an article in the paper, and I saw an attractive woman passing on the street. It was like my whole body got up and went with her, but I could still see my hands holding the paper.

When you merge with somebody, like I do with my wife, and then try to extricate yourself, it can get to where you feel half-melted into the person you love and half-hanging out in space, or disintegrating on a drugstore stool. When I got up to pay, I couldn't tell if the cashier's voice was coming from him, or the ceiling, or someone else in the line.

I've had confusions between myself and people that I love, where if I think that they're judging me, it's like my life tubes start to unplug, it feels like my energy is draining, and I start to disappear to myself, so that I want to check in the mirror or a plate glass window to see that there's still a reflection there.

It's taken most of our twenty-year marriage to get me to see that I am not being dominated by my wife's wishes, that I don't have to be inspired by her music or be swept away by her personal opinions in order to stay in love with her.

Twos eventually come to realize that the fight for freedom from a partner is no more free or independent than desperately wanting approval from that same person. The partner is still the referent point, and whether Twos stay or break away, it does not necessarily follow that they have found themself. Many aggressive Givers look exquisitely independent, but internally they know that they exercise control through giving and are dependent upon the approval of others for their emotional stability. This young woman says it all:

I spent $400 a month on phone calls for over a year to let him know just how much I didn't need him.

Triangulation

The habit of adapting to other people is confounded by the fact that a Two is attracted to people who embody qualities that are of value to the Two's personal growth. By helping the other a Two helps himself or herself by association, but can also identify so strongly with a partner's potentials, that the boundaries between self and other become confused. A Two can become so habituated to checking out a partner's emotional condition, and ignoring his or her own emotional needs, that another person's desires can cause a similar reaction to arise within a Two's own body.

The erotic contact is very important to me. I get intensely attracted, like my solar plexus and my heart are being physically pulled toward someone who has a command over me. The sexual draw isn't so much genital, like I have to sleep with them, it's more like being flooded with feelings that draw you into somebody's atmosphere. You feel cherished, because you sense the best in them and it brings your own best to the surface.

Givers say that they enter triangular love affairs for two reasons. The first stems from implied sexual innuendos in their relationship to one of their own parents, which gets carried into adult life as an attraction to being a secret favorite and the one who really understands. The desire is usually to be special and loved by the married partner, rather than to break up a marriage. The Two is often attracted to the attached partner's unavailability, but has no particular desire to injure the partner's spouse.

Triangulation can also occur because Twos feel that different lovers bring out totally different aspects of themselves, and a confusion sets in as to which aspect is authentic. They can find it difficult to choose between lovers.

Pride

In this worldview, attention is focused outwardly, upon how to please others. As a result, Twos have a tendency to believe that other people are dependent upon what they choose to give or to withhold. Twos live with the ongoing assumption that help emanates from themselves to others, and that without them, the rest of the world would be impoverished. Self-aware Twos will recognize the feeling of prideful inflation that is attached to being honored for what they have given: a feeling of self-importance that, because it is dependent upon the regard of others, can easily be deflated if attention is withheld. Pride can be pricked because the sense of self-worth is dependent upon others. If attention is withdrawn, it feels like being punctured, like being deflated from a posture of importance.

When I go into a new group, there's an immediate assessment of the people. Who's worth being with, and who would waste my time?

It's as if periodically during the evening my mental periscope will go up, and I'll scope out the corners to check how everybody's doing, and to look out for the interesting person that I might be missing.

Intimate Relationships

Challenge is a key word in relationship. A skilled seducer needs challenge in order to be inspired to the heights of his or her capabilities.

I always go for somebody slightly out of reach or difficult to meet. The excitement is in going for it, in feeling what they draw out of me. When I'm around a totally exciting person, I just become animated, and it feels wonderful to be so inspired. When the connection gets going, it's like a flow of feelings between us which has nothing to do with whatever we're talking about. The words aren't important, they're just filling in the space.

The big problem is when they start to like me, I feel that I've offered them the 5 percent of myself that they wanted, and I'm painfully possessive of the remaining 95 percent. It feels like they don't know me at all, and I start to feel like I'll lose my freedom if I commit to somebody who couldn't possibly accept all of who I am.

Twos are at their best in moving toward a challenging relationship. It is a protected posture, in that the focus of attention is on how to get a response from the potential partner, rather than on self-disclosure. They are able to position themselves so as to be noticed, to insert themselves at the junctures of the potential partner's life, and to be on call when help is needed. The most exciting and vital phase of a relationship is when there are still obstacles to be overcome and the chase is on. When a partner is hard to get, a Two attempts to get close, ignoring the fact that real feelings have been forgotten, and replaced by an aspect of the self that has emerged to meet the challenge.

For me, going for somebody who's hard to get keeps the con going. They don't know yet that there's nobody at home, that there's a kind of vacuum inside me, with no fixed center. The chase keeps the show going. "Let me show you the goodies that I've got. Let me entertain you." At the beginning I don't want anything except their love, so all I have to be is somebody's dream girl.

One pinprick and dream girl goes bust. All the guy has to do is look bored for a minute, and it goes from "Wonderful me" to "Poor me, nobody loves me," just because my friend doesn't seem interested. I can be wildly excited about something that happened during the day, and stay high from it as long as he seems to care, but if he seems slightly disinterested, then my feelings about the day go straight out the window.

When the challenge in a relationship is over, a Two's attention shifts from how to please the partner to how it feels to be with the partner. Twos are often so repressed with respect to their own needs that they have a hard time knowing what they want and so feel limited by whatever the partner believes to be important. There is a feeling of fighting for personal freedom, of having only a part of themselves invested in the relationship, and of suddenly remembering all of the other parts that were left standing at the door while the relationship was finalized.

I've had three marriages and literally became a different personality during each of them. I am now alone by choice for the first time since I was fourteen and am committed to finding myself before I risk another relationship where I might totally merge into a new husband's life.

The first marriage was to a rock musician: three children, a commune, and a cushy Victorian in the San Francisco Haight. The second marriage was to a civil rights activist, who hated the flower child image. We lived and worked in a three-room shack in the South, hauled water and wood, and I never thought of San Francisco or the whole rock scene.

The last one was to a businessman. Completely new life, with a whole new style coming out. People from the southern life did not recognize me as a St. Louis matron, and I have to say that the way that I could remember them best was through my children, who had a continuous memory of all of our lives together.

Because Twos mold their identity through how other people react to them, they are always aware that they are dependent upon others for approval. In the first phases of a relationship they tend to merge with a partner's wishes; but once the relationship is secured, that dependent merger begins to feel like being imprisoned by the partner's needs. There is often an up-front rebellion against whatever the partner wants, a rebellion that is fueled by a surfacing suspicion that the real self has been sold out in order to buy the partner's goodwill.

Twos report that they feel fiercely independent during the phase where they fight for freedom from a relationship that has begun to feel terribly limiting. During this phase they are demanding and irritable and will not cooperate to meet the partner's needs. There is a desire to reactivate the interests of the forgotten self, to pursue activities that the partner finds upsetting, and to run out the back door to other love affairs.

On the high side, Twos have a deep commitment to help potentiate other people's better qualities: "When I am with developed people, they inspire the best in me." They can focus goals and strategies to help the partner be successful.

On the low side, Twos become the partner's custodian if they have a strong need to maintain control of the relationship: "He or she will make it through my love." Overgiving that smacks of emasculation and the need to be in control over the mate. Find it hard to let a relationship break up because of the need to be seen as the successful giver and the beloved partner.

An Example of a Couple Relationship: Two and Seven, the Giver and the Epicure

Twos support a Seven's high sense of self-regard, and the couple will flourish as long as personal goals are in alignment with those of each other. Twos can devote themselves to the Seven's plans and merge with the excitement and optimism that Sevens bring to their interests. The Two will want to help potentiate the partner's talents and align themselves with the Seven's belief that the couple is moving toward a future point in time where the plans that they have made together will come to complete fruition. The couple is likely to go out a lot together, present a tasteful public image, and have a good time sharing the best in entertainment and current events.

Both partners will be able to give space for personal interests. Sevens are basically self-absorbed and preoccupied with their own projects. They will do what pleases them whether or not there is anyone else around. This allows a Two all the time in the world to join the Seven for something interesting to do and then to take off to pursue the interests of the many selves. The Two may feel threatened by the Seven's independence, but if paid attention to in public and reassured that the Seven is not philandering during time away, each will give the other freedom. Neither will feel limited, and each will be able to take pleasure in whatever outside interests the other finds appealing.

Both parties are naturally seductive, the Two more overtly so but less likely to follow through. The Seven is less overt but more likely to go in and out of casual affairs. Both enjoy attention and sexy innuendo, and each can take a certain pride in the fact that the other has potential partners available to them. Once the couple decides upon a level of flirtation acceptable to both partners, the couple can make private allowances for the kinds of outside attention that each of them needs.

Both partners will have a limited window for continuous intimate contact. The Seven will want to buffer any prolonged deep feeling by finding other things to do, and the Two will start to feel controlled. The Seven partner's moving away from intimacy is likely to make the Two want to move toward, which keeps the couple together; if the Two wants out of the relationship, the Seven will also move toward the disappearing option. A breakup is not likely to occur from lack of romance or interesting things to do. The most likely basis for a breakup will be the Two's wish to become more central in the partner's life, getting angry and critical, with the Seven holding out for something lighter and waiting for the Two to come to his or her senses. The Two will see the Seven as emotionally lightweight, and the Seven will see the Two as an emotional drag.

Sevens enjoy being listened to and will be pleased to have such caring attention as long as the Two remains aligned with the Seven's purposes. If the Two merges too heavily with the partner's point of view and then attempts to maneuver the Seven into another course of action, the Seven will withdraw, become secretive, or create diversionary tactics to draw the Two away from Seven's real priorities. If the Two begins pressure tactics for more attention, for immediate results in projects, or for more time spent on the Two's personal interests, the Seven partner will again withdraw, become secretive, and create diversionary interests to distract the Two.

Another version of a severe crisis can develop if the Seven starts to feel limited and either becomes evasive, or won't measure up to the Two's image of a powerful mate. When disappointed, Givers are likely to resort to manipulation, which, when the Seven catches on, will create a breach of trust. Givers report the following common maneuvers that occur when they feel unappreciated in a relationship: double standard—"I've been good to you, so you should stick with me; but you've ignored me so badly that I have to find love elsewhere." Proofs—"Show me that you care by filling my agenda first. Do this task. Fulfill this quest." Moods—"Figure me out. I won't say, but you should hang around and guess." Temper fits— Anger arising from being ignored.

Point Two's Relationship to Authority

Twos are attracted to power and want to be loved by powerful people. They are very good at recognizing potential winners and at placing themselves as helpers at the strategic spots of the leader's operation. They know about the relative status and degree of respect between people and will merge with the fashionable trends within the group. While Twos will not admit to needing anything from the authorities whom they help, they are very demanding of an authority's presence and advice. Over time, they will extract status benefits, but the chief benefit will always be that they maintain an inner circle relationship with a power elite.

Twos will merge identities with an authority and adapt into whatever the leader finds desirable. Although Twos have the capacities necessary to be a leader on their own, they generally prefer to be the power behind the throne, a prime minister rather than the king. From this strategic position, Twos will identify their own security with the authority's rise to power. By protecting the authority, Twos ensure their own future while at the same time earning love. It is extremely unusual to find a Giver in an unpopular public position unless there is also an alignment to a power source.

Twos do not waste valuable time on relationship to petty authority. The reaction to meter maids or an important person's secretary is to first try to manipulate through flattery or through being "known." Failing that, the case will be taken over the head of the petty authority, and the Two will push firmly to the front of the line. The reaction to a punitive or an unresponsive authority is to manipulate a behind-the-scenes takeover by a rival who is likely to be more appreciative of a Giver's assistance.

On the high side, Twos see the potentials in people. Willing to work for few material rewards if the quality of human contact is good. Able to go toward others, to make them comfortable, to draw them out. Sensitive to bringing an outsider into the group. Adaptable to any setting, good mixers and socializers.

On the low side, Twos are prone to manipulate others through flattery. People are seen as worth cultivating or not worth the time. Competitive with peers for those who are "worth it." Seductive toward those above, condescending to those below.

A Typical Interpoint Authority Relationship: Two and Eight, the Giver and the Boss

If the Two is the leader, there will be an outer appearance of independently made decisions but an internal attachment to the opinions and goodwill of the important people in the field. The

Two leader will be working as hard for the personal regard of significant people as for material gains. While this moves a Giver toward association with the big wheels of the field, it also makes for a weak command if an action has to be taken alone against a respected authority.

Even in the best of working conditions, a Two is likely to display an alternation of purpose as attention merges with the differing priorities represented in any major decision. The Two boss will also alter temperamentally, at times wanting to be liked by the employees, at times feeling burdened by their presence. The Two's moods will be uneven, and she or he will be prone to temper outbursts quickly forgotten by the Two but not necessarily by the employees. A Two leader is also likely to form an inside circle relationship with "those on my staff who understand."

The Eight employee will tend to see the Two's preoccupation with important people as a form of weakness and capitulation to other people's power. The Eight will want to know where she or he stands in the organization and to have inviolate ground rules and penalties fairly and uniformly enforced. Any special privilege to "honchos" or "insiders" or the boss's favorite clique is likely to be met with a full-out public denouncement, especially if the Eight has not been informed, or feels left out of the boss's clique.

The Eight will want entrance to the inner circle and is usually aware of feeling disadvantaged by people who are more socially graceful and diplomatic. An Eight usually attempts to enter the circle by frontal attack, and she or he will tend to polarize the circle's members into those who agree and those who disagree with the Eight. If the Eight employee is rejected, there will be a short angry statement of differences, and the Eight will withdraw into stony silence, feeling safer because sides have been taken, and friends and foes have been defined.

Eights hate to feel excluded from any special group and prefer to be in a position of control. This puts them in a precarious position with regard to a boss who is capable of using flattery to make the Eight feel like an inner circle adviser. If Eights feel accepted and important, they can easily be seduced into service beyond the call of duty. Eights are also blind enough to social nuances to "not get" that they are being used to fight someone else's battles or to be identified within the organization as an uncompromising heavy that the boss can unleash at any given time.

If the Two boss is wise, the Eight employee will be given a small fiefdom within the organization. The Two can retain nominal control and can be in charge of the overall strategy as long as the Eight retains control of private territory and is free to implement the plans without interference or supervision from the leader. Eights take a lot of pride in making their own operation work and are far more tolerant about other people's procedures if power boundaries are clearly defined.

A mutually respectful relationship will emerge if the Two is able to confront the Eight employee openly. Both types like a good fight, and each can understand the other's desire for control and power. Open confrontation and open competition will lead to productive solutions as long as the disagreement is conducted as a fair fight in which the position of each party is argued publicly. If, on the other hand, the Two becomes intimidated or begins to manipulate the opinions of others, the Eight will feel betrayed, and can become overtly uncooperative, lead an office revolution, or quit the job. The surest way to alienate an Eight in open argument is to resort to an elegant put-down. Eights are unusually blunt and quite blind to nuances of presentation when they are focused on making a point. If they are made to feel embarrassed or condescended to, they will become infuriated and uncompromising. Knowing this, a Two can deliberately provoke the employee into looking bad and force a dismissal or a resignation.

If the Two is the employee, she or he will be likely to understand the boss's needs for control and full disclosure on the part of subordinates. If the Eight boss is perceived as a protective power source, the Two will become his or her right hand, take on a great deal of responsibility, make the organization run smoothly, and report to the boss alone.

Eights are particularly controlling if they find that they are dependent upon other people's performance and will be likely to conduct unannounced inspections and to assert control by becoming overly interfering about the enforcement of small regulations. Rules of procedure will be adamantly stated, and then arbitrarily broken by the boss herself or himself, as a way of stating that the boss is above the rules. Workers may be set against one another as the boss will give out very few compliments, but will publicly assign blame.

If the Two employee is wise, she or he will direct the boss's attention to legitimate areas of concern as a way of both satisfying the Eight's need to control and as a way of getting the boss to stop interfering with the staff. If the boss is kept completely informed and is alerted to real areas of threat to the operation, the lines of battle become clearly focused, and the boss will happily fall into a position of leadership coupled with a reawakened desire to protect the staff.

Twos can become instrumental to their bosses by using their superior social graces to gain access to special information. The literal-minded Boss will see this as an advantage, and if the boss is wise, he or she will offer protection and status to the employee. If the Boss remains tied to a fixated suspicion about falling into other people's hands and periodically asserts herself or himself over the Two by asserting control, the Two employee is likely to manipulate an overthrow by backing another front-runner in the organization.

Attractive Environments

Attractive environments include any situation of assisting or associating with a powerful leader. Devotee of a demanding guru, rock star groupie, the right-hand woman or man who counsels the chief. The president's secretary, who runs the corporation.

Advocate for the underprivileged, volunteer for social causes. The helping professions. Chicken soup: "It's for you, but thanks a lot, I'll have some too."

Triangulated love affairs. The other man, the other woman. A job with a sexual connotation. Makeup artist, chorus girl, personal colors consultant.

Unattractive Environments

Unattractive environments include jobs that do not generate approval. For example, you probably would not meet a Two working at a collection agency, unless he or she was in love with the boss.

Famous Twos

Madonna, whose image of an explicitly sexual woman first appeared on the record jacket of *Like A Virgin*.

Elvis Presley □ Elizabeth Taylor □ Mary Magdalene
Jerry Lewis □ Dolly Parton

How Twos Pay Attention

Attention is by habit focused upon the emotional fluctuations of significant others, guided by the wish to become the object of their love. On the level of physical cues, this would mean something like watching to see who the partner pays attention to, or watching to see whether he or she smiles or frowns when a particular topic of conversation is brought up, and then trying to join with those interests in a pleasing way.

On another level of perception, Twos say that they find themselves altering to become what others want without being aware of any facial or behavioral cues that have caused them to modify their presentation. They say that when their attention is attracted to someone that they find themselves adapting to what they imagine that person's innermost desires to be and that their habit of falling in with another's wishes means that they can become the prototype of what the other believes to be desirable.

It starts out with hating to be rejected. What you do to not ever get rejected is learn how to be the same as someone else. You learn to look at a stranger, sense how the two of you are the same, and then slide into that feeling. It can happen on the street, where I find myself going out to someone and fitting into how we're the same.

At the level of intimacy, it's far more intense. It feels like whatever you want, I also want. Whatever you desire, I feel that same desire. Whatever you wish for sexually can be acted out through me. When the chemistry is working, it's the most wonderful form of intimacy. But when I feel like I'm standing on the street corner, tilting into someone else's life just because I feel insecure that day, the whole idea of merging is a burden to me.

Because attention is outwardly focused upon what others want, there is a systematic lack of attention to personal needs. From a psychological point of view, these repressed needs get satisfied through helping others live out a life in which the Two would like to share. A Two can be helped in therapy by learning to recognize personal needs and by learning to stabilize a consistent sense of self that does not alter in order to meet others' needs.

From the point of view of attention practice, Twos can learn to intervene in their habit of sensing signs of approval from others by learning to shift attention away from others and refocus attention at a reference point within their own body. With practice, Twos can recognize the difference between staying present to their own feelings and allowing their focus of attention to go out to others.

Freedom as a Quality of Higher Mind

Shifting attention inward often produces a great deal of anxiety for Twos. Although they have a much better chance of recognizing their own needs when they are able to pay some attention to themselves, the withdrawal of attention from others interrupts a habit upon which Twos depend for emotional security. Twos commonly report fearing that there may not be a real self at home, that there may be only a black hole in the belly, and that nobody lives in the hole. The fact that real feelings may begin to surface when attention is withdrawn from others is not necessarily good news to those whose security depends upon pleasing other people.

Twos can become so habituated to noticing what others want that they remain unaware of the fact that they get a payoff for the help that they give. They recognize their dependency upon others during those times when they must act alone. Independent action can produce terrible anxiety, especially if the action goes against the wishes of someone a Two would like to please. By not acquiescing to the needs of a preferred person, a Two feels he or she risks sacrificing the other's love forever.

Many Twos report that it is easier for them to know what they want and feel when they are alone than when they are with someone to whom they are attached. They see their task as learning to remember what their own needs are, while at the same time being able to sense what the other wants.

When my second marriage dissolved, I moved far out into the mountains, with the idea of finding out what I really wanted in life. It was like I didn't exist, now that my husband wasn't around all the time. It was upsetting and frightening having to be alone with myself, having to decide what to do to keep myself company every day, and facing that empty hole in my belly when I tried to meditate. I had the dread that there would be no bottom to that pit, that I would keep going inside myself, and that there would be nobody there.

Eventually I found her, I found my own pacing, and I found out how to give myself what I wanted. I lived out there for over three years, and then moved back into town and picked up my old life. The most startling experience of being back with people was that I was quite clear about what I wanted when I was alone, but if I looked fully into someone else's eyes, I would find myself so joined with what they were feeling that I forgot myself.

Intuitive Style

Givers believe that they understand the innermost feelings of others. They were the children who were loved for being pleasing and who as adults are led to believe that they are especially sensitive to what others want. As with each of the nine types, the intuitive style arises from a way of paying attention that helped the child to survive emotionally. As children Twos developed a preoccupation with gaining approval and, motivated by their need for love, became convinced that they were especially able to sense the inner wishes of others.

Whether an individual Two is objectively sensitive to others' needs or simply fantasizing might be described as the difference between merely imagining what it would be like to be in someone else's shoes and what some Twos have described as genuinely sharing another's inner life.

The statement that follows illustrates the distinction between people who believe themselves to be sensitive to others and those who are truly empathic.

When I was in my twenties, I was guided by the idea that I just loved everybody, and that they loved me in return. I was sure that I was everybody's favorite child, and I just wanted to repay them by showing how attentive I could be. With some growing up, and having to survive a few devastating rejections from people that I really loved, I came to realize that I could manipulate people by getting them to like me a lot. What I did was to imagine what they wanted and move in on that tack; or I'd think what it would be like to be standing in their place and would slide into imagining a similar experience from my own life.

For example, if a friend of mine would confide in me about the way they felt about a boy, it might be like, "When I'm around him I'm on a roller coaster, my feelings ride up and down." So I'd imagine myself on a roller coaster and try to imagine that as a way of being in love.

Many more years later, I've become a psychologist and have had experiences of what I would call projective identification, where I feel what my patient is going through in ways that are different from any close approximation to my own life. I have come to value those intuitive mergings as the most direct way in which I can understand my client's situation.

One outstanding example of what I feel was genuine empathy happened when a client of mine was trying to work through a forgotten period of his childhood, where he had been sent to a foster home for a few weeks. While he was sitting in my office and describing the fact that he could not recall any of the events or feelings that he went through during that period of time, I simultaneously began to feel overheated and as if I were about to pass out, although I knew that I wasn't really fainting.

When I described my reactions to him, he realized that his body also felt heated, and eventually his body sensations triggered the suppressed memories of waking up sweating in the basement room that he shared with another foster child in the house. The room was severely overheated, because it was too close to the main furnace, and he had lain awake during nap time, stewing about the fact that he had never been told how long he was expected to stay with the family, and that he was afraid to ask because he thought it might be offensive, and they would turn against him.

The Virtue of Humility

All of the higher emotions have their basis in spontaneous actions of the body that are not directed by thought. As an embodiment, humility is a reaction that is not predicated upon getting something in return. The false humility of a deluded giver would be something like, "I gave you my right arm, but please don't mention it." Humility has nothing to with virtuous thinking or self-sacrifice, which might easily mask unconscious needs to assert control over others by making them dependent.

Those who embody humility may not be aware that they are able to give just the right amount of help, and may not be aware that there is anything special about the fact that they are grateful for what they already have, and harbor no expectation of a return from others.

Humility is the recognition of one's exact needs and the natural inclination to take no more and no less than what is necessary. A person who knows his or her own needs will be likely to extend just the right measure of help to others. Furthermore, such a person's quality of giving will be in just the right proportion to what is required. Humility is like standing naked in front of a mirror and being grateful for exactly what is reflected back, with no inclination to pridefully inflate one's feelings by imagining it as more than what it is, or to be deflated by not accepting what is really there. Likewise, there is the ability to gratefully accept one's objective relationship to other people, rather than to habitually manipulate oneself into a position of importance.

One self-observation practice that is helpful in cultivating humility consists of learning to tell the difference between objective reactions that arise in the body as a result of giving to others and feelings that are directed by ideas about giving and receiving.

Two and Nine Look Alike

Like Nines, Givers are more aware of what others want than they are able to know what they want themselves. Twos behave differently than Nines, however, because they alter personal presentation, with an agenda of asserting control by being pleasing. Nines do not alter and do not control by giving. Nines describe the way that they merge with others as "being like the image of a mirror," absorbing and reflecting back the point of view that others impose upon them. Nines also say that they exercise control by slowing down or spacing out, rather than through manipulation. Another difference between Two and Nine is the fact that Twos actively move toward people with whom they wish to be identified, whereas Nines are slow to put themselves forward.

Both types describe feelings of merger with others. Twos merge with what is similar in the other, or with the aspect of the other that feels inspiring. Twos are selective about those with whom they merge. It has to be somebody who is worth it. Nines would describe their quality of merging as something like "becoming the other and taking in whatever I find there." A Two merges by feeling what is wanted and altering to please and merging with the other as a whole.

Two and Three Look Alike

Like those at its core (point Three), the Two has lost connection with authentic personal feelings. The three points clustered at the right-hand side of the Enneagram, Two, Three, and Four, represent different ways in which real childhood feelings were sacrificed in order to reconcile the conflict between personal and parental wishes. The Two's issues with feelings developed through early adaptation to the needs of others and are maintained by the habit of paying attention to the fluctuation of other people's moods and preferences. Successful adaptation to the needs of others guarantees security and protection.

Two and Three can look alike, if the Two is a high achiever. We would expect a Three to move up the success ladder because he or she has been rewarded for performance, rather than for feelings. A Two can also be energetic and professionally ambitious, but the inner motive of the Two is to be loved for himself or herself, rather than for achievements. The difference between a Three and a high-achieving Two is the difference between the performer who plays to the audience in order to put on a great show and the flatterer who plays to the same audience in order to impress a special boyfriend who is sitting in the front row.

Assets

Twos can make people feel good about themselves. They have the ability to draw out the best in others, and through their enthusiasm they can make difficult changes easier to undertake. They are happiest in a support position to those who seek power and can be a major asset to a friend or associate who is going against the odds. Relationship stands out as the most important facet of a Giver's life, and they are committed to keeping relationships alive whether through fight, seduction, merging with a partner's needs, or making lots of trouble. They are able to get angry and not hold a grudge. They will take time to honor the celebrations that bring people together. Birthdays and holidays will be remembered with a special gift that took thought and effort to prepare.

Subtypes

The subtypes name preoccupations that developed during childhood. They represent strategies that the child resorted to, while attempting to get personal needs met through the agency of other people.

Seduction/Aggression in the One-to-One Relationship

Seduction is based on the preoccupation with being wanted as a sign of approval and entails drawing another to the self. Aggression is the confrontational overcoming of all obstacles to a relationship and means pushing for contact.

I can focus on any stranger in a crowd and know if they are available to me. It's like my body wants to shift into the right fit for them, and there's a physical perception if I connect. When my connection feels secure, I'll move toward them, already knowing that they like me.

Ambition in Social Situations

Ambition involves association with powerful people as a source of protection and as an assurance of status within the group.

I was recently hired to be on the psychiatric staff of a general hospital. I watch myself scouting out the departmental meetings. Who sits next to whom? Who gets respect from the higher-ups? I have to get to know the ones coming up in popularity and to make friends with them.

Me-First (Privilege) in the Area of Self-preservation

The following is an example of the me-first attitude:

"Get out of my way!" is a key phrase. It's a feeling of fury at having to stand in bank lines, or having to be in the middle of the crowd waiting for the cafeteria to open. There's not going to be enough left for me once the others get what they want, and you get so angry at the indignity of being left out that you maneuver yourself to the head of the line.

What Helps Twos Thrive

Twos often begin therapy or a meditation practice with the desire to find the real self. That means learning to recognize the difference between real wishes and the accommodations that take place in order to comply with or fight against what other people want. Typical presentations include relationship issues or illnesses, such as migraines or asthma, that may have their basis in the psychosomatic conversion of repressed needs. Twos need to recognize when attention shifts from real feelings to compliance with the feelings of others. They can help themselves by

- Detecting the urge to manipulate.
- Recognizing real worth to others. Noticing the swings that occur between prideful inflation of importance and exaggerated humility.
- Recognizing flattery as a sign of rising anxiety. Noticing the temptation to give up power to others.
- Encouraging more than the initial emotional reaction. First reactions may be a superficial display that masks real feelings.
- Noticing how attractive getting full attention for one full hour of therapy can be. Wanting to talk about themselves.

- Detecting the desire to appear helpless, to keep therapy comfortable, and to not bring up material that tarnishes pride or a good image.
- Seeing the conflicting priorities between the "multiple selves" and developing a consistent presentation to others that does not alter in order to please.
- Unearthing anger as an indicator of authentic feelings and as a way to unearth the conflicts that underlie psychosomatic conversion symptoms.
- Not pulling others in by flattery and recognizing that the need to retaliate is caused by hurt pride.

What Twos Should Be Aware of

It is helpful for Twos to be aware that the following issues may arise during change:

- Wanting to play at being someone else, fantasizing different ways of being loved.
- Confusion between the several selves—"Which one is the real me?"
- Opting for second best in relationships. Wanting to be with "the best" but, fearing rejection, staying with "the one who needs me more."
- Fear of not having a real self, of being derivative, or of imitating other people. In meditation, fear of the empty hole in the belly.
- Surfacing insecurity about survival without the protection of other people.
- Fears of having bought relationships, of having fooled others into being friends.
- The belief that gaining approval is equal to gaining love. The belief that independence will lead to never being loved again.
- Histrionic outbursts when the habit of seeking approval collides with emerging real needs. The belief that others are trying to limit freedom.

- Fighting for freedom. Refusal to make commitments that appear to limit expression of multiple selves. Demands for unlimited freedom.
- Attraction to difficult relationships. Triangulation. Maintaining control by going after the hard-to-get. Forestalling real intimacy.
- Inexperience with real intimacy. Real sexual and emotional feelings are unfamiliar. Needing time to recognize and stay with authentic feelings that are not influenced by the regard of others. Needing to see the difference between passing likes and dislikes and a deeper level of commitment.

8. Point Three: The Performer

	ACQUIRED PERSONALITY		ESSENCE	
HEAD	Chief Feature:	VANITY	Higher Mind:	HOPE
HEART	Passion:	DECEIT	Virtue:	HONESTY
	SUBTYPE WAYS OF BEING			
	Sexual:	IMAGE OF MASCULINITY/FEMININITY		
	Social:	PRESTIGIOUS		
	Self-preservation:	SECURITY MINDED		

The Dilemma

Threes were the children who were prized for their achievements. They remember coming home from school and being asked about how well they had done, rather than how they felt about their day. Performance and image were rewarded, rather than emotional connections or a deep involvement in other people's lives. Because they were loved for their achievements, they learned to suspend their own emotions and focus their attention on earning the status that would guarantee them love. The idea was to work hard for recognition, to take on leadership roles, and to win. It was very important to avoid failure, because only winners were worthy of love.

Threes seem strangely modern in the context of an esoteric teaching. They are high achievers who have identified with the American popular image of youth, energy, and a competitive life. They adopt the prototype image of any group: the executive with the three-piece suit, the supermom who gets the job done, the bouncy kids in the TV ads, the hippie with hair to his heels. Threes are chameleons, who can turn into the valued achievers of whatever groups they find themselves belonging to, and may unwittingly come to believe that they are whatever image invites approval from those whom they respect.

Because Threes conform to qualities that are valued in the American culture, they present a surface appearance of optimism and well-being. They do not appear to suffer and may live out their entire life oblivious to the fact that they have lost a vital connection to their own interior life. Threes will work for external rewards, often without examining their feelings about the work itself. They identify with a firm's prestigious name, they assign their value to the number of zeros on their yearly income. The work itself may be deadly boring, but an impressive-sounding title can compensate for that. As one Three said, "Don't think about it, just get the job done." Activity is also a natural antidepressant; Threes simply stay so busy that they haven't time to let life get them down.

Work is the preferred area of activity, and because the value of Threes depends upon the job turning out well, they can commit themselves fully to a task. They move immediately from an idea into action, with very little lag time between thinking and doing. Life is high-energy and happy, with plenty of interesting activities, but a life that focuses on personal performance necessarily sacrifices an interior life that stems from intimacy and emotional questioning.

Most Threes are not aware that their preoccupation with doing prevents an emergence of the kind of creativity that can only develop out of prolonged periods of time devoted to being and feeling. Threes keep the schedule packed. There is continuous activity all during the day, with no free time for feelings to surface. Threes want to take work along on their vacation, to fill their play time with a study tour or a five-country sightseeing marathon that ensures that they will be actively engaged for the entire vacation period. Free time without the guarantee of knowing what they have to do next is frightening to those who have been conditioned to believe that worth depends on what you do, rather than on who you are.

Free time is also avoided because personal feelings will come into awareness, and feelings can interfere with efficiency in getting the job done. Threes rarely find that illness or personal life get in the way of the ongoing work schedule and are intolerant of underachievers and those who let their emotions pull them down.

The word *performer* brings to mind a person who is personally vain and, in fact, Threes are vain about what they do. These are people whose self-esteem depends upon product recognition rather than upon being personally adored. Threes say that they are so focused on the task when they go into action that their feelings are suspended and that if they receive a compliment that they take it as given to the product rather than to themselves.

In intimate relationships Threes find that they alter into what an intimate person should look like and say the things that an intimate person would say; but they are often simultaneously aware of projecting an image of how an empathic person is supposed to act rather than being connected to the feelings that intimacy implies. In the midst of an emotional moment, a Three's attention can shift off to other things. The nine o'clock appointment or the power lunch suddenly come to mind when feelings are expected to surface. Emotions have been suspended for years in the interest of effective job performance, until they have become incompatible with getting the job done.

Love is expressed through action, and family life proceeds through a series of picture-perfect images. "We travel together. We play a lot of tennis. We talk about the kids." Attention is on activities and schedules, rather than on free time to hang out and be together. A Three has a relationship that runs efficiently; a marriage "that works." Jobs and income will be well accounted for. It is important to keep projects and prospects alive; it is important to avoid failure and to maximize success.

A sense of inner optimism is often bolstered by paying selective attention to positive achievements. Failures are reframed by turning them into incomplete successes; mobilizing for deadlines and competition is preferable to rest. With time, a Three develops an ability to adapt to job roles, to embody the image and characteristics appropriate to a professional presentation. This chameleonlike ability to take on the mannerisms of a successful role model serves to impress other people so that they will rely upon the Three's abilities, but can also be a source of deep self-deception on the part of the Three, who replaces real emotions with those feelings that successful people are alleged to have. The unrecognized self-deception deepens if a Three begins to identify with the mannerisms of "an effective leader" or "my partner's ideal lover," to the point where the adopted image can replace authentic needs.

Threes suffer from the habit of deceiving themselves and others by taking on the images that guarantee respect. The word *workaholic*, for example, brings to mind a driven overachiever, unable to stop, unable to rest; and in its pathological extreme, that image would be correct. The Threes who are quoted in this section recognize themselves as driven by their neurotic need to excel at those times when their attention becomes so immersed in the task at hand that they seem to become the ideal prototype of their job and can no longer tell the difference between that image and themselves. These Threes are also able to observe and describe how their minds work during their calm, nondriven periods. Because they are able to shift their attention to an observing state of mind and are able to reflect upon the workings of their own internal habits, they are well on their way to growing out of their neurotic style.

Point Three's habitual preoccupations include
· Identification with achievement and performance.
· Efficiency.
· Competition and the avoidance of failure.
· The belief that love comes from what you produce, rather than for who you are.
· Selective attention to whatever is positive. Tuning out of negatives.

- Poor access to personal feelings. Emotions are suspended while the job gets done.
- Presentation of an image that is adjusted to gain approval. A high-profile public persona.
- Confusion between one's real self and the characteristics that are appropriate to one's role or job.
- A way of paying attention that is called convergent thinking, in which a multitrack mind is focused upon a single goal.
- Intuitive adjustment of self-presentation, often to the point of believing that the image is one's true self.

Family History

Threes were prized for what they could produce and achieve, rather than for themselves. They eventually learned that the way to approval and love was successful performance, so they became adept at self-promotion and at projecting an image that incorporated the ideal characteristics of a role.

There has never been a time when I haven't been measuring my value in terms of something tangible that other people could look at. I had a mother who was definitely interested in prepresidential material, and there were four siblings, close in age. I had a conventional middle-class upbringing, where there was a lot of talk about love, but not much contact. So achieving became like a horse race, with a very limited amount of recognition for me as being special, different from everybody else. The way to get that recognition was to ace the piano recital, or make the calendar that was selected for the class billboard, or whatever else would get people's attention.

When I was performing I was being noticed, being fed from that small well of love. So it became a cycle, every achievement became the benchmark for the next success. Achievements weren't cumulative, you had to keep on doing more, so my value came to mean what I had done that day, or on that test, or in that interaction.

The characteristics of a type are most exaggerated during the late teens and the twenties. The following statement was given by a seventeen-year-old high school senior and is typical of a young Three's preoccupation with competitive achievement and the avoidance of failure in other people's eyes.

Besides having to get straight As in school, I'm featured in the big dance performance that we're having, and I'm trying really hard to lead a successful social life. I work every day from one to five, besides going to school from eight to twelve. I go home and do my homework, and make up dances, and stay up until two in the morning. Basically I do it because if I don't, then nobody's going to like me. I want to do really well in school, but I can't say that it's because I'm gung ho about the classes that I'm taking. I most want to come up with a good report card, because then people think that I have everything. So going to school is more for being recognized than for a purpose.

I did gymnastics for six years, four hours a day, six days a week, from six to ten every night, and for the last three years that I did it, I hated it. I didn't know that I hated it at the time, I didn't know that I hated it until I quit. It was just go. Go home, do homework, go to gymnastics, do more homework, go to sleep, go to school, just go, go, go. You don't have time to stop and think, Do I really enjoy what I'm doing? I'd go to competitions, and I really wouldn't like them, but who could afford to sit around complaining? And I'd win, and my father and mother would think it was great, and I'd think, More, more, go for more.

It got to the point where I had problems watching the Olympics on TV. It got seriously down to either quit or have a nervous breakdown. Finally what persuaded me to quit was that a friend quit, and it was okay and nobody hated her. So one day I just gave up. So then I don't have anything to do, so I have to fit all this extra stuff into my schedule, and I go out and find myself a job, and start dancing, and I'm class president, the whole thing. Now I have to get into Stanford.

So I don't tell anybody that I'm applying to Stanford, or at least nobody who'll be around to find out if I don't get in. I can't describe how bad it feels to go out for something and not be sure you can win, so if it turns out badly, even my best friends won't find out that I failed, and I'll try as hard as I can to forget it. I'm gone, I've got other stuff to do.

Threes become the ideal prototype of whatever group they value. If they are raised in a family that thinks highly of public performance, then they will strive in that area. If the family values other kinds of achievements, then a Three child will work hard to conform to that image. A woman who was raised in the country describes her family situation.

From the time that I was little, my mother told me that I was going to do something special. Not that I was special, but that I was going to *do* something really special. She was a single parent, and pretty unstable emotionally, so how I pleased her was to pretty much raise my younger brother and sister. Academics was not what I was encouraged for, it was more for being a helper around the house, for taking care of people. I created my own boutique and sold it after six months at a profit. It was a success from the instant that we opened the doors. My businesses have always come easily, because I know exactly what people want, and I give it to them.

In terms of productivity, I could take a couple of classes on a business topic and get myself hired to teach. Once I've got the surface elements, there's an internal challenge to get in there and be accepted as an authority, be respected by people whom you admire. As a child I didn't feel loved for who I was, but got stroked for a job well done. It's a weak spot for me that I have to watch. Almost anybody can get my time if there's strokes and recognition involved.

Polyphasic Activity

Because love has been given for product rather than for the real self, activity and production eventually develop into a form of control. Keeping busy ensures a constant stream of product and also effectively absorbs any free time in which feelings of anxiety about potential failure might surface. A Three is used to doing several things at once and will advocate keeping as many balls in the air as possible as an efficient use of time. Outsiders, however, tend to see a Three's need for continuous polyphasic activity as a way to not have time for an emotional life.

I can talk on the phone, feed my daughter, make an appointment, and listen to a conversation all at the same time, and track all of it. It's an extension of having two or three jobs going at the same time, so there's always the next thing to go on to before you finish the task in hand. There's a real sense of security in having the time filled, with no dead spaces.

Relaxing has the purpose of getting ready for the next round. The hot tub is on the schedule, because it saves my body, and while I'm in there, I've got a tape recorder sitting on the tub deck, and my mind on the next day, the next conference, the next deal. If I'm cut off from the contact of people telling me how well I'm doing, and there's no good feedback coming my way, there's a great temptation to run to the gym, or run off to someplace where there are people who will give me a little praise.

Image

Because approval depends upon successful performance, Threes are likely to exert such force of attention upon the mechanics of a job that they forget their own feelings and begin to project an image that is suitable to the task at hand. Threes modify their outward presentation easily and often find that they have intuitively adjusted in order to embody an image that gets their message across, or that helps to promote occupational visibility in their field.

To the extent that Threes are aware that the image they project does not necessarily represent their emotional point of view, they are able to alter their image without the danger of identifying with some prestigious facade that gets attention from others. Self-aware Threes know that they suspend their emotions while they work and that they can abandon themselves by becoming what other people want them to be. They also say that they have to watch out for their capacity to deceive others by projecting an image that will make people believe whatever they say.

To the extent that Threes are not aware of their habit of suspending personal feelings while the job gets done, they are vulnerable to believing that they and the image that they project are the same. It can be painful for Threes to recognize that they have needs that run counter to a high-profile image that maximizes the effectiveness of a role.

It switches with whatever group I'm with. It's like a quick change artist, I can feel myself go into whatever the group would like me to be. On a superficial level you have three or four different changes of wardrobe in your closet so that you'll fit in wherever you have to go. For about ten years I'd go from a three-piece suit to full motorcycle leathers to evening dress in the course of a single day; and I'd change as many times internally, according to the crowd that I was running with.

I immediately know how I'm coming across to other people. I can feel a kind of thrill in my body, like I'm alive when I'm connecting. If I'm not connecting, if I haven't scored in some way, I feel it as a not-energy, like nothing's there. I know when I'm accepted, because I can feel in my body that I'm meeting expectations and making an impression.

Advertising agencies embody classic Three qualities. Advertising people are in touch with the images that others value and are able to package and promote those images in an appealing way. Threes, however, are adept at taking on and becoming the image that is most valued by their particular social group. The competent professional, the ideal civic leader, the perfect mate. Work is the preferred area of interest, but if a more laid back way of life is what is accepted, then a Three will be likely to adopt that style and can spend years living out an image rather than getting in touch with real emotional preferences.

I'm living in suburbia with my two sons and my part-time therapy practice, in an ideal setting with what I always knew I wanted in life. It's difficult, however, to say what I'm feeling most of the time. What I'm aware of most is the appearance of things. Are my children clean and looking happy? Hard to just be with them and spend time, without making everything into an activity. What I realized is that I'm cultivating the image of the perfect New Age woman alternative therapist, living with her sons in the suburbs.

A Performer will adapt into being the prototype of whatever cultural norm is valued. A surfer will have a hot board and the perfect tan, a manager will exhibit a charismatic leadership style. Attention is focused outwardly, on any cues that indicate positive attention from others, to the extent that a Three withdraws awareness from personal feelings and works hard in the interest of projecting an impressive personal style. The self-deception is complete if real feelings submerge and are replaced by a pseudoself that takes on leadership positions by adopting a presentational style that other people trust.

The major decisions of my life were made in the light of image. Choosing to be involved in a certain relationship because of the image that the woman would project. Choosing a college, the kind of work that I would do, the kind of fraternity house that I would be in, based on prestige.

These decisions are also made in reaction to image, in thinking that I do not want to be seen as an outsider, as counterculture, I do not wish to live out that image. So being with the most attractive woman at the dance, or having the most honors in the group can become a compulsion.

The replacement of real feelings with an acceptable performing self can be particularly painful to Threes when they realize that they can make honest and enduring commitments to their intimates, couched in all the appropriate nuances and an engaging presentational style, without being truly connected to the emotions that they hear themselves describe. A personal crisis can develop if a Three wakes up to the discrepancy between real feelings and the fact that they have been fooling others by projecting an appealing facade. A Three can feel like a phony, like someone who has been getting away with a fraudulent story and not been found out. The realization that real feelings do not always match the roles that others value can be accompanied by real rage. Threes are angry with the fact that others fall so easily for a good front and that they have not been valued for themselves.

If you're in a situation that makes you uncomfortable, you can show emotion, but you don't show it because you feel it, you show it because you're supposed to be feeling it. Like if somebody says that they care about you, you say the same thing back, because that's what your friends do, it works out as the right thing to do, whether you truly feel it or not. You can put out an image of being emotional, when in fact your head can be off a million miles away, doing something else.

You could be on the threshold of death and still have to look cool. If I were starving, and you put a bowl out, it's dicey as to whether I'd reach out if you were looking. You're so sure that it's instant rejection if you look bad in the eyes of someone you respect.

Threes are identified with the images that they project: beautiful images of youth, intelligence, and productivity. It can be a shocking realization when a young Three discovers that outsiders can tell the difference between who the Three really is and the pseudoself that the Three believes will win a little love. Stemming from a childhood where only the successful were held in high regard, adult Threes live with a compulsion to be front runner, to be that winner who is worthy of love. From an outsider's point of view, Threes can also be perceived as pressed, as being in struggle and as having sold themselves out for personal gain.

The attention of Performers is focused on comparative status and on the acquiring of status symbols that are the tangible evidence of success. They are vain about their achievements, about their honors, about having won out over their competitors. They strive to be in positions where they have power over other people's lives. They are narcissistic in the sense that they are convinced of their own competence and superiority and are self-centeredly focused upon the projects that give them value in their own eyes. Their vanity, however, is based on their ability to perform, and to earn, rather than on a deluded sense of innate natural worth. Threes work for what they get; their power is in being able to outlast the competition and to finish the project. Unlike true narcissists, Threes are quite aware that the world does not owe them a living and they experience severe anxiety if they are unable to earn status and respect. They live with a sense of confidence in their capacities but not with a belief that they do not need to earn their way.

So much is invested in success that if an objective failure does occur, Threes redefine the failure as a partial success, or pin the blame on others. There is an urge to escape a shaky project or a sinking relationship and move quickly on to better things.

There will be no feeling of failure if another promising opportunity can be mobilized quickly enough. Threes can change jobs and change identities without breaking stride, and as long as there is enough activity and enough hope for a better future, negative feelings can be kept at bay. Their extreme adaptability is both a blessing and a burden. The blessing is that they can move quickly and efficiently under pressure. The burden is that real feelings are suspended in the interest of getting the job done, and that as a consequence of their ability to take on new opportunities and become the image that the new role suggests, they are perceived as people who can change hats for self-serving purposes.

Deception and Self-deception

We see examples of the power of appropriate image in the political arena, for example, in the personal appeal of Ronald Reagan and the comfort that the nation takes in being assured and led by a man who emanates qualities of sincerity and good intent. Skilled performers are able to take on characteristics that are particular to a role and to become the identity that they have chosen. In the movie *Pumping Iron*, Arnold Schwarzenegger, the many-time world champion of bodybuilders, and a likely Three, describes his competitive edge as a psych-out technique: he projects the impression of himself as an unbeatable winner to other contestants before they pose together on stage.

Threes commonly report that they are aware of the manipulative possibilities of deliberately projecting an image that will generate trust. They also say that they get so immersed in their role that they deceive themselves by paying selective attention to support and discarding negative feedback as sour grapes from poor losers. As long as image needs are being met, Threes will want to press excitedly forward for a win.

I will go for the person who models whatever I am interested in. It could be anything from Latin American politics to an academic subject to something in the fine arts. High-profile people who look really together. Successful people who've got all the externals solved. Money, position, and power are very attractive. It's wonderful to keep moving toward your ideal image and very painful to see through to the falseness of images, to see that you've worked so hard to keep the front up and that there may not be that ideal job for you at the end of the line, or that not everybody loves a winner. Like a fantasy cookie that crumbles to sawdust because of what you had to do to get it.

You wake up to the fact that you're focused on image with a sense of self-betrayal. You betray yourself by juggling to stand out in whatever group you're with. There's a great pain in realizing the degree to which I will adjust myself to be the most perfect woman that somebody has ever met, or to be the one who leads and is looked up to by the crowd. Right now it is more important for me to be friends with an old lover, and to know that they like me for who I am, than to be trying to get something out of them in terms of the fantasy image that I thought I was when we were doing our relationship together.

Intimate Relationships

The schism between the real self and the performing self that developed in childhood is particularly apparent in intimate relationships.

Feelings have always seemed incompatible with getting the job done. You can either sit around and be emotional, or you can get on with it. As a result I've had a lot of people tell me that I step on them, that all I care about is their output, rather than their feelings. It's quite true, in a way, because I'm applying the same yardstick to them as I do to myself. It has, for example, been hard for me to recognize that other people slow down under pressure, or that they get disoriented if their private life isn't working out.

When I try to stay with my own feelings, there's a sense of real confusion. Do I have the right one? How am I supposed to tell the difference between my own and the ones that my image thinks it should be feeling? When you've lived your whole life fitting into other people's expectations, and all of a sudden you get hit with your own experience, it can be alarming. Real likes and dislikes come up. You try to come up with a different barometer, how things feel, rather than how they look. Focusing on yourself rather than others terrifies you, because you don't know what you're going to find out about yourself, or even if there's anyone at home to find.

Threes can project the image of being an intimate partner, while at the same time being aware of performing a role. If sensitivity is required, then sensitivity is presented, but not necessarily felt. They are vulnerable to "performing" intimate partnerships, to becoming what they suppose a potent partner should be, or "doing" the perfect mate. When real emotions emerge, there is a sense of inexperience: "I have only one or two clear emotions. Where are the rest?" Or there is a sense of jamming up: "If I let any feelings come, I'll be overwhelmed and immobilized." The most common questions from workaholic types who are opening up to feelings for the first time are, "Do I have the right one?" and "Will I get stuck in my emotions and be unable to produce?"

Anger is the most difficult to deal with. I've disappeared for months and realized afterward that it was because I was deeply angry, and it took that long to get it under wraps. It's the emotion that blows image and turns everybody off, and rather than deal with it it's easier to switch jobs, switch image, and create a new world that will protect me from that kind of situation again.

At this point in my work on myself, I appreciate someone who's going to get me onto my feelings. In looking back I see many situations that would have resolved differently if I had dealt with those feelings in the moment. It seems to me that I can't get to what I'm feeling in the moment, that I need space and time to figure it out. But then if I get too much space I know that I'll have the time to develop a script that sounds genuine even to me. The safest strategy seems to be for me to ask for time to figure out what I feel and to agree to a discussion at some definite point in the near future.

On the high side of relationship, Threes show extraordinary support for the goals and aspirations of family members. They work hard to provide and take great pleasure in the successes of those with whom they are identified. They are great at getting others out of seclusion or off negative emotions and into emotionally constructive activities. If they are identified with family life, they will spend time and energy on the family. If they are identified with the idea of intimacy, they will work hard to be an intimate partner. If they are identified with work, however, there won't be much time for either family or love.

On the low side, they can get easily distracted from feelings by projects, which Threes take on in the spirit of working for the family, but which translates to others as a craving for personal success.

They are greatly concerned with the physical appearance and the external accomplishments of a partner, which can replace depth of feeling.

I feel that I'm great on the first hit, a great date, mutual admiration, I'm at my best when the attention spotlight is on. As the relationship progresses, I want to go into work, and my partner feels ignored. A big problem has been wanting to come home late because I'm working to earn money to be successful for us, and finding hurt feelings when I get there.

When feelings come up that are too much for me, I have ways of cutting them off that drive my partner crazy. When the emotions heat up, I just check out with work, or find myself mentally redoing a project while our serious talk is under way. Or it just feels like it's time to leave. When I say, "Back off," I mean it, I can't stand being pushed. I need time to cushion any bad opinion or sense of failure in private, and when I know that I'm going to survive it, and that I'll still be able to face myself, then I'll want to come back.

An Example of a Couple Relationship: Three and Five, the Performer and the Observer

Both Three and Five have an issue with emotional intimacy: for Three, it is being seen for the self rather than for achievements; for Five, intimacy brings up fears of exposure and humiliation. There is an initially limited window of emotional contact. Three buffers intimacy with too much to do, and Five buffers intimacy by withdrawal. The usual scenario places Three as pursuer and Five as pursued. Three makes things happen, and Five does not resist.

A Performer will move toward intimacy when image needs are being met and will move away when self-esteem is low. An Observer will move toward intimacy in short bursts, under guarantees of noninvolvement. Each has a delayed reaction to sudden emotional encounters and needs to withdraw in order to figure things out. Each must be sensitive to when the other is available. Three needs to respect privacy and not take over by becoming managerial. Five must build up tolerance for spontaneous contact without needing to move away.

A Three keeps looking for things to do to make the relationship work, and in this he or she is unimpeded by any counterforce from Five. Because there is no control issue to fight about, Three is often attracted to setting up a picture-book life and then starting to take on projects. If they develop a home routine, then Three and Five often collude to lead otherwise separate lives. The Observer compartmentalizes: he or she keeps activities and friends separated from one another, puts intimacy into a box, and withdraws immediately afterward. If the household becomes tense, a Five's withdrawal can turn into long periods of closed doors and minimal communication. If Three is busy enough, he or she may not notice. If Three's projects interfere with home routine and meals, Five will respond by sulking and, if feeling safe enough, by fierce Eightlike anger (security point). Anger from an intimate is deadly to a Three and will cause a swift retreat.

In terms of social life, Three wants to project an appealing image, likes to go places, and feels safe and loved when performing. Five is more retracted, likes to be alone, and will not accompany Three to unpredictable public situations. Five wants to know the concert program and who will say what to whom. Three will organize and carry the ball socially and will often cover for the Five in public encounters. A project-related partnership places the Five as the invisible thinker who operates through the Three by remote control. The Performer makes all public contact, negotiates the decisions, and phones progress reports back to the Observer, who has never left home.

Authority Relationships

Threes want to be the authority. They can prioritize and compete well and enjoy the recognition of success. They most commonly compete for a personal win, for example, they may strategize to take on leadership of a group. If they become identified with a team effort, however, Threes are forceful in rallying the group and will assume an unacknowledged leadership role. A Three on the team guarantees forward motion.

On the high side, they are an example of the personally committed authority and a rallying point for others. They can offer unqualified commitment to the task and an optimism about future success. They move directly from an idea into action and are willing to take on other authorities with opposing views.

Threes are able to wing it through difficult interactions, with a fix-it-next-time-through attitude, and to support others in moving into exposed, high-risk positions, without getting bogged down in cautionary fears.

On the low side of authority interactions, Threes are likely to take control by working around the existing authorities. They get jobs done by cutting corners, with an appreciable loss of quality control. There is a likelihood of exaggerated self-promotion, or a habit of relating to others through a work role rather than through feelings. "My image talks to your credentials."

An Example of an Authority Relationship: Three and Six, the Performer and the Devil's Advocate

In a good relationship the Six will be the idea person and troubleshooter, and the Three will promote the project and provide the follow-through. If the Six can set the idea and refine the scheme by giving full scope to the Devil's Advocate habit of questioning and seeking out hidden flaws, then the Three will be in the perfect position of promoting an ethical and solidly based product. If the Six feels respected for ideas, then the Three will be welcome to most of the public spotlight and public presentation.

If the Six feels neglected, however, then suspicions will arise about a power takeover by Three. Six will assume that Three is aware when presentation is deceitful or exaggerated and will suspect Three of deliberately scheming for personal self-advantage rather than acting for the general good. This puts Six in the underdog position, and Six may then look for allies behind Three's back. The Three will be focused on getting to the goal by whatever means necessary and will be oblivious to Six's concerns. Once focused on a goal, a Three's emotions are suspended, and he or she is therefore insensitive to what coworkers are feeling. A Three is so identified with an image that is composed of the best features of a successful authority that he or she is unaware of the fact that others are becoming exhausted. Three tunes out negative comments, interprets Six's questioning as interference, and tries to assume control: "Watch out for my tracks on your back."

If a project is in trouble, Three will want to work harder and Six will want to talk. If the project continues to look shaky, Three will want to veer off to a job with better prospects. Six will see this as betrayal and will want to hold on to turn the project around. If a project is successful, a Three will want to expand and franchise, whereas a Six will tend to become cautionary and to procrastinate in a successful stance. The Six will become concerned about possible threats stemming from the jealousy of others and will counter the threat by becoming preoccupied with the values and ethics of success.

If the Three is able to share decision-making power, and to inform others fully before taking action, Six's paranoia level will decrease considerably. It is also helpful for the Three to provide long-distance vision at those times when Six falls into procrastination and doubt. The authority relationship will be greatly improved if the Six learns to question openly, rather than allowing suspicions to build that may be based on faulty information.

Assets

Point Three embodies an infectious enthusiasm for projects and future goals. Coupled with immense capacities for hard work, its exemplars can inspire others to high levels of personal excellence. There is a desire for lifelong learning and an antidepressive ability to find interesting things to do. Threes possess a natural ability to present themselves and their projects in an effective way. There is an interest in supporting social programs that help people to rise materially by their own efforts and in developing future leadership.

Attractive Environments

Attractive environments include small businesses that have been built up through effort and long hours. Managers. Salespeople. Media. Advertisers and image makers. Jobs that require the consolidation of known ideas into workable systems. Packaging, promotion, marketing, and sales.

Threes become the model of their habitat: the prototype radical on the left, the prototype conservative on the right. They gravitate toward environments where they can excel and avoid those where they cannot achieve. High-profile jobs with room for advancement. The corporate ladder, the person at the top. Politicians who get voted in on media image and personal style.

Unattractive Environments

Unattractive environments include jobs with a limited future. Work that is not prestigious. Anything that entails a public image that runs counter to a Three's social sphere. Creative projects that require introspection or periods of trial and error before a product emerges. Threes are journalists rather than novelists, magazine art directors rather than serious painters who need months to develop a piece.

Famous Threes

Famous Threes include *Werner Erhard*, the supersalesman of consciousness, who packaged the growth movement under the banner "est works."

Ronald Reagan □ Walt Disney □ Farrah Fawcett
John F. Kennedy

How Threes Pay Attention

To an observer, a Three looks like a highly focused achiever; Threes report, however, that they are only trying to keep up. If someone else is good, the Three has to be better, because a Three's self-esteem is riding on a win. Activity is a form of control, and personal value and security depend on how much you can get done. A Three habitually does several things at once, a way of paying attention that is called polyphasic thinking.

I'm in the car and slightly late. At the same time that I'm driving, I'm conversing with the back seat rider, scanning mirrors for cops, moving back and forth over the speed limit, eating a sandwich, and checking in and out of the radio. There's a sense of well-being with it all going on at once; like being on top of things.

Polyphasic activity has its counterpart in an internal habit of attention that is largely focused on tasks. Attention rarely stays with the project at hand, but moves rapidly on to the next thing to do. There is practically no space between thoughts for reflection, for reconsideration of priorities, for paying attention to personal feelings about the job.

You've got to be best, because otherwise you don't exist. The sense is that you're perpetually number 2, trying to be number 1. There are always three or four projects under way, and you're running through the physical motions of one, with your mind on the mechanics of the next. By the time I'm near the end of the first project, I'm so involved in the next that I hardly realize the first one is over. It's like the present doesn't exist, because I'm always ahead onto what to do next.

As a way of understanding this stance of attention, you might imagine yourself established at permanent high speed, gravitating toward stress and competition as a preferred way of life. You are sensitive to anything in the environment that will contribute to your current goal, and you see people in terms of what they possess or what they can do to help the project materialize.

As goals become more focused, your interest increases and so does the speed at which you want to work. Attention narrows to those cues in the environment that will support forward motion toward the goal, and people start to look like automatons who are either blocking forward motion or who have something that will serve the work. If they are automatons who are in the way, you either ignore them or walk around them. If they are automatons who can serve the project, you seek them out for what they can give.

Obstacles only serve to increase your focus of attention. Focus increases under pressure because if you fail to achieve the goal, or somebody else gets there first, you will feel anxious about being an unlovable failure. Runners-up are unlovable. You either take first place or have no place at all.

If obstacles continue, then you go inside yourself and brainstorm every similar situation that you can remember, ferreting out every relevant past solution that has any bearing on the current case. This narrowing of attention to all the bits and pieces of environmental cues, old memories, and past solutions that relate to a current goal is called convergent thinking. It is a state of mind that Threes are particularly suited to and that helps them find creative solutions when routine solutions have failed.

I've turned several businesses around to where they've become extremely profitable. Some of my best saves have been when I've geared up for a deadline by pulling out every half-feasible idea from all the other projects I've been on. My saves have been through a bizarre combination of ideas that worked successfully in other contexts.

Identification

When a project becomes successful enough to hold a Three's attention, all of her or his mental effort converges upon the goal, and she or he begins to embody the characteristics that are particular to the job. This meeting of image and attention is called identification; it is a defense mechanism by which we become like people or prototypes that we are exposed to when we are young. For most of us, psychological identification means something like, "I am like my mother" or "I am an American." For a Three, identification can mean "I have become the prototype of what I do." When identification takes place, a Three has difficulty separating personal worth from the worth of the Three's product, and if the product comes under question, then the Three feels personally attacked.

Threes have a lifelong habit of shifting attention from real feelings in the interest of efficiency and in order to "do" the image that a task requires. They are particularly susceptible to identification, because they look to others for approval and can therefore mobilize a lot of energy to change into what other people want. They are often unaware of the fact that they do not stop working long enough to ask themselves how they feel about what they are doing, or if they would prefer to be doing something else.

Once identification takes place, a Three can become persuaded that she or he has always been that ideal doer. The self-deception is only partial if the Three feels fraudulent, like a person who is hiding behind a mask, acting out a role in order to make a good impression. Identification can be pervasive enough, however, to cause a Three to take on a role and live it out for many years; perhaps until an illness or a midlife crisis forces a work stoppage that allows time for feelings to surface. If there is a title, an impressive image, or a lot of money involved, Threes may well work until they drop "for the firm," "for the corporation," for whatever role they have become identified with, without ever stopping to ask whether their lives are fulfilling.

Identification Exercise

This is an exercise that can help you understand the shift of attention that Threes undergo when their attention merges with an image.

Sit facing a partner. Designate one of you to be the observer, and the other to be the Three. If you are the Three, you are the active partner in the exercise, so close your eyes so as to be undistracted by the observer's reactions. Keeping your eyes closed, choose a quality with which to identify. Choose a quality that you don't believe you actually embody. For example, you could choose to identify with the quality of beauty, or handsomeness, or intelligence, or compassion, or joy; but try to pick one that feels alien to you.

Imagine feeling that quality within yourself. It will help you recognize the quality's feeling if you remember a time when you actually did feel that way. Notice the shifts of attention that you go through while you "make up the quality." Notice the fact that the quality comes and goes. When the quality is present, you are feeling like a Three who is becoming identified with that quality, and when you have to exert effort to keep the quality present, you are feeling like a Three who is holding up an image.

With your eyes still shut, focus fully on the imagined quality and let it permeate your body. When you can stabilize your

attention on the sensations or feelings that the quality stimulates in your body, open your attention to include the observing
partner, and pretend that she or he is an important person in
your life; someone such as a boss or a spouse, who has the
power to affect you, and who you are going to pretend is susceptible to the quality that you are embodying.

Now open your eyes, and while keeping your attention focused inwardly on the presence of the quality, simultaneously
carry on a simple conversation with the observer. Notice the
shifts of attention that happen as you attempt to identify internally with the quality to which your partner is susceptible.
Threes would recognize these internal fluctuations of attention
as the difference between times when they are faking an impressive image and times when they have become so immersed
in an image that they are the quality that the partner values.
Threes habitually shift their attention to identify with culturally
valued images and begin to project these images as themselves
without remembering to question the difference between an
adopted image and their own internal feelings.

When a Three can successfully personify an image, she or he
will become acutely aware of other people's reactions. If the
image is effective, the Three will remain identified with it. If
the public does not approve, then self-presentation will tend to
be unconsciously modified.

Intuitive Style

As a child, Three's security depended upon being best at activities that were valued by others. A child whose well-being is
linked to image and performance is also likely to develop sensitivities to information that supports those emotional needs.

When I enter a new situation, I'm immediately aware of how I'm coming across to others. I can sense myself "shooting for the middle" of
however the group feels to me. It's not so much an emotion that I feel,
it's that I can sense what the group will accept, and start to behave
that way.

I depended a lot on that in promotional work. I was going from group to group with the same product line, and each time the story came out in a slightly different way. I'd stand up to give my talk, and sometimes hear myself redirect the pitch in midsentence, without knowing exactly why I was doing that. Or I would feel my body going into its own performance that was different from what I had planned.

If this sales representative did not know that his real position was replaced when he slipped into a presentational style, he would experience considerable confusion between the two. There are several interesting outcomes that could develop from his learning to tell the difference between his own feelings and the adjustments that he undergoes when he tries to make a sale. The first outcome is likely to be emotional. He would either become anxious about lying to his audiences, or he might have the desire to deceive them more effectively by developing his intuitive ability to make people want the products that he has to sell.

Another outcome could be a step toward telling the difference between what he wants for himself and driven activity that does not serve his personal needs. Yet another outcome could be that he trains himself to voluntarily reenter the state of mind in which he can intuitively adjust his presentation in order to match the wishes of a group and find out what other information is available in that state of mind.

Hope as a Quality of Higher Mind

Performers measure their value in terms of what impresses others. They are vain about their accomplishments, but believe they have little value separate from what they do. When Threes begin to work compulsively, when they push the river to make a project happen, they have forgotten themselves by immersing their attention in the neurotic habit of finding identity through a task.

The positive aspect of compulsive doing is that Threes feel alive in the midst of activity and become adept at sensing the energy requirements of different jobs. Our exemplars certainly remember the times when they were exhausted and drained by the hurry habit; but they also describe times when they have worked and felt themselves aligned with the pacing and flow that is natural to a particular task.

Threes say that it's like being suspended in the midst of an inexhaustible energy; you are aware that work is being carried along, rather than that you have to direct. They say that time slows down, although you may be working at top speed; that worry drops away, and you enter a frame of mind where what needs to be done presents itself without counterthought or question. In that state of mind, a project's positive outcome seems assured. Anxiety about the project drops away because you are aware of the fact that each stage of the work inevitably leads to a correct conclusion.

This statement, given by a San Francisco restaurateur, who sees himself as a confirmed workaholic, describes an experience of hope:

I'm often working alongside people who are half my age, and it's still a source of pleasure for me to do it and do it well. There are times in the kitchen that are so frenzied and so fast, that you're literally elbow to elbow in a kind of ritual motion in a tight space where you might get hurt, or you could blow an entire menu item for the night. At those times all I can think is, "God, I hope this turns out okay."

There are times when I fight the work, and times when it goes so well that my mind gets quiet at high speed. Then I could be hours on the line and feel great, because I know that it's going to turn out right.

The Virtue of Honesty

Threes get a good deal of validation in the American culture. In fact, they receive so much validation that they can easily mistake a neurotic style of being for genuine health. Why set personal goals when you can deceive yourself that society's goals are really your own? Why run the risk of rejection when acceptance can be bought by projecting an image that brings you respect? Why have a self if it's going to suffer? The saner approach might be to identify with the cultural standards, suspend your emotions, and abandon yourself.

Threes are often convinced of their own psychological soundness. Emotional distress is for losers, for those who have time on their hands or who can't keep up the pace. Neurotic Threes may have lost all awareness of the fact that there is a difference between the highly achieving pseudoself and their own emotional wishes. They are likely to be aware of the fact that they do not like sticky emotions, or do not like to feel that they have emotional needs; but the fact that their range of feelings is very small is likely to be overlooked, because Threes are energetic and need to project an image of optimism and success.

Performers commonly face their honest feelings during an enforced slowdown. They usually stop because of a job layoff, or an illness, or the intervention of a spouse, rather than making a voluntary decision to cut back. The enforced inactivity can be terrifying to a person whose worldview depends upon earning merit through work and typically brings up fears about self-worth and the realization that emotions inevitably come into awareness as soon as attention is withdrawn from activity.

Unless you're in action, there's a real sense that you do not exist. Unless I know what I'm supposed to be doing next, I start to get anxious that there's nobody home. Last year I got seriously ill from a clear case of overexertion. I was only forty and I had a coronary and lay there staring at the ceiling from a hospital bed, counting the days until I could get up and go.

The enforced quiet was worse than the heart attack. I thought that I was going to lose it in that bed, from the fear of not being physically able again. I could barely grasp what was happening to me when the feelings started to come. Sometimes there'd be just nothing, and then I'd freak out because there was too much, and then I'd numb out again.

Performers are used to doing, not feeling, and habitually suspend their emotions while an activity goes on. Feelings will have to be brought into awareness slowly, because their presence is experienced as threatening to a way of life that depends upon producing like a machine.

Threes who commit themselves to presenting honest feelings will have to learn to recognize the discrepancy between what their body is really feeling and the habit of shifting presentation in order to get a win. Their question of existence then becomes, Do I go with what I feel, or do I stay with my habit of knowing what to do? The risk in following feelings is that Threes inevitably lose the recognition that achievement guarantees; and the risk of not following feelings is that Threes live out life as a fraud.

For Threes, the shift in awareness from deceit to honesty (veracity) could be described as a gradually emerging side effect that stems from learning to tell the difference between truthful feelings and the need to do well in the eyes of others. In the process of making that shift, Threes are likely to experience a period of voluntary suffering, in which a protective habit that developed in childhood is given up in order to become psychologically free.

The following statement was taken from a highly successful career woman.

At the beginning of my therapy I thought that I was fine. It was my husband who had the problem because he wasn't as interested as I was in getting ahead in life. The first impulse was to run, to not feel anything, because as soon as I'd have a lot of free time, the only thing I'd feel was that I was afraid. Sundays were the worst. A whole day of nothing to do. It was ironing, and making calls, and getting myself together for the week, but all the time in between I would feel afraid.

I had to put my "emotion lessons" on a schedule. I had to remember to stop in the middle of a job and ask myself what my likes and dislikes were; and I had to find out if I was feeling anything. The hardest part of the exercise was to stay with a feeling while I went back to work, because as soon as I'd start an activity, my feelings were totally gone.

With time I built a repertoire of genuine emotions, which I am very proud about. I can be touched by people, my own reactions matter to me. I can tell if I'm happy, and if I like what I'm doing, and I'm living in a dimension of life that used to entirely hidden from me.

Subtypes

The subtypes are preoccupations that were formed in childhood as ways to reduce anxiety. For young Threes, any situation that could provide money, possessions (security), prestige, or an enhanced female or male image helped to lessen the fear of being unworthy in the eyes of others. With experience and self-observation, these same preoccupations are seen to be instrumental in producing an image, rather than being true to the feelings of the real self.

When Threes become aware of the fact that their honestly felt feelings may be different from socially valued norms, a crisis of decision can set in. Which way to go? Toward success or toward the self? Threes often recognize this dilemma when faced with retirement, when immobilized by illness, or when dealing with what seems like far too much free time. A conscious decision to give up image, or social prestige, or a secure financial base can feel life-threatening, because the self does not seem separate from these supports.

Masculine or Feminine Image in One-to-One Relationships

Threes tend to adopt a sexually appealing image and are often aware of performing a role. Being recognized as physically appealing or as sexually potent is taken as a sign of personal value, and Threes can compete to be attractive in other people's eyes. Some Threes report that the need to project a winning sexual image masks a deep confusion between the masculine and feminine aspects of themselves. This confusion commonly takes the form of feeling split between a "masculine driven self, and a more feminine 'other' self." An exaggerated feminine image can therefore act as a mask for confusion about "acting as competitively as any man." None of the Threes who report gender confusion are homosexual, nor do they think that their preoccupation with being seen as attractive is a mask for sexual ambivalence.

My greatest self-deceptions have been through intimacy. At the end of a ten-year marriage, I realized that I was feeling the qualities that I believed a perfect woman would embody, without being able to tell if they were my own. If my husband had fallen in love with a billboard model, I would have adopted the look, and the habits, and the dress that she wore.

Prestige in Social Groups

Threes are preoccupied with presenting a good social image. Their personal presentation will alter to assume the valued characteristics of the group. Threes want to lead the herd.

Early on it was important to have the most affiliations listed under your picture in the high school yearbook. Later on I became a clinician and I am always alert to who is giving workshops in my part of the country, and how well respected they are, although I may have no idea what their workshops are about.

I have also come to realize that the reason that I strive to be well known stems from the feeling that I am obliterated as a person if someone whom I see as influential and valuable disagrees with my approach.

Security in the Area of Self-preservation

Threes are caught up with money and material ownership as a way to reduce anxiety about personal survival. Threes work hard to produce the money and status that provides security.

It's the kind of terror that doesn't go away even if you're working to make as much as you can. You can have $50,000 in the bank and still be worried that there isn't enough, or that you should get a job that pays more, or that you should have a couple of backups just in case. There is a feeling that if someone criticizes your job performance, that your life is being threatened.

What Helps Threes Thrive

A Three often enters therapy or begins a meditation practice because a physical breakdown or a personal loss has made it impossible to maintain the pace that kept feelings at a distance.

The emotions that emerge as the result of this enforced slow-down can, at first, be experienced as threatening. Real feelings often interfere with the capacity to perform and can be confusing to a person who has never realized that he or she has a wide range of internal signals.

Contact with physical and emotional reactions should be encouraged, especially those disowned by Threes, such as fatigue, fear, and confusion about what to do next. Performers need to recognize those times when commitments and tasks begin to control feelings and to learn to wait until real responses surface.

They can be helped by
· Learning to stop. Leaving time for emotions and real opinions to surface. Contacting the fear of feelings that creates the desire for constant activity.
· Noting when actions become mechanical. Acting mechanically. Producing like a robot while feelings are suspended.
· Recognizing when real abilities are replaced with fantasies of personal success.
· Not veering off from problems by introducing new projects, reframing failure into success, or discrediting sources of criticism.
· Recognizing the postponement of emotional happiness. "I'll be happy after the next promotion."
· Recognizing a profound difference between an emerging private self and the public, performing self. Sense of being separate from the image.
· Noting feelings of being a fraud. Putting on a show. "Nobody looks behind the mask. I am not seen; only what I do is seen."
· Seeing your own participation in having to do so much; in feeling surrounded by incompetents and lazy people.
· Noting the desire to be the perfect therapy client. Producing Freudian dreams for the analyst, pounding the pillow for the Gestalt therapist. Reporting energy experiences to the

guru. Therapy becomes a job to master. Meditation becomes a task. "How many minutes did I sit perfectly still? How many mantras did I recite today?"

· Recognizing the existence of feelings by first finding and then naming the sensations that underlie feelings. For example, if it is hard to identify an emotion, begin by naming any physical sensations that you feel in your body. "My face is hot" or "my belly feels tight." Naming physical sensations helps you recognize what you feel.

· Learning to tell the difference between doing and feeling. Remembering to shift attention from task to feelings about the task.

· Starting meditation and attention practices on a scheduled basis, with a definite time limit. Sit for forty-five minutes and then go back to work. The "not doing" of meditation generates resistance that needs to be handled in therapy. Do not stress results for meditation, other than health benefits.

· Noticing when meditation becomes an activity such as a perfect score at counting breaths. Controlling the activity of a meditation practice prevents being acted upon by the state of mind that the meditation evokes. Learn to allow yourself to be moved, to be affected, to be acted upon.

· Supporting yourself in opting for feeling choices over status choices.

What Threes Should Be Aware of

As attention is redirected from preoccupations related to image and a workaholic way of life, Threes should be aware of reactions such as the following:

· Confusion about feelings. "Do I have the right one?" "Which one is real?"

· Confusing an idea about an emotion with the real thing.

· Overactive fantasy life. Imagining success when direct action is blocked or when negativity surfaces.

- Manufacturing a fantasy image about being enlightened or "being an evolved example of a Three." Bypassing the feeling state by believing that these qualities are already present. "I'm already there."
- Wanting quick results, feeling better when replacing feelings with work, desire to quit therapy before real change can occur.
- Needing proofs of success. Wanting to become the teacher in order to feel like a meditator.
- Habit of detaching from feelings when talking about personal issues, or having these issues arise in meditation. Believing that these issues have been solved once they are named and talked about, without having to experience emotions.
- Tendency to pick an omnipotent therapist or spiritual teacher, one who embodies the external values that are appealing to a Three. Identifying with therapist's values without finding your own.
- The fear that nobody's at home when meditating; that the real self does not exist.
- Feeling like a saint when others criticize. "I've accomplished so much that I don't have to listen."

9. Point Four: The Tragic Romantic

	ACQUIRED PERSONALITY		ESSENCE	
HEAD	Chief Feature:	MELANCHOLY	Higher Mind:	THE ORIGIN SOURCE
HEART	Passion:	ENVY	Virtue:	EQUANIMITY (BALANCE)
	SUBTYPE WAYS OF BEING			
	Sexual:	COMPETITIVE/HATEFUL		
	Social:	FEELING SHAME		
	Self-preservation:	DAUNTLESS/RECKLESS		

The Dilemma

Fours remember abandonment in childhood, and as a result they suffer from a sense of deprivation and loss. Their inner situation is reflected in the literary prototype of the tragic romantic who, having attained recognition and material success, remains steadfastly focused upon the lost love, the unavailable love, a future love, and a picture of happiness that only love can bring. To understand this worldview, you need to project yourself into a state of mind where decisions are based as much upon the shifting chemistry of mood as upon the perception of actual facts; and where conversations are remembered as much for their feeling tone and innuendo as for whatever words were actually expressed.

Depression is a frequent mood. It can bring life to the kind of halt where days are spent in bed, the mind regretfully attached to some unalterable past mistake. "If only, if only." Attention locks, like a record needle stuck in a deep cerebral groove. "If only I had acted differently. If only there were one more chance."

Fours are unanimous in their understanding of the black mood of depression. Some accept it fatalistically, succumbing to prolonged periods of self-isolation. Others fight their depression through hyperactivity, staying constantly on the run. Still others channel their emotions through a profound artistic exploration of the shadow side of human experience. The Fours quoted in this book have known depression, but they also describe a mood called melancholy, which is attractive to them, like a twisted emotional refuge that springs from loss and pain.

Melancholia creates an atmosphere of sweet regret. Like depression, it stems from a perception of loss, but here sadness is transformed into a mood of mistiness along bleak shores. Fours feel intensely alive in the shifting emotional mists; nothing is permanent because one's mood may change tomorrow.

The core issue is loss and a subsequent lowering of self-esteem. "Would I have been abandoned if I were more worthy?" Fours live with the conviction that there was an original source of love that was taken away. "I was loved once, where did it go?" There is often a history of literal abandonment and the need to grieve for early loss; however, feelings of abandonment are painfully recreated in adult life by a compulsive attraction to the unavailable and the (usually unrecognized) habit of rejecting whatever is easy to obtain.

Fours unconsciously focus their attention on the finer points of what is missing, so that by comparison, what is available seems to lack appeal. They particularly yearn for a passionate, fulfilling relationship; they assume the stance of the lover longing for the beloved. One of the sweetest shades of melancholia is the coupling of sadness over the loss of love with the romantic anticipation of an ideal future mate. There is the sense that the present is only a rehearsal for the future when "my authentic self will be reawakened through love."

When real life gains start to materialize, though these may be the fruits of years of anticipation and effort, attention will predictably shift to that which is missing in life. If you get the job, you want the man. If you get the man, you want to be alone. If you are alone, you want the job and man again. Attention cycles to the best in what is missing and, by comparison, whatever is available seems dull and valueless.

Romantics are likely to sabotage real gains. When attention is brought to bear on the day-to-day events of a real life love affair, Fours can become angrily disappointed at having to pick up their partner's socks and having to tolerate another person's idiosyncrasies. The image of a splendid future that was to emerge through love is threatened by the fact that an actual relationship contains some very boring moments. Small quirks in a partner's presentation turn into major irritants. "She is politically illiterate." "He has no ear for music." "How insensitive to leave a toothbrush in the glass!" There is a rage at having to accommodate to someone else's tastelessness and a fierce need to protect oneself for the future reawakening through love.

When it appears that intimacy may require a sacrifice of elite standards, Fours will want to drive their partners away, to force them to leave before the image of a precious and authentic relationship is corrupted by a negative influence. It becomes clear that the partner is to blame. Feeling bitterly disappointed, Fours will want to say the worst, in order to make it perfectly clear just how much they've been let down.

Once the relationship is driven back to a safe distance, the Romantic will begin to miss it once again. There is a push–pull pattern to relationships: pushing away what is available and pulling for what is hard to get. The grass is always greener at a distance, as attention shifts to the high points of an absent partnership.

Fours keep life at a safe arm's length. Not too far away, lest the familiar edge of longing turn into black despair; but certainly not too close. For although there is great yearning for intimacy with another, actual intimacy triggers the fear of being found deficient and potentially reabandoned. If the partner tires of being at arm's length and threatens to leave, a sudden illness or intense recrimination may follow, as the Four once again pulls for the relationship. Fours pull out all the emotional stops when abandonment looms. There are theatrical scenes and wild accusations, suicidal gestures and deep despair as the original loss is recreated in a highly dramatized way.

Fours say that the highs and lows of their emotional life open up an intensified level of existence that is beyond ordinary happiness, a level far richer than that for which other people seem to be willing to settle. There is the sense of being an alien outsider to ordinary reality, of being unique and strangely different, of being an actor who is moving through the scenes of one's own life. To give up the suffering of a heightened emotional life would mean sacrificing the sense of being special that drama tends to generate. For a Four the prospect of becoming happy can also threaten to close access to an intense emotional world. Worst of all, there is the risk of settling for a pedestrian vision and an ordinary life.

The preoccupations of point Four include
- The sense of something missing from life. Others have what I am missing.
- An attraction to the distant and the unavailable. Idealization of the absent lover.
- Mood, manners, luxury, and good taste as external supports to bolster self-esteem.
- An attachment to the mood of melancholy. Depth of feeling as a goal rather than mere happiness.
- Impatience with the "flatness of ordinary feelings." Needing to reintensify one's feelings through loss, heightened imagination, and dramatic acts.
- The search for authenticity. The feeling that the present is not real, that the real self will emerge in the future, through an experience of being deeply loved.

- An affinity with what is real and intense in life. Birth, sex, abandonment, death, and cataclysmic happenings.
- A push–pull habit of attention. Focus alternates between the negative features of what one has and the positive features of what is distant and hard to get. This attention style reinforces
  - Feelings of abandonment and loss, but also lends itself to
  - A sensitivity to other people's emotionality and pain. An ability to support others in crisis.

Family History

The underlying theme is childhood loss. Fours describe many variations of being abandoned by someone important in early life. They often describe a literal abandonment, the most common example of which is a divorce, in which a beloved parent went away. Another theme is having been born into a grieving family, in which the child was valued for identifying with a close adult's misery. The following statement was given by a talented dancer who has spent most of her adult life without relationship, entirely dedicated to her art.

I was an incubator baby, and so frail that my parents were told that I would not be likely to survive. I think that they withdrew from me to protect their own feelings, so that although I was not literally abandoned, that image feels correct for me. Then when I was a baby, my father began to die. I always think of myself as a person with a casket in the front room and scented flowers in the house. There's an attraction that I have to people who are around crisis and death, because they are far more in touch with their deep self and willing to be honest in some soul way.

Another childhood situation is described by Fours who felt abandoned because a parent came and went, or was alternately cruel and kind. The child became attached to the promise of affection and love and became angry when it was taken away.

When I was born my father took my mother on a trip around the world in celebration of my successful birth and left me behind with a nanny.

I adored him and did everything I could to please him. He was dash-
ing, popular, and unavailable, except when Mother was also there. He
would go away on long trips, and before he'd return, I'd be frantic
about getting him to stay. It would feel like this would be my only
chance to hold him. He would bring presents and tell stories, and then
he'd be gone again or, worse yet, he would be gone with her, and
there I would be left again, getting ready for the next time around.

There are several theories of depression that are anchored in
the idea that childhood anger was turned inward against the
self. Romantics commonly describe early feelings of loss that
have resulted in recurring depression during their adult life.

This statement was given by a man who traveled around the
world for ten years in search of the perfect companion. At different points in his journey he idealized radically different types
of women, both for their physical appeal and for certain qualities of being that he attributed to the culture in which he found
himself. Predictably, as he would begin to fall in love with one
of his women, he would also begin to miss the special qualities
of the rest. At the time that he gave this statement he had made
millions of dollars as an importer and was totally preoccupied
with his continuing search for a wife.

I asked my mother if she breast-fed me, and she said, yes, she did for
a while. My guess is that I had satisfaction as a baby, and then one
day it was missing; which is, incidentally, the same way that I feel
treated by her: she's there for me and then she's not. That's become
like a life stance: "I was happy once, where did it go?" For my whole
life I've been in search of it—where did it go?

Yet when people ask what I'm missing in life, and what it is I think
I'm seeking, it doesn't place itself as seeking "that thing, or that person, or that money." I'm searching for *it*, that feeling of connection
with something wonderful that is always hidden and always out of
reach.

Anger and Depression

There is often a feeling of rage at having been deprived, of
anger at the abandoning parent, who has caused such grief,

when others have been given more. This anger is likely to appear as biting sarcasm, as a need to verbally cut others down, to even the score for having been so badly hurt. More often than not there is no practical opportunity to get angry at someone who has either vanished or is likely to withdraw under fire. As a result, a Romantic's anger is usually directed inwardly as an intense self-criticism for not being worthy enough to have merited love.

This inwardly directed criticism makes Fours feel helpless and produces long periods of inaction, during which there appears to be no possible course of action toward happiness. Depression is based on feelings of sadness over having lost a basic and valuable human connection. It is the stance of the separated lover, yearning for a way to reunite.

Depression and Melancholy

Fours liken depression to being imprisoned in a black pit. They withdraw into themselves, move into a solitary part of the house, and gradually eliminate outside contact. There is the feeling that life has never been this bad before and a conviction that the situation will not change. If the depression deepens, offers of help begin to sound absurd in the face of the difficulty. Help is refused and one is powerless to act on one's own behalf. Activity stops and eventually there is a loss of hope that anyone could possibly understand the inner situation.

Romantics are not alone in experiencing sadness. We all mourn our own failures, or grieve when something precious has been lost. Depression is different from grieving for something that has been taken away, in the sense that there are stages of acceptance in grief, where eventually the pain lessens, and attention can be returned to rebuilding a workable life. In a severe depression, everything worthwhile in life is replaced by pervasive sadness, and the movement through the stages of acceptance is unusually slow.

I'm still on the divorce that happened eighteen years ago, because my mind is dominated by the idea that I've made an irreversible error that has altered the course of my life. The feeling is that you've blown your only chance for happiness, and you're desperate to pick up some thread of understanding so that you can get a way back in.

So you go over it and over it, trying to understand the intricacies of all the phases of what you've been through, which makes me so preoccupied with past mistakes that I've been oblivious to some really promising love affairs.

The mood of melancholy stems from the same sense of loss that produces a wretched depression. It is a sensibility that transforms the conviction that one has been deprived into a bittersweet yearning for things that are impossible or that can never be. Fours say that they prefer the richness of melancholia to what other people describe as happiness. It is a feeling of sadness that calls up imagery and metaphor, and the sense of being connected to distant things. Melancholy is a mood that elevates the life of an abandoned outsider to a posture of unique temperamental sensitivity.

It's like being a character in a story, a character who's been put under adverse circumstances. I'm in this world as an outsider, and no one understands who I am, which makes me feel different and misunderstood. It also brings on a kind of contained desperation. Nobody gets me, I'm an outsider and therefore tormented by not belonging, but I'm also intense inside because I am tormented. I live at the outer edges of whatever human beings can stand in the way of feelings. I remain mysterious to myself, and I am absolutely different from anybody else.

It is very easy to spot a Four who has become depressed. There is an ongoing lamentation for whatever is missing in life. The lament has become so self-preoccupying that it is impossible to turn attention to more productive things.

Melancholy, however, although it is also based in yearning, casts ordinary events into the dimensions of the aesthetic. Yearning takes on the quality of search, and depression is transformed into a poetic appreciation for the human condition.

Melancholy evokes the sense of being young and wrapping a cloak of invisible drama around myself. You never just walked, you walked with the swish of the cloak. You didn't walk for pleasure, it was for the feel of the costume and the electric air, and the stranger who was walking toward you who would change your life forever.

At home I felt like a victim, but the sense of being abused got ennobled into a fictionalized, dramatic character. She got to put on her cloak and her magic and wasn't interested in fun or being happy, because she sought the extraordinary instead.

I remember walks where the image of a flying bird would stay inside me for a mile, or a wet flower would become reason enough to go on for one more day. Melancholy is a place I choose to be, it's the place of making your life an artistic experience, and although it is centered around the search for something yet to come, it is the search that makes me happy.

Pain and Creation

There is a fine line between living one's life as an artistic expression and becoming preoccupied with pain as a way of supporting an aesthetic self-image. The connection between deprivation and artistic expression is as old as the image of the artist who starves in a garret rather than compromise the creative life by selling out to a lucrative livelihood. Life as art and life as pain are often intertwined, in that suffering can sensitize one's appreciation for what is most essential in life, and mobilize an atmosphere of inner tension that can be made meaningful when expressed through a creative act.

The following statement was given by an aspiring young painter who recognized herself as a Four when she was unable to attend her own gallery opening because she was incapacitated by love.

When a depression comes on, it replaces anything else that I have going. Life just stops. There is no point, no purpose, no hope. What I hold onto is the passage of time. Everything passes with time, and in time I'll be released, seemingly by just having waited it through. When you've been as confined by grief as I have been, your whole body feels as if it's being played by whoever you are grieving for. You literally give yourself over to be played upon by another person. After an experience like that, you feel like you've just recovered from a long illness. You appreciate small things, like weather and the colors that you want to wear. You feel privileged to have lived out so much. Tragedy will set you apart, in some way it will single you out, because you've looked at death and survived.

Loss places one outside the ordinary crowd. It makes one temporarily tragic and different, and somehow special in the sense that for that time one feels more deeply than other people do. The experience of one's self as unusually sensitive can also develop into a tenacious attachment to personal moodiness, particularly if loved ones happen to be attracted to intense displays of feeling, or if genuinely creative expressions well up during periods of emotionally charged sensitivity.

The dilemma of a creativity that is stirred by pain is exemplified by the life of the poet Rilke, who suffered deep psychological distress yet remained unwilling to enter analysis. He was certain that if his devils were driven out, his angels too would receive a shock.

Four is the Enneagram's place of the artist, which taken literally means that many working artists are Fours, but which also refers to a temperamental preference for evocative feeling states. Bouts of longing and despair are bound to produce an intensification of ordinary emotional climates. This intensity, and the sense of special purpose that it generates, can make the shifting moods of melancholia far more attractive than the range of ordinary feeling.

Mood Swings

Romantics live at the extreme poles of emotional life. There is a tendency to swing between depression at one extreme and hyperactivity at the other. Fours describe themselves as gravitating toward one or the other of the emotional poles, or as having lived out their lives swinging between the two extremes.

There are three kinds of Fours: basically depressed, basically hyperactive, and basically swinging in mood between the two extremes of feeling. All three kinds feel that something vital in life has been taken away and that they are seeking to regain what was lost, but the different kinds of Fours go about the search in radically different ways.

The basically depressed Four tends to withdraw into self-preoccupation in the search for meaning. The basically hyperactive Four does not look at all depressed on the surface and can move through activities and love affairs quite quickly, trying to extract meaning from the same external sources that appear to make other people happy. The Four whose moods swing between the poles of depression and hyperactivity presents the clearest picture of the inner intensity that all Romantics describe. There are radical shifts of emotion. Love turns into hate and passion turns into apathy. Attractions to unavailable or destructive lovers are likely to form, attended by dramatic outbursts and the discharge of intense feelings into suicidal fantasies.

Normal Fours say that suicide comes up in their thoughts as an "option" for them if life starts to get too bad. Fours lean toward a biting, sarcastic black humor, which reveals their inner anger. They describe suicide as "a little something you can count on if life pushes back too hard." What they mean by this is that they think of "bailing out" as an option, very much like a Two might think of seduction as an option, or an Eight might imagine blowing someone away as an option, without any deep-seated intention of acting it out.

Dramatized Emotional Life

Fours say that others find them too intense, that they have to hold their feelings back because their passions are so strong. They are very hurt by social oversights: a missed birthday leads to deep disappointment, casual remarks lead to alienation from friends.

A single overdue phone call can attach itself to the feeling of abandonment in a very dramatic way, and I react by overamping and alienating the people that I most want to be with. It's like the pain attaches itself to all of my past pains, and it becomes overwhelming. One late phone call can turn into a profound feeling of abandonment that will make me hate my friend by the time that the call comes in because I've been hurt so badly.

By *intensity*, a Four means living at the extremes of emotional reaction. One extreme is suffering and the other extreme is the fantasy of total fullfillment. There is not much experience with the range of feelings in between.

A thought such as, "Do I love him?" can attach itself so quickly to the imagining of what it might feel like to be utterly loved that there is no time to catch the real response to the question. A Romantic in an empty room can get so caught up in her own reveries about "what it felt like when he hurt me," or "what it will be like when he loves me," that she can lose touch with how she feels about "him" in the present moment.

Fours are not alone in their tendency to amplify their feelings. For example, we all tend to imagine the worst when we are in pain.

In natural childbirth or pain control training, patients learn to direct their attention exclusively toward the actual physical sensations that they are experiencing, rather than allowing themselves to slip into imagining how bad the next pain might be, or how the pain might feel at the worst possible extreme. Any real pain that is truly felt in the body can, unfortunately, be made intolerable if it becomes overlaid with sensate memory or imagination.

Here is a statement by a man who is describing his state of mind during a bad accident. The way that he reacted during his crisis does not necessarily indicate that he is a Four. Romantics, however, are especially vulnerable, on a daily basis, to the unconscious shift of attention that he describes.

I'd been a ski pro since my teens, and had never had a real accident until one day, on a totally familiar slope, I wiped out and broke a leg.

By the time I got to the hospital, I was out of my mind without knowing it. I had a lot of pain that I thought I could handle, but when someone tried to touch my leg, it got so bad that I'd fight them off.

I actually bit one nurse who tried to sedate me. All I could see was this needle in her hand and feel how much it was going to hurt when she stuck it into me. By the time my boss arrived, it was a standoff between me and the emergency room. The leg needed surgery, they were ready to go, and I wouldn't let them. He did me a great favor by grabbing me by the hair and threatening to punch me, unless I took the medication.

I thought that punch in the face was what snapped me back to myself. It did not compute that his fist was raised but that he hadn't struck, or that the needle that was grinding into my hip was clear across the room. I felt a blow in the face when I hadn't been hit and felt the needle when I hadn't been touched. In fact, I felt them strongly enough to forget the real pain in my leg while I believed those things were being done to me. When I got back to where I really was, in the emergency room, it felt like snapping out of a place where any touch was pure pain, back into myself, inside my head, with a hell of a pain that was localized down in my leg.

Fours are prone to intensifying their emotions in the same way that the young skier amplified his physical pain. The habit of unconsciously exaggerating real feelings effectively jettisons a genuine emotional life in favor of emotional intensity. Access to real feelings is blocked to the extent that an individual Four identifies with the exaggerated feelings that stem from an excitement of mood.

One can sometimes observe the times when Fours lose touch with real feelings if one watches the changes that their faces go through when they become emotional. If a Four is asked a question, such as, "How are you?" the first reaction, possibly the most authentic, gets bypassed as the Four goes through a series of what appear to be internal considerations about how he or she really does feel. The answer is the result of a series of remembered imaginings about different qualities of feeling overlaid on the genuine reaction. This habit can change a simple reaction, such as, "I'm okay," into "Well. . . I've been going through a lot of difficult changes."

Intimate Relationships

A tremendous amount of internal attention is directed toward preparing for the arrival of the lover. It is as if the present exists as a time to get ready for the future awakening through love. If there is no actual relationship going on, then the future meeting is imagined with great feeling. If a real relationship is happening, then it is necessary to withdraw in order to savor the imagination of reunion with the beloved. The following statement was taken from a New York City schoolteacher.

My best relationships have been long-distance romances. I've done New York–Boston and New York–San Francisco, and a couple of long-term affairs that were a few hours' drive from the city. The best part is the time in between, where you get to have your own life, and be totally looking forward to seeing your friend, and feeling how special it's going to be when you finally meet again.

The build-up in the days before is like dressing for your wedding. Like you might shatter from how romantic the hours feel before you get a call on the phone. You finally meet, get each other's news, make a lovely dinner together, and move in together for a few days.

The strangest thing is that although I've dreamed of our meeting, I am not really there when it gets played out. I seem to go away in my mind when we are together, because I want to imagine him again; so that I can be in bed with him and blank out that I'm there.

Within a short time I'm starting to feel the strain. Small things about him start to bother me. If he leaves a dresser drawer open in the bedroom, it makes me see his negligence. The open drawer stays in my mind as a symbol of all the other ways he might be neglectful. I think, how could I live with a negligent man?

But all I have to do to love him again is to imagine him gone, to think that we'll be separated soon, and then I can be with him again.

Relationships are afflicted by the Four's habit of focusing attention on the negative aspects of whatever is present. When attention is focused on a present situation, the unexpected negatives stick out, those less-than-beautiful features of the beloved's personality that simply did not exist when she or he was romantically far away.

I've been married for a number of years to a woman who seems slightly out of reach and always slightly out of commitment. Being with her has been like looking at a splendid sunset, knowing at the time how much I'll miss it when it's gone. I feel that she's a soul mate, that through her something ultimate will happen to me. At the same time I know that when she wants to be close to me, small things start to become visible that were not apparent before. Her peculiarities of speech start to irritate, and her features start to re-form in a less intriguing way. Everything seems less meaningful, diminished in some way. I have the compulsion to set everything right, to not have it be spoiled; so of course there's a fight, and she withdraws, and then I'm painfully aware of how much I miss her and want her again.

There is the belief that the real self will emerge through being loved, that the internal drama will lessen, and that a very simple, satisfied person will emerge, who feels whole and complete, without the need to yearn for something more. In order for such a feeling of completeness to develop, however, attention would first have to stabilize in the present. The Four would have to find the good that is there and accept it as enough.

An attractive saleswoman came to the office a couple of times last week. My fantasy script immediately got going, the vibes were great, my juice got moving, but thank God I've been around long enough that I knew that it was a fantasy I was into, rather than starting to invest my future in her.

Ten years ago I would have believed the vibes, I would have believed that this was mutual, that this was *the* one of my life. Her product spiel would have sounded like double-meaning promises. It would have driven me crazy until I'd have had to have gotten her. Life or death, more important than anything.

I know enough now to predict exactly how I would have felt if I'd gotten her. She would've been flawed, she wouldn't have dressed quite right, she wouldn't have been intelligent enough, it would have been a real shock to see what a mistake I'd made. The fantasy would go up in smoke and there I'd be, remembering the great things about other women that I'd be losing forever if I committed to her.

At this point I'm clear enough to recognize when I'm starting to fault a lover that I'm afraid of two things. I'm for sure afraid that I'll get stuck with a woman who isn't up to snuff, and I hate it that she might have to be the *only* one in my life, but I'm also realizing that I'm scared to get in any closer, because she'll start to see what's wrong with me and maybe ditch me first.

So I freak out and break it up. I wreck the whole thing, and then she's at a distance again, and looks wonderful, and I need to have her back. The whole thing is like a rubber band, she pulls back and I go forward.

The rubber-band relationship pattern places a Romantic in the position of being reabandoned, over and over again, but in a controlled way. If intimacy becomes too frightening, then the partner begins to look a little off, which justifies a fight and withdrawal into the familiar stance of separation. With distance, the partner's better features stand out again, and the Four becomes reattracted to the relationship. The possibility of getting love is so linked to the possibility of abandonment that it is safer to reject rather than run the risk of another loss.

Keeping intimacy at a safe distance is an art form for Fours. Not too far, not too near. Far enough to be able to selectively attend to the better features of a partner, near enough to wish for more. A safe half-distance, where it is possible to maintain interest, to maintain the hope that something real will emerge with time, but without any pressure to commit to the present.

On the high side, Fours want the relationship to remain intense. They are ideally suited to seeing others through crisis and will not buckle under fierce emotionality or under someone else's grief. They understand the aesthetics of a relationship; the love of beauty, innuendo, setting, and presentation. They know that people change with time and can allow a relationship to develop through many stages. They can want to start all over again and are able to bury a negative past.

On the low side, envious comparisons arise between the self and what other people seem to be getting from their relationships. Their sadness leads them to believe that other people's neglect has caused them to be sad. They will lie in wait to get back for having been hurt.

An example of a couple relationship: Four and Three, the Tragic Romantic and the Performer

Both types share an attachment to image, and so the couple will present well publicly; the Four as a dramatic figure, the Three as a successful figure. If the Three relies heavily on a conformist image, the Four is likely to upset the image by publicly announcing a controversial or outrageous position, or by becoming darkly emotional in the face of the Three's need for a smooth public facade. Threes are likely to respect the Four's unwillingness to be controlled by public opinion and will become more tolerant of the Four's emotional presentation if others seem to be impressed.

Fours want to be central in the emotional lives of their children and their mates. They want to talk about experiences and feelings and to be sought out and consulted with on family affairs. The Three partner is far more task-oriented and wants to be central to a project rather than being tied down by emotional demands.

A Three's preoccupation with worldly success can either cause the Four partner to feel abandoned in favor of the mate's profession, or it can act to create the necessary distance that will ensure a Four's continuing interest. The discrepancy between the feeling versus doing styles will be compatable if the Three is willing to periodically disentangle himself or herself from commitments in order to spend some private time with the Four. In that way, Three gets to work a lot, and Four gets to anticipate the intimate time together and to appreciate the partner in lovely small episodes that are not prolonged enough to stimulate the need to reject.

If the workaholic Three is too busy, or too emotionally remote, the Four can either hang in and become depressed for long periods of time or become dramatically angry over being abandoned. The Four partner could easily garner attention by becoming productive in an area that the Three thinks is valuable, especially if the Three is installed in the capacity of expert adviser and protector. If the Three is suspected of "dumping" the Four, using business as a covering excuse, the Four will become competitive in order to win the partner back. Competition may include theatrical scenes, threats against the partner, and suicidal gestures. If such tactics fail, the Four can become depressed and vindictive for many years. The Three partner is likely to move quickly on to another relationship.

The couple's children will be likely to see the Three parent as the go-getter who is proud of the children's successes, but has limited time and toleration for spending time with the family. If the Four parent relates well, the children will see him or her as emotionally devoted and willing to spend time. If the Four parent relates neurotically, the kids will feel drained by the Four's demand to be emotionally understood and will be likely to say that the Four parent competes with them for the attentions of the hard-to-get Three.

Point Four's Relationship to Authority

Fours tend to ignore petty authority and to give "grand" authority an enormous amount of respect. Petty authorities—the police or the shopkeeper who makes you wait in line—are to be ignored and gotten around; but grand authority, such as kings and queens or critically acclaimed people, are to be viewed with respect. Fours tend to believe that ordinary rules and regulations do not apply to themselves. They are rebellious in the sense that they do not obey, but do so by disdainfully forgetting to take the rules and regulations seriously rather than out of a need to bring authority down. If the authority is punitive or restrictive, the Four will be likely to break all the rules of behavior and "get away with" as much as possible.

Grand authority, on the other hand, is greatly admired, particularly if the situation supports a Four's image of specialness and elite presentation. A Four wants to be selected for having unique abilities and to be mentored and nourished by the best people around. They become patients of world-class analysts and confidants to eccentric geniuses. There is a need to be recognized by distinguished people and to be loved by those that a Four believes are in touch with authentic depth.

On the high side, Fours are able to sense genuine talents and qualities of feeling in others. They see through an imitative or derivative presentation. They understand the distinction between "the best," and "the best known." They will turn a tacky presentation into something beautiful and unique and can see extraordinary possibilities in a common business situation. They reach out to join forces with the very best people in the field.

On the low side, Fours compete with peers for the respect of grand authority. They become spiteful if not recognized and do not like to be in a servile position or to work in an ordinary setting unless this is in the service of "my real work as an artist" or "my true calling as a mystic."

A Typical Interpoint Authority Relationship: Four and Two, the Tragic Romantic and the Giver

If the Four is boss, he or she will set an example of distinctive personal style, both in a striking physical image and in the look and mood of the business place. This is likely to be supported by the Two employee, who will fit in well with the boss's image needs. The Two will try to please, figure out what is wanted, and accommodate to that. On one level the Four will appreciate the support, and on another, may subtly begin to sabotage things when the enterprise starts to run smoothly. The Two will be left to mind the shop, as the boss's attention turns away from the successful area of life and begins to focus on what is missing. The boss may become emotionally wrapped up in something completely separate from the office, leaving the Two without the personal contact that helps a Two to function well.

If the Two employee likes the boss personally, or believes in the boss's programs, he or she will take up the decision-making gap as the power behind the throne. As long as the Two is personally committed to the situation, either through affection, or through the belief that the work is important, the boss will be well covered and protected. The Two may be able to delegate and organize better from the second-in-command position than if placed as the front runner in the same post.

If the Two employee loses personal contact with the boss, or if the boss starts to criticize the employees, the Two will feel unappreciated and a severe power struggle is likely to develop. For example, the Two may want to take over the boss's post or will assist someone else in becoming the new leader of the enterprise, and the Four will feel betrayed. The situation can be greatly helped if either one can admit to the emotional basis for having injured the other. Both Two and Four will open if they are able to understand the emotional wounding that underlies defensive behavior.

If the Four is the employee, the situation will go well as long as the Two boss extends special recognition. The boss should not count on the goodwill of a Four employee who has been made to feel deprived. If Tragic Romantics feel put into a servile role or find themselves working in a situation in which others have better advantages, they may try to "catch the other out" in terms of a competitive win, or will scheme in order to publicly humiliate the other, or will strive to gain the favor of an outsider who has potential power over the situation.

A competitive standoff can be eased if either party will give recognition to the other. A Two-Four competitive struggle may well be acted out as an argument about business procedures, but is likely to have its origins in hurt feelings. Each needs to feel respected by the other. Both types thrive on being important in the lives of other people, and if each can be given special duties and special attention, they will be more likely to support each other in their separate areas of expertise.

Elite Standards

The sense of being victimized by loss makes for lowered self-esteem. There is the sense of little children who, having been deserted, feel that they would not have been abandoned had they been winning or more worthwhile. There is a feeling of having lost in life because of some fatal flaw of personality that makes a Four less valuable than those who have been given love. The childhood stance of believing oneself to be the unloved outsider to the family develops into a mystique of being the outsider, of being different, of developing a unique personal style.

Fours often develop a dramatized personal image as a way to compensate for feelings of low self-esteem. There is a unique elegance in personal presentation; an expression of the fact that one is different through costuming and being ahead of the current style.

When I'm over at a friend's, I'm mentally redecorating the rooms, and redoing people's makeup and clothes for a more distinctive look. For the first two or three weeks after I move into a new place, I do little else except find the proper arrangement of objects in the space. Does the vase go here or there? There's a great deal of importance in ritualizing the space; it feels like a setting in which I am rehearsing for the events to come. The sense is that I'm building and containing my forces for the future; the physical supports and the appropriate mood for a major life event. The whole thing starts to feel like a magical preparation for the special meetings of people that are going to happen, all of which is symbolized by some critical placement of lighting, and couches, and chairs.

The pages of high-fashion magazines are filled with dramatically fashionable Fours. They are elegant and thin, draped and angled in exclusive creations that were never intended for the common crowd. They present an outer image that is often diametrically opposed to internal feelings of shame at having been unloved and abandoned in the past.

There is an urgency to find a style that is unique enough to emotionally transmute the rejected outsider into a prestigious individual who is not subject to ordinary rules. Matters of taste can become critical to survival. You'd commit suicide before you'd appear in pink polyester pants. If you own only one silk blouse, then it becomes your uniform until you can afford another. The touch of commercial fabrics is unacceptable, whatever is on sale is not what you will wear. The compulsion to be extraordinary can be easily mistaken for refinement of tastes and aesthetic sensitivity, and the fear of abandonment can be sidestepped by discounting the importance of those who tastes are less refined. An extreme version of the preoccupation with aesthetic image appears in anorexia nervosa and in other psychological disturbances where there is an attempt to ruthlessly force one's body to conform to an elite standard.

Elite Nonconformity

I have a talent for escaping the ordinary. In a way I've made it my life task. I've never had a boring job in my whole life, mostly because I will embellish them to the point where they aren't ordinary anymore. I would have a job selling books, for instance, and I would take as many as were appealing to me. Then I wasn't a clerk anymore, I was a criminal, a much more interesting thing to be. They were always art books, useless in a way, but wonderful to take a risk for. I developed such a foolproof method that I was delighted to have a party given for me when I left, at which they presented me with a book which I had already taken home.

A kind of amorality can develop as a Four's self-image shifts from being a rejected outsider to being someone who stands aloof and slightly above the ordinary crowd. There is an attraction to breaking the social rules, which, following a Four's adherence to elite standards, can get played out as kid-glove criminality, like shoplifting only white angora sweaters.

Fours delight in "getting away with it." They like the thrill of secret mischief and playing at the edge of scandal. There is an excitement in courting disaster, in being eccentric or difficult, and therefore getting special treatment. Being difficult also satisfies a kind of masochistic need to be revealed as that flawed and despicable child who is still unworthy of being loved. These feelings of unworthiness are coupled with an angry wish to even the score with people who appear to be getting more out of life. The coupling of masochism and anger could be encapsulated in the image of the society matron who serves a perfectly appointed dinner and lies in wait for the proper moment to announce that she is in support of a controversial cause that most of her guests despise.

This statement was given by a San Francisco socialite who stated that she became entirely absorbed with the task of getting the best people to attend her parties, only to feel instantly turned off when their RSVP was marked "accept."

I cannot stand to be ignored. It brings up terrible feelings of being left out, which quickly move to hate. Being publicly humiliated makes you want to erase the shame by finding a way to get back. I either negate the importance of the people and leave, or I notice myself becoming sarcastic, and I find that underneath I'm terribly angry that attention has been taken away from me.

It's equally dangerous for me if a situation gets too predictable or quiet. I want to break the mood by saying something shocking, which gets my message across that I think the conversation is a bore, and is also my kind of attempt to draw out some special stranger who would instinctively recognize that I was trying to upgrade the level of a poor conversation.

Envy

Envy is fueled by the belief that others are enjoying an emotional satisfaction that is being denied to oneself. Unaware Fours will try to ease feelings of deprivation by a change of scene, by adornment, or by surrounding themselves with lovely things. Fours also vie for the attentions of a popular person, with the hope that they will feel more worthy if they possess what appears to have made other people happy.

It's a moment-by-moment feeling that something is missing. "Is this all there is?" It starts out as, "If I only had that lover, or that place to live, or that piece of art," and you spend a lot of time chasing around after these things, and as soon as you get them, you're onto the next acquisition.

When you get older it's looking out at reality and finding it sadly lacking. But what is it lacking? And how is it that other people seem to hold hands and smile a lot? "What do they have with each other that I don't have?" You get on a Holy Grail search to find the something more; grasping for something that satisfies my friends, but which misses me entirely. I sense the good feelings that other people have toward each other, and their having it makes me feel the absence of it in myself.

The bottom line of my depression is when I've lost the hope of something more. It's been incredibly hard to give up the desire for more and to settle for "This is enough."

Envy is also a powerful motivator. When Fours describe their feelings of despair at being deprived of something that appears to hold the promise of happiness, they say it is like being squeezed between "I can't have it" and "I must have it." The squeeze of envy can transform despair into the kind of action that will cut through any obstacle in order to achieve happiness. There is plenty of energy to move forward until success begins to materialize. Paradoxically, when results begin to appear, attention often shifts to different interests.

I play in a band that's become successful over several years. At the beginning, before we made our first record, I'd hear other bands on the radio and get furious that we weren't being heard. I moved heaven and earth to get that first one made. Once we were recorded, music started to seem irrelevant. I began to lose interest and returned to an old relationship. We parted and returned to each other over and over again, until the band started to collapse, and then I made another record happen. It's like the action is always where I'm not. When the band's together, there's a man I want. If he starts to come around, I start to wonder if I'm making a mistake.

Assets

Their lifelong familiarity with suffering makes Romantics particularly suited to working with people going through crisis or grief. They have unusual stamina for helping others go through intense emotional episodes and are willing to stick with a friend through long periods of recovery. Fours often say that by focusing on someone else's needs, they are able to shift attention from their own.

Mourning and abandonment are the keys in which my life is set, however, those are not depressing experiences to me. The dark moods are what interest me most and have given me a real talent for the shadows inside people's minds. If something dramatic, or dangerous, or deeply disturbing happens, then I find myself immediately present.

My husband has had an assistant for several years, and I've been cordial to her, but have never been attracted to knowing her. Suddenly her marriage dissolved when she was five months pregnant, and with that news, she has become a central figure in my mind. I am much more likely to become disturbed when life gets too predictable than I am when a disturbing event occurs.

The search for depth of meaning often misleads a Four into the belief that lighthearted relationships are lightweight and therefore not worthy of consideration. There is a great attraction to people who are caught up in the most intense human experiences, such as birth, and death, and encounters with the dark unconscious. Fours feel far more real at those moments when life and death are close companions, because those events are so intensely demanding that their full attention is brought into the present moment. The following statement was given by an organizer for suicide hot lines.

Happiness is incidental. Is a moth made happy by the flame? I am a counselor myself and was in analysis for years. I faithfully tried to see myself that way, but I have developed a suspicion of my insights, and an impulse to resist what other people see in me. I feel that passion holds a greater possibility, that I truly exist only at the center of my deepest feelings.

As a counselor I'm attracted to crisis work: to battered women and people on the borders of sanity. I have started a hot line for our county and find an instant rapport on the phone with some stranger who's out there on the edge with a revolver or a bottle of pills in his hand.

Attractive Environments

Fours often have two jobs: "my money job and my real job as an artist." They are attracted to environments that require body discipline as a way of conforming to special standards. Dancer, chanteuse, magazine model. They are atelier owners, interior decorators, antique collectors, and owners of excellent secondhand stores.

They are metaphysicians and depth psychologists; they search for a connection to higher planes of mind. They are grief counselors, feminists, animal rights activists. They are attracted to religion, ritual, and art.

Unattractive Environments

Unattractive environments include mundane jobs in ordinary settings. "I work in an office, but that's not me." Close work with people who earn more or have more. Service jobs, anonymity. A job where special talents are not seen.

Famous Fours

Martha Graham, the most famous name in the modern dance movement, is a Four. Dedicated to the expression of mythic themes and the human unconscious in grand-scale presentations. She initiated a school of dance organized around the bodily contractions that visually convey the inner drama.

Keats □ Shelley □ Alan Watts □ Joni Mitchell
Orson Welles □ Bette Davis □ Joan Baez
Marlon Brando

How Fours Pay Attention

Fours rarely live in the present. Their focus of attention travels away: to the past, to the future, to the absent, to the hard-to-get. There is a background preoccupation with whatever seems to be missing: the absent friend at the dinner party, the missed connections in an intimate talk.

The preoccupation with absent things is flavored by a highly selective remembrance of the positive aspects of whatever is missing. "The evening would have been complete if only John had been there." John's better aspects are remembered when he is at a distance, and a tenuous connection of yearning is set up that acts to draw a Four's attention away from what is actually going on in the present. If John were present and accounted for, his less-than-interesting aspects would begin to surface, and the Four's attention would tend to drift away to one of the other pieces that seem to be missing from life.

Romantics say that they feel an intimate connection with absent friends, that, in fact, their feelings of affection can get stronger with enforced separation. They say that in any relationship, there must be time away in order to reawaken the true feeling of connection that occurs only with distance and separation.

When a Four is forced to focus on the actual events happening in present time, there is a feeling of being let down, of seeing the negatives of the situation, perhaps for the very first time. It can feel like a blow in the face, because there are so many disappointments, and they all come at once. It's as if the light goes out of a lover's face, and all that is left is a set of mismatched features.

Fours unwittingly engage their imagination in such a way that the missing positives become devastatingly desirable and, by using the same shift of attention, they imaginatively amplify the present negatives so that they look far less appealing than they actually are.

This shift of attention can be illustrated by way of the false self-image that people can create of their own face, depending on how they feel about themselves when they look into a mirror. The same face can look quite different, depending on the way in which we selectively pay attention to the strengths and weaknesses of the features and how we imagine the strengths to be more or less than what is actually there. An ordinary face can become positively radiant if we imaginatively heighten the colors of the eyes and soften the textures of the skin; and that same face can appear to be grotesque if we focus on, and imaginatively amplify, its plainer aspects.

An unfortunate example of negative amplification can be drawn from the reports of Fours who are predisposed toward anorexia nervosa. It is striking to note that a high percentage of Fours report that they have what could be called an anorexic self-image, where, when they look into a mirror, their bodies appear to be shapeless and fat when, in fact, they are quite thin. Some Fours report having developed a distaste for their own bodies, such that their own objectively attractive physiques have become mentally preoccupying and repulsive.

The same unconscious attentional shift that serves to imaginatively alter physical appearances can also act to amplify emotional reactions. This shift of attention serves to exaggerate a Four's authentic emotional responses in the same way that visual imagination can overlay and enhance a reflection in a mirror.

For example, the thought of a distant friend can quickly summon wonderful feelings, an emotional counterpart for the thought of being together again. If attention then shifts from the authentic response that develops from thinking about the friend into imagining the greatest possible warmth that humans are capable of, the authentic reaction has been lost in an imaginative and unrealistic overlay of false feelings. Likewise, a small oversight by that same friend could stimulate powerful feelings of rejection and hatred, which would quickly overlay the authentic, small reaction that the oversight actually warranted.

In order for real feelings to emerge, it is first necessary to stabilize attention at a neutral reference point and to learn to pay attention to real physical sensations being experienced in the present moment.

Intuitive Style

On the neurotic side, Fours tend to exaggerate their emotional climates; however, the habit of focusing attention on a distant person and yearning for feelings of connection can also have some striking side effects. Fours say that they feel as close to someone at a distance as when that person is physically present in the room. They also believe that their own mood adjusts in order to resonate with what the absent person feels.

Fours say that they take on other people's emotions, that their vast experience with shifting moods allows them to match the feeling tone of other people as a way of staying connected to them. There are many recollections of Fours who wanted to be with an absent parent and who came to believe that they could sense how the parent was feeling about them at a distance. Fearing abandonment and hating to be ignored, Four children learned to internalize a felt connection to loved ones who, it was feared, might go away.

It is as if a sensing mechanism developed within the growing child through which it was possible to match the moods of significant people as a way of staying connected and never being left behind. The intuitive task for Fours who believe that they can accurately register other people's feelings would be to learn to tell the difference between a projection, based upon neurotic fears of abandonment, and the possibility of a genuine attunement.

Intuitively inclined Fours often feel burdened by the habit of taking on other people's emotions. They say that they are vulnerable to picking up pain and depression without realizing it and can go through an entire day before they realize that the mood that they are carrying may not be their own. They report that once the feeling connection is made that they cannot tell whether the mood has its source within the other or within themselves.

On the high side of this way of paying attention, Fours can be unerringly sensitive to matching the feeling tone of clients, family members, and friends. This is far more than an idea or a hypothesis about what a friend might be feeling; it is an actual following of the fluctuations of another's moods within one's own body. Highly intuitive Fours can resonate with other people's emotional state to the extent that they know when the other is available to being reasoned with or loved, or when it is safe to express negativity and to talk things out. The following statement was given by a Four who has been able to use his intuitive talent in the practice of psychiatry.

All during my life I felt drawn to the intensity in other people. It was like I felt my own emotions spark when somebody had been moved or struck deeply or become desperate in some way. I call it my leap of the heart, and have learned to welcome it, although it first came to me in what seemed like irrational ways. Like walking into a room feeling one mood and suddenly realizing that I was feelingly different when nothing came to mind about why that should be happening to me. I could also become gripped by what I supposed was my own emotionality, only to find that someone in the clinic or the family therapy session had just had the identical shift.

I eventually found that my signals were sometimes projections and sometimes direct hits. I was often right on when the leap of the heart happened. At other times I was dead wrong, because I was merely confirming through my feelings what I intellectually assumed somebody was supposed to feel.

The Original Connection to Higher Mind

As with each of the types, the dominant neurotic preoccupation can be seen as indicating the search for a particular aspect of essence. From a purely psychological perspective, the concept of a depressed individual's return to essence is something like the completion of grieving and a maturation into a happy life. From the point of view of a psychological/spiritual system like the Enneagram, a Four's return to essence implies something quite different from emotional satisfaction.

A Four's sense of childhood loss continues onward into adult life as a background awareness that some crucial factor for hap-

piness is missing. The original milk was lost and has been replaced with a tacky substitute. The rewards that flow from the
material life do not recreate that original connection for a Four.
The Romantic can have it all and know that something is missing.

Because objective life does not produce satisfaction, there is
often the sense of two realities: the objective world and the one
behind the scenes. Objective reality does not hold the promise
of fulfillment, yet there are indications to Fours that other realities of experience occasionally coexist with the objective world.
There is the sense of a plane of existence that is beyond ordinary reality, that can be particularly sensed at the intense con-
cordances of emotional life; at those junctures where tragedy
forces an upwelling of unconscious feeling, or in affairs of the
heart, where love is lost or gained. Fours report that at such
moments a connection can be sensed to that which is missing;
that they experience a felt connection to an eternal source of
support.

On the neurotic side, Fours are fiercely determined to hold
onto the dark side of feeling. They want to remain unique and
resist being remade into an ordinary happy person. On the
mature side, they are quite correct in sensing that their nature's
more than merely psychological; and by their tenacious resistance to becoming adjusted to ordinary life, they remind the
rest of us about that felt connection to our own higher awareness.

A person who feels chronically deprived might first sense the
connection to essence as a moment of complete belonging, moments that remind one of being held in the safety of a mother's
arms, or of the surrender of one's being to the hope of an enduring love. This connection to what Fours would describe as
"my real self" is often felt during nonverbal moments of artistic
reverie, or meditation practice, or being in love, those very con-
tacts to which Fours feel themselves habitually drawn.

The Virtue of Equanimity (Balance)

Envy describes a compulsive attraction to the unavailable. Fours can exert a great deal of time and energy trying to obtain something appealing only to find fault when it comes within reach. For severely fixated Fours, the desire to possess and the need to reject can arise almost simultaneously. They report being attracted to unavailable people whom they know immediately will not be good for them or to people unwilling to commit themselves to a relationship. So the dance goes on. "You move backward, I move forward. If you move forward, I dance backward."

Balance is the resolution of the suffering caused by being pulled to what you cannot have and repelled by what has come to hand. It is the recognition of having enough of what you really need. Like all of the higher impulses Balance is an embodiment, rather than a thought, or an idea about what it would be like to be fully satisfied. It depends upon being able to stabilize attention in the present and feeling the satisfaction of having enough.

Embodying the virtue of equanimity begins with strengthening the capacity for self-observation to the point where one is able to recognize when attention drifts off to the past, the future, the distant, or the hard to get. Fours will experience equanimity when they are able to gently return their awareness to the present and pay attention to the bodily satisfaction that is here.

Subtypes

Competition in One-to-One Relationships

Fours often compete because of a need to be worthy in the eyes of a desirable mate. In a heterosexual one-to-one relationship, this often gets played out as a woman competing against another woman for a man; or man against a man for a woman.

In a nonsexual relationship, competition gets played out as "wanting the respect of the best people."

I was a trial lawyer for six years before my career took off. The takeoff was inspired by a behind-the-back remark that I overheard in the hall one day. The guy said I was a mediocre defender, and it so infuriated me that I took off. What had just been cases before became tests of manhood. I waited him out for months, and finally I got to nail him in court.

Shame in Social Relationships

Shame at not measuring up to group standards.

It's that all eyes are upon you when you walk into a room. They are not adoring eyes. It's never that you do anything improper, it's that they can see that you're wrong inside.

Dauntlessness (Recklessness) Regarding Personal Survival

Recreate the possibility of loss through reckless actions. The excitement of playing the edge of disaster.

I was in real estate with my husband for years. My approach was to borrow to the limit on everything we owned, and take a chance on expanding the empire. His approach was cautious and when he'd go for safety, I'd want to confuse the paperwork and go ahead without him, because it felt like our best chance was going down the tubes, and that if anything went wrong, it was worth it, and could be handled when the time came.

What Helps Fours Thrive

Fours often begin therapy or a meditation practice in order to break a depression or to stabilize intense mood swings. The presenting issue is typically the primary relationship. Tragic Romantics need to recognize when attention shifts from real feelings to either idealizing the unobtainable or finding fault with what is possible to obtain. Fours can help themselves by

- Accepting the fact that early loss was real; that it needs to be mourned and finally set aside.
- Recognizing the self-absorption that occurs during intense mood shifts. Breaking self-absorption by moving toward others and focusing on what is important to someone else.
- Building a habit of completing projects. Seeing ways in which beneficial projects are sabotaged or left as incompletes.
- Seeing how feelings of victimization are perpetuated by rejecting whatever is easy to obtain.
- Finding a version of qualities within oneself that are enviable in others.
- Trying to stay aware of the habit of pulling others into dramatic outbursts. Recognizing the secret attraction to those who do not allow themselves to be pulled in.
- Accepting sadness rather than trying to make happiness happen. Knowing that the mood will shift.
- Informing others that intimacy will produce an angry attack along the lines of being misunderstood. Asking others to hold a consistent position under attack. Knowing that a steady presence provides reassurance that others will not abandon under attack.
- Honoring the ability to empathize with other people's pain but learning to detach attention at will.
- Returning attention to the present situation. Notice when attention drifts. Noting how selective attention is paid to negative aspects of the present situation.
- Building multiple interests and friendships as interventions for depression.
- Building a physical exercise habit as a way to shift mood.
- Noticing when real feelings get buried in the habit of dramatizing emotions. Above all, noting when a presently felt emotion shifts to "it's going to get awful again."

What Fours Should Be Aware of

Progress toward happiness will probably be slow. Satisfaction with a real relationship in the present represents giving up the connection to the original loved one that has been kept alive and recreated through loss. Fours should attempt to feel satisfaction with life in the present and pay special attention to the difference between real feelings and dramatized emotions. As patterns change, Fours should be aware that the following reactions may occur.

· Wanting to go over a million angles and approaches to the same problem as a way of not moving on.
· Not wanting to be categorized, to be seen as having an ordinary problem. Feeling that others do not understand the uniqueness and severity of the psychological situation. Fearing that one might be wrongfully altered by therapy.
· Wanting a magical cure. Wanting to be "taken somewhere" by meditation.
· Impatience with the flatness of ordinary feelings. Wanting to reintensify emotions through loss, fantasy, and dramatic acts.
· Regret. "It's too late to change." Or "If only I had acted differently."
· Suicidal thoughts and gestures. A cry for help. "If only they knew how I feel." Or, "They'll see how I suffered after I'm gone." This reaction needs to be carefully watched for signs of a potential attempt.
· A desire for luxury. "Doing laundry is beneath me."
· Envious comparisons between self and others. "She is prettier." "He has good clothes."
· Seduce and reject. Finding fault with others before they reject you.
· Intense self-criticism. Faulty self-perception of own body as distasteful in some way. Sometimes an anorexic image of self as fat when this is not objectively so. Anorexia or bulimia as symptoms.

· Biting sarcasm, cut the other down. It's their fault that you suffer.
· Asking for advice and then rejecting it. Not able to give up the intensity of suffering.

10. Point Five: The Observer

	ACQUIRED PERSONALITY		ESSENCE	
HEAD	Chief Feature:	STINGINESS	Higher Mind:	OMNISCIENCE
HEART	Passion:	AVARICE	Virtue:	NON-ATTACHMENT
	SUBTYPE WAYS OF BEING			
	Sexual:	SHARING CONFIDENCES (SECRETIVE)		
	Social:	SEEKING TOTEMS		
	Self-preservation:	SEEKING THE CASTLE (HOME)		

The Dilemma

The Observer's ego is like a castle, a high, impenetrable structure with tiny windows at the top. The occupant rarely leaves its walls, watching who comes to the door in secret, while avoiding being seen. Observers are very private people. They like to live in secluded places, away from emotional strain. They are often at home with the phone unplugged, and they watch the action from the edge of a crowd, making tentative effort to join.

Fives felt intruded upon as children; the castle walls were breached and their privacy stolen. Their strategic defense is withdrawal, to minimize contact, to simplify their needs, to do whatever they can to protect the private space. Fives say that they invent elaborate ways to create safe distance, because once someone gets too close, they have lost their primary defense. The outside world feels invasive and dangerous. Consequently Observers take what little comes their way, rather than risk taking leave of the safe walls of home.

They can be hermits, leading a reclusive, and usually mental, life, within the confines of a small house, venturing out only as far as the library and the store. They can also be quite public, but from a position of remote control, where frontline interactions are handled by others, who will probably make reports by phone. When Fives appear in public, they are likely to be hiding in a pose, which means that they have minimized their feelings while blending into a scene.

Fives prefer to not get involved. Financial interactions feel dangerous. Obligations are coercive. Anger and competition are to be controlled, and emotional attachments are felt to be a drain. Fives can also feel coerced by people's positive expectations. Safe distance means *not* getting involved, and unless intimacy and affection are approached with guarantees of continued independence, Fives will find ways to hide, or to isolate the intimate contact into one regularized sector of their total life.

Fives are particularly sensitive to interactions that make them visible to others. Self-promotion, competition, and demonstrations of love or hate all make Fives feel as if they are playing into other people's hands. Fives remain aloof from interactions in which they could be judged; a self-protective habit that is often masked by feelings of superiority over those who crave recognition and success. They believe that desires and intense emotionality indicate a lack of control, and when feelings are painful they should be let go. There is a sense of accomplishment in being able to so easily detach from the needs that dominate other people's lives.

It is quite true that Fives are independent people. They can live happily alone, have very modest needs, take great delight in their own fantasy life, and don't get sidetracked into spending time and energy on trivial concerns. Their independence, however, is based on their ability to detach attention from their emotional and instinctual life, which has the expensive secondary effect of forcing them to live in their minds.

The love of privacy turns into loneliness when a Five becomes isolated and unable to reach out. When the hunger for contact is aroused, Fives realize how difficult it is for them to move toward people, and how often they stand watching as their own life goes by. They live in an atmosphere of scarcity, preferring "independence" to satisfaction, wary that their own desires might cause them to become attached to others. Inwardly empty and unable to ask for more, they become extremely attached to the little that they have: a few mementos to fill the empty space, and a few incalculably precious ideas to feed the hungry mind. "When I want to reach out, it's like starving at a feast. I crave the feelings that I see others have. I can't reach out, I can't pull back. My hand feels frozen between the table and my lap." Detached from emotion and desperate for connection, Fives will spend endless time and effort on finding a mental link back to their own humanity. Having centered their existence in the mind, Fives seek connection through special knowledge.

Observers are strongly attracted to models and systems that explain universal principles of interaction, particularly human behavior. By mastering a system, such as mathematics, or psychoanalysis, or the Enneagram, they can form a mental concept of the way that interactions take place, and they can locate themselves within the system in an emotionally detached way. Their interest is rarely attracted to wealth or material things. Money is good only for the privacy it buys and for the independence of having free time to study and pursue their other interests. Fives will not spend their limited energy in acquiring quantities of worldly things. If they inherit money, they will be likely to hoard it for the independence that it guarantees but will continue to live in modest luxury. If they are born without money, they will not work for others in order to accumulate it.

They will, however, put endless time and effort toward study and other mental pursuits.

Fives say that their feelings are more available when no one is around to see. They say that it's hard to let the real self out with other people in the room, that solitude is their staging ground for a private fantasy life. They say that they are detached from their feelings during much of their day, that they need the time alone to "sort things out, and find out what I really feel." They say that they feel more connected to people when they are alone, remembering what was said, than they are during a real life talk. Their enjoyment of life comes most easily when they are alone and free to retroactively savor what was left unfelt during the course of their day.

A short meeting can mean a lot to a Five, who is going to enjoy the interaction later, in the privacy of his or her home. Fives get attached to sharing a special interest or a special bond of understanding with each of their different friends. The friends may never be introduced to one another, or be informed about what else is happening in the Observer's life, but their presence will be treasured within the limits of the special bond of trust. Fives can feel closely connected in a nonverbal way, needing only minimal contact to keep a relationship alive. Small rituals of friendship are honored, and if the friends are wise, they will make a Five their observer-adviser, rather than expecting demonstrations of emotion or hoping the Five will be the initiator in the relationship.

Five's habitual preoccupations include
· Privacy.
· Maintaining noninvolvement; withdraw and tighten the belt as a first line of defense.
· Fear point. Afraid to feel.
· Overvaluing of self-control. Detaching attention from feelings. "Drama is for lesser beings."
· Delayed emotions. Feelings withheld while others are present. Emotion comes later, when safely alone.

- Compartmentalizing. Commitments in life are kept separate from one another. One box per commitment. Time limit for each box.
- Wanting predictability. Wanting to know what will happen ahead of time.
- An interest in special knowledge and analytic systems that can explain the way that people work. Want a map to explain emotions. Psychoanalysis. The Enneagram.
- A confusion between spiritual nonattachment and a premature emotional shutdown to keep out pain. The unenlightened Buddha.
- An attentional style of focusing on life and oneself from the point of view of an outside observer, which can lead to
  - Isolation from the feelings and events of one's own life.
  - The ability to maintain a point of view that is detached from emotional bias.

Family History

There are two family patterns that commonly make children want to withdraw. The first is described by those who felt so utterly abandoned that they accepted their fate, but learned to detach from feelings in order to survive. The second, and the more commonly reported childhood, is one in which the family was so psychically intrusive that the child closed down emotionally in order to get away.

The following statement was given by a man with a classic Five profile. He has made a great deal of money in an obscure business specialty in which he is the lone expert in the field, but he prefers to live in a rundown section of San Francisco, because the rent is cheap and the Chinese restaurant where he takes all his meals is half a block away.

What I remember is the silence and liking to be alone. It was like five people spinning on separate orbits in different rooms of the house. Not much talk and definitely no touching. Our parents had both been born deaf and, like all deaf people, they couldn't modulate their voices. So you'd be in public with them, with this weird shouting, which drew a lot of glaring and made you try to disappear into a pea on your plate.

The main feeling was not wanting to be seen, so I got expert at blending into the potted palm, and distracting myself by fading into the pictures on the wall when I was out with them, trying the best I could to disappear from being there.

The second childhood prototype was given by a computer processor who likes to work at night, when there is no one in the office except occasionally cleaning people and more than a hundred silent machines.

I grew up living with seven people in three rooms. There was no way to be alone, unless you were outside or in the bathroom. So I invented my own place on a tree platform. I would go up there to space out, read, and spy down on everybody else.

I had to keep changing trees when my brothers found my spot. I was desperate to be alone, because it was the only time I could be by myself, instead of having to try to get away from people making me do what was good for them.

Then I started to grow up, and the terror was parties or anything to do with meeting people and dressing up. I just wouldn't be there on time and have to get into small talk and say predictable things. The first thing I'd look for on the way in was the location of the exits, and I'd chart my flow pattern from the front door to get into position near one of them. The worst would be getting pinned into a conversation, particularly with someone who wanted to get something out of me.

Emotional Distance

Children who feel that they have to escape are going to find ways to distance themselves. One way is to stay in your room and close the door. Another way is to put up a wall of emotional distance by removing yourself from your feelings. Eventually you can learn to stand directly under the gaze of someone who is trying to pry into your life and not feel any reaction to their intrusiveness. As one exemplar put it, "They could try to control what I did, but they could never get to me."

We were at a restaurant, and my mother began reading the menu aloud to us: "They have snow pea beef, and spicy eggplant, . . . and so on." She has always done that, and it's always been a pain. The way that I can decide from a menu is by reading the item and checking it against my inner reaction, the taste, the feeling; but when I'm bombarded by Mom about the choices in a way that doesn't match my internal pacing, there's no time.

It takes a lot of internal concentration to create the distance, the wall, behind which one can read the menu and make one's decision. Meanwhile, there's the feeling of invasion, of powerlessness. Later we're at the zoo and the Rose Garden, and Mom is describing and interpreting everything: "Look at that. Oh, that's beautiful. Look, there's a Joseph's Coat rose. That one's called Pink Peace." Again, no space to feel the roses without being directed.

I found myself acting like I had in grammar school, falling behind or walking ahead, trying to get space away from her, and still not having it because I'm watching to see how she's responding, and waiting to have my concentration interrupted. Am I making a scene? Will she interpret this as rudeness? I'm so wound up with her that I'm not in the garden, and feel that I must be alone to appreciate the roses.

Autonomy from coercive influence can best be maintained in the absence of strongly felt connections. A Five's version of controlling a situation is to cease reacting to it, rather than to try to take charge of the problem, or to try to control the other people involved. Controlling personal reactions usually means that feelings are suspended during the time that an interaction is happening and are sorted out later, in the privacy of the home.

When I was younger I had become such a loner that when I had to be around people, I would imitate their faces and mannerisms to fit myself into their scene. I liked being alone and didn't find anything inside myself that wanted company, so for when I had to be around people I developed a system of watching how they acted and trying to behave the same way. I would see people making out on the street and sometimes that would make me lonely, thinking about what was going on inside them.

Later on, I started to hate the isolation. I wanted to share some of what I had found out while I was alone, but the real enjoyment of being with someone would only come afterward, when I was by myself again. It was like remembering the meeting was a lot more vigorous than actually being together. I was trying to match up the feelings that came with the memory to find out which ones fit.

It's taken years to be able to feel something on the spot, when something intense is happening, rather than getting really fascinated with an interesting blot on the wall, and starting to disappear into that.

Fives commonly report a perceptual shift that keeps people at a distance. There is a sense of watching others, as if there is a vast empty space between themselves and the other people in the room, or as if they are engaged in a conversation from the perspective of standing on the invisible side of a one-way mirror. Being invisible, they can watch dispassionately, without having to insert themselves into the conversation or react in an appropriate way. Fives occasionally report that when pushed to talk, they not only see others as physically far away, but also as "caricatures, like aliens from another world."

It happens under pressure of not wanting to be seen. If I can't get away or distract myself with art books on the coffee table, then there's always blending into the room, removing my presence so that no one knows I'm there. I've been able to go into a wall so well that a good friend who might come looking for me can walk right past without finding me there.

Going into the wall works best if you've got a drink or a cracker in your hand and can mix into the general atmosphere. But the main thing is to deflect all of your attention behind yourself, until you know you can't be seen.

From that perspective things look a lot more interesting. You're watching a room full of partying grotesques walking around, like the bar scene in *Star Wars*, or some other weird alien flick.

The defensive tactic of not getting involved in emotional entanglement extends to positive as well as negative emotions. To want something is to open the door to loss, and to want something badly means to suffer the consequences of allowing yourself to become attached to, and dependent on, others.

My idea of safety was to unhook my feelings before they got hold of me. I could always manage by myself, so why let things get to the point of jealousy and betrayal? So the idea was to never pick up enough cards to get caught into a game.

Four years ago, after almost ten years of seeing each other on a three-times-a-week basis, my girlfriend announced that her biological clock was running out, and that she would leave me to find someone else unless we married and started a family.

I started to miss her even when I was alone. I couldn't marry her and I couldn't let her go. I finally agreed, because it looked like I would lose something either way. In the months before the baby came, I panicked. I didn't know if I could take the constant interruptions and the demands on time.

About a month after the birth, I realized that I had changed. The baby would cry and I would just go and pick him up, rather than fighting myself because I wanted him out of the room. But my feelings didn't unhook. I managed to stay feeling whatever it was at the time, rather than disengaging and holding out until I could be alone.

Previewing and Reviewing of Feelings

Fives commonly report that they try to get full information about an event ahead of time, so they can prepare by previewing everything that's likely to happen. The desire is to be forewarned about any unpredictable or potentially embarrassing encounters. Anything unexpected, or any strong demand on the part of others is likely to panic a Five into having to feel in a situation where he or she does not wish to.

The habit of previewing an interaction allows a Five to remain relatively detached during the time when the event is lived out. The strategy is to privately view an event beforehand, imagining how it would be best to behave, and to then detach from feelings while the event is played out, often with the sense of

"I've been through this before." When safely alone again the Five will later bring the event and its feelings together, a little piece at a time, in order to figure out an emotional stand.

Being unprepared is frightening. I always get myself filled in about the details of a dinner date, and who's going to be there. Then I view myself going through my part, what's on the bill of fare, and the backgrounds of who's been invited. I usually get it down so well that I'm really not at home when the time comes to live it out.

I teach ancient languages at the local university. It was both exciting and frightening at the beginning, but as soon as I got used to the material and the classes, I found myself detaching mentally, often to the point where I would be located somewhere above and behind myself, watching myself deliver my talk.

It would take something totally unexpected, like a student suddenly yelling, "Fire!" to get back to knowing that I was really being seen by twenty people in a class. When I've shifted out, the feeling is that my real self is standing outside and above it all, watching my proper, professorial self be amusing, or intelligent, or whatever I've rehearsed him to be.

There's a real irritation at the predictability of it all, like wishing that someone would notice that I'm not where I seem to be, or that someone would be stunningly bright and ask me a question that would interrupt the monotony of observing myself, like a bystander who's watching someone else's life.

Observers are more emotionally available when the limits of an interaction are clear. When they know the limits of the agenda, and how long the meeting will last, they are freed to express themselves fully and passionately within the topic and within the frame of time. They may be well rehearsed, but they are more likely to be in touch with feelings on the spot when they understand the agenda, and more likely to shift out to observe when anything unpredictable comes up. They will want to go home when the agenda is completed and the time for small talk comes around.

Many Fives report that they are far more extroverted, and reach out easily to others, when they are traveling. The situation is ideal for them to reach out, because there is the sense of being an observer of a different culture, and they can control how long they're going to stay. Consequently, they can enjoy a unique situation fully, wanting to condense as much experience as possible into a small amount of time and store up memories for later enjoyment.

I was a botanist and taught in the field for several years. One day I left it flat and have been traveling continuously ever since. There's a compulsion to exist minimally, a great excitement at entering an alien place, with minimal language and about $20 to survive. I've done it over and over again, forcing fate to give me something. I have to extend myself in order to make it through the day.

Once I establish friends, a lover, and a base of support, I'll start to plan to leave. There's a tremendous intimacy for an intense period of time, and then I'm away again. As soon as I know exactly where I stand with people, there's the dissatisfaction of knowing what they expect from me. As I withdraw, it all vanishes, and I'm left with a kind of nostalgia for what happened to me back there which doesn't leave my mind, and will stay inside of me forever.

Compartmentalizing

The first line of defense in an elaborate attempt to create safe distance is to physically withdraw, unplug the phone, and become incommunicado. A more internal way of maintaining distance involves unplugging attention, so that potentially charged experiences are walled off from one another. Fives separate the different sectors of their lives from one another. There are different friends for different sectors, who will never be introduced and who will not be told about the other people in the Observer's life. Fives can develop passionate interests within the confines of a specific time and place, which are then set aside until it is "that time" again. The compartmentalizing of life into isolated sectors will read as privacy to an Observer, rather than as an aversion to being totally known. It is as if Fives have so little defense against others in an open arena of negotiation or conflict that the preferred defense is to not come to attention at all.

I feel like if someone gets in my door, they can take my shirt. It's a declawed-cat defense: you have to leave and shut the door to everything, because you haven't got the resources to make a fight. Rather than fight, I'll leave, which means they get everything, and I'm once again going to have to do without.

The other thing about them getting my shirt is that I have so little, it might be the only one that I have. But I'd rather give the shirt off my back than have to wrangle with someone about whose it is.

Another way to create safe distance is to section off memories from one another, so that what you did this morning seems discontinuous from what you are doing this afternoon. Discontinuous memory doesn't really mean that you can't remember what you said this morning; it is more like the events of your life seem to occur in little pieces, without any continuous feeling state to glue them all together.

I have a mantle full of mementos, and the reason why I hold onto these little things is that they pack a great amount of memory into a small object that brings back a whole time of my life to me. I have a box with some threads from the sweater that I wore for four years in graduate school. I have the tip from the pool cue that I used to help me through that school by betting on myself; and I have the umbilical cords from the births of my two sons. There's also some tokens of the trips that I've taken, which help bring back the memories of those wonderful times.

I also collect facts. It's what I call flypaper mind: an amazing array of disconnected facts about whatever I'm interested in. They pile up like specks, and I'm always hungry for more, but I can lose the thread of how they're all supposed to hang together.

The Joys of Privacy

Fives come alive when they are alone. They often need to get away from people in order to recharge their batteries and to let out the feelings that were suspended while they were in the presence of others. A Five's private time is filled with reverie and interesting things to think about. They love the company of their own minds, and unless privacy deepens into feelings of isolation, they are rarely depressed or bored because they have nothing to do.

Although Observers can appear to be lonely and socially isolated from the point of view of the more extroverted types, Fives themselves prefer to be alone. They are, in fact, remarkably independent. They do not look to others for approval, they prefer to be economically self-sufficient, they insist upon being able to come and go as they please, and they want to remain free of the emotional drains of dependency relationships. Because Fives do not seek recognition, an entirely autonomous life can be built within the home, in which Observers can live happily with the companionship of their own projects and fantasies. The following statement was given by a young filmmaker who originally took up photography because he felt comfortable in public behind a viewing lens.

I am known as an outgoing and gregarious fellow, which is totally different than the way that I feel inside. The outgoingness is because when I shoot I'm totally in love with my script and I know exactly what I want everybody on the set to do to get that vision captured on celluloid. Because everything is premeditated and as strictly controlled as I can make it, the small improvisations on the part of the actors, or the unexpected visual improvisations that show up when the reel is developed are very precious to me. The happiest times of my life are when I'm alone in the screening room, watching my own imagination come to life.

Ways to Hide in Public Places

People who prefer to be alone, but who find it necessary to appear in public places, will develop ingenious ways to distract attention from themselves. An obvious tactic is to shift a conversation to a topic of mutual interest, or to shift the spotlight to someone else's story line. Fives can be supportive friends, as long as they are in the advisory role to people who are moving ahead independently in their own lives, rather than hoping to extract an emotional connection from the Five.

Another way Fives deflect attention is to be familiar with a method that encapsulates the complexity of human behavior into a comprehensive mental system. Fives can relate to others in depth, and understand about emotional upheaval from a purely mental place, by studying a system such as psychoanalysis or astrology. By learning how people work emotionally, they can speak easily about patterns of feeling, without having to get personally involved. An outsider may see a Five's preoccupation with systematic abstraction as a way of hiding from personal connection by replacing feelings with ideas about what one is supposed to feel.

Fives are specialists at another form of public hiding: disappearing into an appropriate pose. The pose is adjusted to suit the circumstances. For example, a Five exemplar who was an excellent rock musician managed to perform with a number of big name bands by positioning his attention slightly outside of himself and going through a well-rehearsed routine. The pose he might adopt at a cocktail party would involve a costume, a drink, and the right placement of his knee as he crossed his legs. His hope would be that if he could deflect enough attention to the shell, he need not inhabit the shell for the duration of the party.

Intimate Relationships

The central issue for Fives is the fear of feeling. Intimacy is a strain on the basic defense of detaching attention from powerful emotions; which means that an Observer in love is caught between being affected by strong positive feelings and the habit of not wanting to feel at all.

Fives struggle with the fact that they are more emotional about people when they are alone and recreating an encounter than when those same people are physically present. They say that they are often frozen during a face-to-face meeting and that they need to be alone to figure out what they feel. The fact that Fives can feel more in retrospect, when they are safe from intrusion, is particularly obvious when they retreat into isolation directly after a deeply intimate encounter. Easily drained by powerful or continuous contact, Observers will withdraw in order to figure out where they stand. The immediate withdrawal from intimacy is bound to affect the partner, who may not have the same capacities for detachment. Because Fives rarely talk about it, their friends are generally not aware how much they focus on the significant people in their lives during their time alone, or how much time is spent in previewing or reviewing their meetings with people who are important in their lives. A powerful mental connection can be formed on the Five's side without the other party involved being aware of how central he or she has become in the Five's interior life.

When a relationship is mentalized, it can be enjoyed a little bit at a time, in an abstract way. Observers try to match up their feelings with their thoughts when they are alone, so that they can eventually be reunited with what they really feel. Because they detach attention from intense emotions, and because they mentalize their affections, Fives are often seen by partners as permanently withdrawn, and therefore emotionally cold.

On the high side of intimate contact, Fives do appreciate people on many abstract levels of connection. Commitment is made first mentally, and then emotionally. Once made, the commitment can be enduring, although always with clear limits of time and energy.

On the low side, the split between wanting to feel and wanting to detach becomes extreme in intimacy. There will be a strong avoidance of situations that bring up spontaneous feelings, especially confrontation. Eventually any partner will feel that he or she is in the role of active agent: the one who has to initiate, the one who has to move toward the Five.

An Example of a Couple Relationship: Five and Nine, the Observer and the Mediator

Both types share an awareness of nonverbal communication. There will be many evenings at home where the partners will feel secure and understood by each other, but without having to say so directly. Each will naturally give the other the private space that is necessary to make decisions and to come to an authentic personal stand.

Sexuality can develop into another important nonverbal communication for the couple, with the Nine likely to unconsciously merge with the Five's sexual style. The Nine will reach out to the Five in an attempt to merge with the partner's wishes, which (in an interesting meshing of energies) turns the naturally withdrawn Five's unspoken wishes into a major focal point for action. The domestic routine will also be an area of nonverbal contact, with each valuing the familiar day-to-day meetings in the kitchen and at dinner time as a secure, familiar way to spend time with each other.

It is unlikely that either partner will interfere with the other's interests. If the Nine wants to divert energy into multiple activities, it will not bother a Five unless this upsets home routine. If the Five partner wants to compartmentalize activities, that will also be acceptable unless the Five becomes secretive and withdraws the bond of confidentiality. As long as each partner is able to tell the other what is going on in his or her respective lives, the couple can give each other a great deal of space with minimal interference. However, both types have a tendency to withhold information as a form of self-defense, and both can become extremely jealous. Difficulties will arise if one partner creates distance by withholding sex or personal information from the other.

If the Nine exerts energy toward personal projects, the Five partner will move into an advisory position and begin to see the Nine's activities as interesting bridges to the outside world. However, if the Nine begins to get too dependent on the Five's support, or attempts to pull the Five into taking part in the activities, a severe rift can develop in which the Five feels crowded by the partner's dependency and the Nine feels abandoned by the Observer's withdrawal. Nines can become dependent on approval and demonstrations of affection, in which case the Five will stonily maintain that the partner should know that she or he is important without having to be told too often and will start to put limits on the time spent with an emotionally needy mate. The Nine will feel doubly abandoned if the Five begins to withhold sex as well as reassurances of affection. The way out for the Nine is to focus on outside interests as a way of bringing vitality back into the relationship. Once direct attention is removed from the Observer, she or he will feel less crowded and begin to refocus on the couple's interests.

Boredom can be another trap for the pair. Each looks to the other for juice, and each is concerned about the lack of juice. With boredom will come criticism: the Nine will criticize because she or he has merged with the wishes of the partner and finds no inspiration there; and the Five will criticize because anger surfaces strongly when the home environment feels safe enough to express negative emotions. A Five's anger is usually expressed by pouting, or a stony negative silence that will make a Nine feel very uneasy.

If either partner threatens to leave the relationship, or begins an outside affair, a great deal of unexpected jealousy will arise. If the Five has become attached to the mate, although this may be intellectually denied, then losing the partnership will feel like losing one's own life. Similarly, the Nine will feel that the aspects of the self that have merged with the mate will be cut off and lost forever. In another interesting meshing of emotions, either fight or jealousy will move the couple out of boredom and into an awareness of how important the relationship has become.

It can be painful for either a Nine or a Five to be drawn out to the point of real commitment. When a Nine makes up his or her mind to commit, and a Five develops a continuous feeling for another person, the connection can be solidified by making and remembering small demonstrations of affection. The Nine needs emotional and erotic merger and the Five needs reassurance when feelings appear.

Relationship to Authority

Fives have an aversion to having their time and energy put at the disposal of other people. They live with a sense of having limited resources of energy and of being easily exhausted by personal interactions. They feel especially drained if they are unclear about what others are going to expect from them, or if their duties at work are subject to change on short notice.

Motivated by the reluctance to have their limited supply of energy used by others, Observers resist by withdrawing from authoritative control. They prefer minimal supervision, and especially dislike supervision by a boss who shows up unexpectedly or who wants to be constantly informed. Contact with strangers feels intrusive, unless the limits of what is going to be discussed can be made clear in advance. They commonly view rewards like titles and salary as entrapments that authority uses to seduce workers into allowing their time and energy to be drained away. Fives prefer to do without such recognition, if it means being able to set the conditions under which they work.

Fives will, however, be willing to work hard under an authoritarian system that allows them to set their own time schedule and gives them freedom to choose the conditions under which they interact with people. They can be outgoing and friendly if informed in advance about what will be expected of them. For example, Observers usually want to know something about the people who are going to attend a gathering and what the likely topics of discussion will be, so as to be prepared.

Petty authority is likely to be seen as an extension of the controls that Observers like to avoid. Their level of concern about potential invasion of privacy from petty sources can range from a neurotic reluctance to answer the telephone to elaborate and time-consuming efforts to avoid interactions with neighbors, landlords, and public agencies, like the IRS.

The underlying reason for avoiding contact is that Fives have practically no defenses against confrontation. Once an authority can mail a letter directly to them or, worse yet, request a face-to-face meeting, Fives feel themselves hard pressed to negotiate against whatever the authority might demand. The preferred line of defense is to withdraw from an authority's sphere of influence and to forgo those luxuries that lead to entanglements with society's system of payments, mortgages, and debts.

On the high side of authority relationships, Fives are often able to focus clearly on difficult decisions, because they can detach their attention from interfering fears and desires. They are often the brain behind the scene who stays cool while others are distressed. They have a natural bent toward detached planning and long-range projects that demand a broad-based theoretical overview. They are willing to initiate important but obscure projects and to work behind the scenes on projects that will never lead to public recognition. They are far more effective if protected from confrontation and used as a mind, rather than being made responsible for follow-through or picking up the pieces.

On the low side of authority relationships, they can be evasive when feeling overwhelmed, and will become physically unavailable. They can suddenly announce a vacation just when the project heats up, or schedule barriers of time and people between themselves and the heat.

A Typical Interpoint Authority Relationship: Five and Four, the Observer and the Tragic Romantic

If the Five is boss, she or he will feel most comfortable working in a private space with a clear time limitation on all personal interactions: the fifty-minute hour, the meeting with a set agenda, the scheduled conference call. The Four employee will be expected to filter out all unnecessary intrusions and to deal directly with customers or clients whenever possible. As long as the employee makes deadlines and acts as an efficient interface, the boss will have no desire to supervise. The operation is likely to run smoothly if the Four likes to take on responsibility and only confers when necessary. The boss will be happy to let the employee become indispensable as long as no conflict arises.

If trouble does develop and it comes to the boss's attention, a Five boss tends to withdraw rather than confront. The Four may misread this as lack of personal attention, especially if the boss uses memos or intermediaries to deal with the employee rather than attending to the problem personally. A severe situation is likely to develop if the Four employee feels ignored and the boss withdraws, with the employee either becoming depressed and negligent or escalating troublesome behavior in order to force a response. The boss might prefer to fire the employee rather than negotiate, which is likely to make the Four hang in and fight what is perceived to be an unfair dismissal.

This kind of a standoff can be averted by a show of concern from either side. The Four wants recognition from a special source, and the Five wants to be the brains behind a smoothly running operation that doesn't depend on personal presence. If the boss will show interest in investigating the causes of disagreement, the Four will become more cooperative. If the employee is able to offer workable suggestions to remedy the

situation that do not require confrontation or emotional encounters, the Five will be appreciative. The employee will have
to move from a primarily emotional stance into a more logical
one, and the boss will have to move away from a primarily
mental stance into paying attention to the employee's feelings
about the job.

If the Five is employee, she or he will have more difficulty
being happy with coworkers than with the tasks involved. It is
difficult for some Fives to work at a desk in an unpartitioned
room in the presence of other people, and it is difficult for all
Fives to stay in contact with their feelings if not protected by
privacy. Many Fives report that they hide themselves behind
the pose of an appropriate-looking worker while feeling internally detached from their emotions. A direct line of communication with the boss would help so that instructions cannot be
interfered with by outside sources.

Five employees can develop an appropriate pose that allows
them to take on such jobs as receptionist or entertainer in which
they have to deal with the general public. The key mechanism
to a Five's work pose is that it is rehearsed and is supposed to
provide the Five with a safe hiding place in public places. The
pose is safe only insofar as a Five can reliably predict how other
people are going to react to the pose. Jobs requiring a real ability to deal with the public—such as salesperson or politician—
that depend upon spontaneous meetings and shifts of personal
presentation would not attract a Five, who prefers to meet new
situations from the safety of a fixed pose.

If the Four boss has confidence in the Five's capacities, she or
he should set about developing a private relationship that puts
the Five in an advisory capacity. Fives enjoy a private relationship with someone whose expertise they can respect and contribute freely when attention is focused on an objective project
rather than on themselves. The Tragic Romantic boss would be
wise to take on the responsibility for public presentation and
follow-through while leaving the Observer employee to advise
and strategize. If protected from direct confrontation, the Five

employee will be able to think clearly during a project's difficult phases and aid a Four boss, who will move through alternate periods of depression, elation, and destructiveness with regard to personal projects.

How Fives Pay Attention

A Five's isolation does not depend solely on withdrawal into privacy, or even on putting up emotional walls. The psychic isolation of the type can be seen as the habit of disengaging from feelings in order to observe. This habit of attention can become particularly obvious in stress, intimacy, or unpredictable situations that demand a spontaneous response. In extreme cases of detachment, a Five can attempt to disappear by freezing attention at a spot located just outside of the physical body.

I was a literal hermit for most of my twenties. No phone, few friends, and a long drive down a bad country road. By the time that I decided that I wanted to study photography, I couldn't remember how to hold up one end of a conversation. The first year of school I got into therapy. They recommended bodywork. I shut down so completely during the breathing exercises that I couldn't feel my body at all.

In one session I went through a full body convulsion and found that I had detached and was watching myself go through it without any feeling in my body. I am periodically aware of being outside and watching ever since. It comes up when I have to "go onstage." Even if I'm rehearsed, I can suddenly find myself separated, watching my body going through the motions of what I'm supposed to do.

Besides providing a buffer to the immediate experience of a strong emotion, the habit of detaching from feelings in order to watch can produce a dramatic experience of what meditators recognize as the separation between the object of attention and the inner observer.

I sometimes feel like I'm one of my old paper dolls, with a nice dress that's hung on my front, with little laps over the shoulder. Nobody sees me, just the front of the dress and my paper-doll face. Meanwhile, I'm standing behind myself, like a third party to my conversations, watching the face of whom I'm talking to and myself, standing there in the dress.

When I was seventeen, and first started having sex, my mind would flip, and I'd be outside watching myself. Making love is the clearest example of where I go when I'm under pressure. Basically, I want to avoid pressure, but when I have to face up to it, I will find myself detaching from the feeling. The harder my own life gets, the more fascinated I become with watching myself. I keep wondering what I'll do next. I got married because I wanted to see what I would do, and I've let the wolf get really close to the door, because I want to see how I'm going to get out of it.

Attention Practice

This practice can give non-Fives a taste of what it's like to detach and observe an object of inner attention. This is the placement of attention that Fives learned in childhood as a way to feel safe in threatening situations. There are *differences* between a Five's habit of separating attention from objects that frighten him or her, like intruding people or strong sexual feelings, and a meditator's awareness of the separation between the observing self and the object that is contemplated. One *significant difference* is that a Five gets frozen in the detached stance, compelled by habit to watch as a frightening event transpires, and constrained to keep attention separated from the feelings connected to what he or she sees. If the Observer merged with the feelings generated by the frightening event, Fives would lose the defense of keeping mind and emotions separate. The Five would then be vulnerable to being affected by others and to feeling his or her own desires.

In contrast to the frozen watching of a Five, who is avoiding feeling, a meditator's inner observer is able to merge, and become one with, inner objects of attention, such as body sensations, the resonance of chants, images, and pure emotions.

Imagine yourself standing in front of someone who tried to intrude into your life. It might be the mother who checked your dresser drawers when you weren't home, or the brother who broke into your diary and read it for months before you became aware of it. Get the feeling in your body of how you felt about being violated in a way that you couldn't control, and also imagine what it would be like to have to live with this person in your house day after day.

Now find a way to isolate yourself from being affected by what that person has done. The emphasis in this exercise is on protecting yourself from having to feel by isolating yourself from the intruder, rather than clamping down to hold back the emotion. Fives report a sense of control and even pleasure in being able to detach from being affected by outside influence.

Some Fives say that they move deep inside themselves to where there is no emotion. Others say that they separate themselves from an intruder by moving behind a wall or a one-way mirror, or they shift attention to a safe place just outside of the interaction. From that vantage point they can observe what is going on without becoming emotionally involved.

Intuitive Style

When Fives are drawn to meditation, they almost invariably find a natural inclination toward detachment practice. Vipassana and Zen are examples of such a practice, and they both emphasize cultivating the power of inner observation by letting go of thoughts and other intrusions upon an empty mind. The attraction for a Five can, unfortunately, be the desire to become a master of noninvolvement and to become protected from ever having to feel the fears and desires of ordinary life. Because of this desire for premature mental detachment, Five has been called the unenlightened Buddha.

Consider the difference between the premature detachment of a Five who meditates in order to become more immune to feelings and this report from a Five who has always used the detached state of mind as a way to become more aware of what he feels.

I have always been a runner, and for many years I considered it a metaphor for wanting to get as far away from home as two legs would carry me. No matter what went on in the house, I could count on flushing it as soon as I was about half a mile out. My thoughts would drop away, and I was free of everything but nature rushing by and my body moving, which seemed to go on without me making it happen. Distance is my thing. Working up for a fifty-mile run, and doing that every year, is a high point in my life.

I also use my running as a way to get to my feelings. I can count on a run to clear out whatever I'm jammed up about, and when I'm clear enough, I try to become aware of my question and let the feelings come and go. I call it running with a problem, and I have learned a lot about myself that way.

On several occasions I've had real intuitive flashes into a decison I'm running with, like once I found myself sprinting down a canyon toward a potential partner in my firm and away from two other strong contenders, although, of course, there was no one in the canyon but me. Another time I believed that my ankle was going to have pain, but I knew that a fellow would help carry me back, which was a pretty accurate description of what later happened in the negotiation I was running with.

This runner has found a way to allow his feelings and impressions to surface while he is in a detached state of mind. He is in no danger of getting "caught" by his emotions, in the sense of not being able to let them go. What is unusual for a Five is that he is able to let himself feel, to let his reactions come up spontaneously before he has prepared for them.

When he runs, his attention becomes attuned to the inner observer, and because he is willing to deal with his problems rather than intent on putting them aside, he focuses on his questions, rather than detaching from them for the duration of his run.

Avarice

During hard times an Observer would rather make do with less than risk reaching out to others in order to get more. The preferred reaction is to withdraw, to institute an economy move, to reduce personal needs to bare necessities, and to minimize dependency on other people. There is a feeling of independence in mentally noting, I don't need that, I can do without.

There's more pleasure in minimal living than in accumulating a lot of junk that you have no use for. My portables are a cot, a cat, some very important books, and a couple of changes of clothes. Breakfast is always the same: a granola bar and a cup of tea. There's a great delight in the little bit that I take, a real appreciation for having enough air, and enough food, and enough time to be by myself.

I do not feel deprived by living on very little. I am out of the rat race that runs my friends' lives. More money means more taxes, a big house means being tied like a slave. For me, luxury is something like having dessert after dinner, but dessert every night would make me feel like I'm run by dessert, and I would give it up and go on a fast.

Wealthy Fives also like to do without. There's often a feeling of being impoverished; an inner atmosphere of emptiness, as if whatever is offered is not nourishing and can be done without. Wealthy Fives adopt the same minimalist way of life as their poorer compatriots and suffer from the same sense of inner impoverishment, but the refusal to put their energy at the disposal of other people, or to make efforts to earn money for extras, is not as obvious as the Five with his precious books and his cot.

Howard Hughes, the billionaire Five who lived without luxury and eventually withdrew from most human contact, is an example of a Five showing pathological schizoid traits. He headed his empire by remote control, through intermediaries and the telephone. He managed to avoid contact and conflict, but did not partake of the luxury that he acquired. It was his habit to sit at the table but not extend his hand to eat.

How then could Observers be afflicted with avarice? If doing without gives a sense of pleasure, and even superiority over those who toil to gain material wealth, how could those with minimal physical wants ever feel the pangs of greed? The fact is that the detachment of Fives is compulsive, rather than chosen. It is based on the fear of losing the little that they have, of sacrificing independence by becoming involved with those who commandeer the source of supply, of being invaded by people, as they have been in the past.

It is as if a Five's independence rests on being able to mentally note, I can do without that. The situation becomes impossible when a Five gets hooked on something he or she cannot do without. When something becomes so valuable that it pervades a Five's private space, when a Five is caught by the wish to possess a person or a thing, then this inner poverty is intensified by the invasion of desire.

Because Fives rely so much on foreknowledge for protection, their chief attachment is to knowledge rather than to people or to things. They report that their inner sense of isolation is relieved when they feel close to knowing how the universe works or understanding human behavior. It is as if they can be included in the world machinery without having to be emotionally involved, and that by obtaining the keys to the machine, they can watch others get caught by the perils of love and hate without feeling left out.

I followed a guru all during my twenties and gave myself over to the study of yoga. The asceticism had great appeal. I got up at 4:00 a.m., kept a vegetarian diet, fasted regularly, and I was also celibate for seven years. I think I saw one movie the whole time I was at the ashram. I loved the schedule and found some power in myself to survive happily and to renounce.

Then my teacher told me to leave and reenter the world. I was not to come back for at least two years. I left the ashram with about $500, looked for a job, and started to live alone. I have to say, my teacher had been on the mark: the Laundromat, and my bills, and having to interview with strangers for a job brought up enough reaction in me that I plunged into yoga in order to survive.

The Virtue of Nonattachment

Nonattachment is obviously the opposite of attachment, and attachment stems from a sense of frustrated desire. When we can get as much as we need of something, we can let it go, knowing that, if necessary, we can have it back again. A Five's false detachment is based on an aversion to the possibility of feeling desires, rather than a sense of fullness at having enough. Fives will quite correctly point out that most of us are addicted to having far more than we need to survive comfortably and that we expend enormous energy in the pursuit of status and material wealth, because we have become enmeshed in our own cravings and desires.

But the compulsive need to *not* get involved, to *not* feel connected, and to *not* be coerced can lead Fives to believe in their own superiority because they can do without, but not to a feeling of satisfaction in getting what they want. Real detachment, of course, requires that you have a full range of feelings available to you, and that you are able to accept any impressions that need to surface into awareness before you let them go. The Buddha himself lived through many different life experiences before he sat and had his realization about the natural emptiness of mind. He began to teach the practice of detachment only after having had a bellyful of joy and suffering and his fill of some marvelous desires.

The Omniscient Quality of Higher Mind

What would pacify the fear of one who is afraid to feel? What would satisfy the need to be forewarned, to save oneself from a potentially invading world? For a personality type that has retreated from the body into the mind, the best defense is knowledge.

Like all the higher abilities indicated by the Enneagram's teaching, access to omniscience is gained through a nonthinking state of mind. It is not a question of knowing all the facts about a given subject, or developing a brilliant conceptual framework within which to arrange the facts. It is more like being able to engage the inner observer in such a way as to merge one's own awareness with impressions of the past, present, and future of all possible events.

Assets

Observers can carry on personal interests without the support of others. Their ability to reduce contact with feeling to a mere thread allows them to assist others in times of stress. The same capacity for emotional detachment makes them good decision makers, because they can think clearly under pressure. Fives make lifelong friends if the conditions of the friendship allow them complete independence and the freedom to retire when necessary. They can express a great deal of affection nonverbally and appreciate others on many abstract and nonverbal levels of connection.

Attractive Environments

Fives are often scholars of obscure but important fields of study; the inner circle of the ones who know. The psychologist's psychologist. The shaman's shaman. A slim book of data, that took a lifetime to complete.

The definitive dictionary of remote tribal language. Academic cubicles, the library stacks. Computer programmers who prefer to work the night shift. Those who run the stock room at the back of the store.

Unattractive Environments

Unattractive environments are any job that requires open competition or direct confrontation: salesperson, public debater, smiling political candidate.

Famous Fives

The billionaire *J. Paul Getty*, who is famous for multiplying his wealth rather than using it for pleasure. Getty had a pay phone in his home and was famous for being willing to wait an hour for a lift in someone else's car, rather than spending money on a cab. Eyewitnesses say that he habitually put his hand in his pocket after lunch and would not remove it until after the bill was paid.

Emily Dickinson □ Jeremy Irons □ The Buddha
Meryl Streep □ Franz Kafka

Subtypes

The subtypes describe preoccupations that developed from the need to protect personal privacy from outside influence.

Confidence in the One-to-One Relationship

Fives experience private bonding in the one-to-one relationship through the exchange of a confidentiality. The sexual subtype experiences more confidence in nonverbal sexual communication than in more public ways of relating. He or she feels the intensity of a secret bond.

Sexuality has been the freest part of my life. You don't have to talk, nobody else has to know, there's immediate intimacy, and the bedroom was the one place my mother wouldn't walk in on me.

Totems in the Social Arena

Fives feel a need to align with the source people of the tribe, to give advice to, and get advice from, the inner circle. Totems can also extend to seeking the knowledge contained in governing symbols, such as scientific formulas or esoteric paradigms.

I teach mathematics in an engineering school and would have quit years ago, except that it supports my real interest, which is editing a scholarly journal. We have a world readership of less than one hundred, all theoretical mathematicians. Most of us have never met, yet I am devoted to them personally through our mutual passion.

Castle (Home) in the Area of Self-preservation

Fives see home as the secure refuge from an invading world. There is a preoccupation with the control of private, personal space. "A womb with a view."

I can't withdraw into myself if there's a friend in the room. I'm so aware of what they're doing that if they're quietly reading a book, it feels as loud as a band playing polkas. My only hope for concentration is to get them out or to get myself out to a coffeehouse where nobody knows me and I won't be disturbed.

What Helps Fives Thrive

Fives often enter therapy or begin a meditation practice because they begin to feel isolated and lonely. Cut off from feelings, yet aware that others can feel, Observers will place themselves in situations where they can be drawn out. Typical presentations include difficulties with social relations, the loss of a person or an object to which a Five has become attached, and phobias that limit freedom of movement. Fives need to learn how to tolerate their own feelings without detaching. Fives can help themselves by

- Noting the desire to withhold when others expect a response. Giving up the control of withdrawal and strategic giving as a manipulation. "I'll come through when I want to, but not when you expect it."
- Noting when emotions are replaced by analysis or when mental constructs become substitutes for experience.
- Realizing that access to feelings does not equal always being hurt.
- Noting the desire to be recognized without exerting effort.
- Noting how easy it is to give up. "I tried once and it didn't work."
- Working with the three Ss: secrecy, superiority, and separateness.

- Learning to tolerate spontaneous happenings. To risk, to reach out, to activate private dreams.
- Seeing the discrepancy between how much can be felt when others are present, and what can be felt when safely alone.
- Recognizing the intense needs for control of personal space and control of time spent with intimates.
- Learning to finish important projects and to let them go public. To let oneself be seen.
- Realizing that feelings and self-disclosure might actually effect a change.
- Realizing how little one is willing to settle for.
- Questioning the minimalist way of life.
- Seeing the ways in which others are made to be the active agents. The ways in which nonaction forces others to move first.
- Learning to capitalize on the search for special knowledge and symbolic thinking.
- Learning to tolerate other people's needs and emotions.
- Being willing to bring emotions into the present moment with methods such as Gestalt, bodywork and artwork. *But at the same time* not seeking out a premature cathartic release. Allow time for delayed emotional reactions to connect with insight.

What Fives Should Be Aware of

Fives should be aware of the following behaviors during times of change:

- Leaving the body and retreating into the mind.
- Wanting to hoard time and energy. Saving rather than putting out.
- Trouble with self-disclosure. Censoring conversations that reveal the self. Withholding information.
- Not giving; feeling imposed upon by other people's needs.
- Intensification of need for self-sufficiency. "I can do without you," directed at therapist, friends, family.

- Feeling drained by commitment. Letting others have only a little bit.
- Withdrawal by mentalizing experiences. Increase of loner's stance. Bringing people into fantasy life, rather than dealing with real life.
- Fantasy of being specially selected, of being recognized without putting oneself forward. "If God wants me, he will come to me."
- Hiding in a pose. Manners suitable to therapist's office as mask to avoid placing attention on immediate feelings.
- Believing oneself to be above having to feel. "Anger is for lesser beings." "Why can't they control themselves?"
- Paralysis of action concomitant with emergence of desires. Can't reach out, can't pull back.
- Partitioning off of emotional life. Secrecy. Nobody gets it all.
- Confusion between spiritual detachment and the need to withdraw from emotional pain.

11. Point Six: The Devil's Advocate

	ACQUIRED PERSONALITY		ESSENCE	
HEAD	Chief Feature:	COWARDICE	Higher Mind:	FAITH
HEART	Passion:	FEAR/DOUBT	Virtue:	COURAGE
	SUBTYPE WAYS OF BEING			
	Sexual:	STRONG/BEAUTIFUL		
	Social:	DUTIFUL		
	Self-preservation:	WARM/AFFECTIONATE		

The Dilemma

Sixes lost faith in authorities when they were young. They remember being afraid of those who had power over them, of being unable to act on their own behalf. Those memories have carried over into adult life as a suspiciousness of other people's motives; Sixes try to ease this insecurity by either seeking a strong protector or by going against authority in the Devil's Advocate stand. There is both the wish to find a leader, to give one's loyalty to a protective organization, such as the church, or the company, or the university, and an equal mistrust of authoritarian hierarchy. The dutiful posture and the Devil's Advocate stance both stem from the suspicion of authority.

Because they are afraid to act on their own behalf, Sixes have problems with follow-through. Thinking replaces doing because attention shifts from the impulse to act on a good idea, to an intense questioning of that idea from the point of view of those who might disagree. The motive behind pervasive doubt is the childhood need to ward off interference from powerful people. Doubt leads to procrastination, which forestalls a resurgence of the fear of punishment that the Six child endured for acting against authority.

Because they take a mental "Yes, but . . ." attitude toward their own ideas, Sixes move toward success in fits and starts. There is usually a history of job changes and unfinished projects. Anxiety tends to peak as goals materialize, which means that self-doubt and procrastination intensify as Devil's Advocates move toward exposure and success. They vacillate, not because they are confused about their task, but because they question their own capabilities, and are convinced that an open success will draw the attention of hostile authorities, who will try to stop their efforts.

The antiauthoritarian stance makes Sixes gravitate toward underdog causes. They come to the fore when the odds are against them, and they can sacrifice heroically for a cause or for a friend in need. They are extremely loyal in the us-against-them position, because duty demands a clear-cut action and once sides are taken, an authority's intentions are made perfectly clear.

Devil's Advocates are convinced that they can see through slick images and false presentations. Afraid of being disadvantaged by others, they are wary of being taken in by compliments or seduced by calculated praise. They are likely to become more vigilant if they are treated affectionately, because when they trusted in the past they were hurt when their guard went down. Their way of paying attention is to scan the environment for signs of anything harmful and to watch people closely for indications of what goes on in their minds. Sixes want to be forewarned and prepared, and this need makes them want to discover what lies beneath an image and what might be hidden by a pleasant smile. Sixes can often spot the weak points in an argument and recognize a hidden power play.

When Sixes become alarmed or feel inwardly threatened, the habit of looking outward intensifies. The more distress they feel within, the more they tend to look without, with the result that Sixes can easily mistake the source of their alarm. There are always things to be afraid of, and those who are predisposed to think that their uneasiness is caused by the ill intentions of others will be vulnerable to hearing innuendos in innocent conversations, or believing that they know others' real intentions despite what the others might say. The following statement, given by an extremely frightened Six, describes the habitual way of paying attention that perpetuates a paranoid's concerns.

It's hard for me to work around people I don't know. I've waitressed since high school, and I am still plagued by the feel of eyes boring into my back. It's worst when I have to draw beer at the bar. The customers pass by, one by one, and I'm wondering what they think about me.
   If I raise my head to look at the faces, I'm gone. Each of them seems to be thinking something, or holding back what they really want to say. I have to tell myself that it's okay, that these people are not mad at me, that they are not really thinking badly of me. But I have gotten so pulled off by what I see in them that I've lost track of what I'm doing, and the beer spills, or I forget to center the glass under the tap.

The waitress is clearly attributing motives to her customers that are unlikely to be true. Her interest is not in the physical reality of the restaurant, with its conversations and its beer. She is more concerned with the reality of people's thoughts and inner intentions and believes that she can recognize that inner reality by what she sees in a customer's face. Given her fearful state of mind, the Six is more than likely to misread the intentions of others, but she may, in fact, have developed an acute sensitivity to the small range of information that supports her neurotic concern. She has had a lifetime of experience in looking for people's hidden negative intentions, and within that small slice of reality, she may indeed have found ways to recognize discrepancies between the image that people project and the way that they really feel inside. Unfortunately, she may be so preoccupied with looking for that small discrepancy that it may dominate her perceptions, as if it were an established fact.

Phobic and Counterphobic Types

There are two kinds of Sixes, or paranoid worldviews. A phobic Six looks furtive and frightened about life. Like Woody Allen's self-characterization, a phobic type will vacillate, replacing action with analysis, filled with contradiction and self-doubt. The waitress is a phobic Six, because she hangs out on the sidelines rather than challenging her fears. If she was counterphobic, she would be more likely to engage the customers, to talk, to check them out, to reduce her anxiety by getting them to like her.

A counterphobic Six might also make the customers uneasy by probing for their real intentions. People often feel misread when under the gaze of paranoid attention, and if they become annoyed, the Six will "know" that they were untrustworthy all along.

When the waitress splits her attention between her job and her fears, she sometimes makes mistakes. As a phobic type, she is likely to continue wondering what the customers are thinking about her, without daring to check it out. A counterphobic Six, equally terrified, reports that he ran straight into the dragon's mouth by making himself a skydiving champion in order to master a fear of heights. Both phobic and counterphobic styles stem from the same psychological roots.

The habitual preoccupations of Six include
· Procrastination of action. Thinking replaces doing.
· Issues with work and incompletion.
· Amnesia with respect to success and pleasure.
· Authority problems: either submitting to, or rebelling against, authority.
· Suspiciousness of the motives of others, especially authorities.
· Identification with underdog causes.
· Loyalty and duty to the cause, to the underdog, and to the strong leader.
· Fear of direct anger. Attribution of own anger to others.

- Skepticism and doubt.
- Paying attention by scanning the environment to look for clues that might explain the inner sense of threat.
- An intuitive style that depends upon a powerful imagination and single-pointed attention, both of which are natural to the fearful mind.

Family History

Sixes report that they were raised by authorities who were untrustworthy. Lack of trust commonly centered on punishment or humiliation by parents, particularly when the parents were unpredictable and erratic in how they dealt with the child. Very occasionally a Six reports that the family lived with a secret that had to be kept quiet. Young Sixes had to predict the behavior of adults who were likely to flare up without any clear indication about what the child had done.

The more hyperalert Sixes say that they were often punished because their parents were personally disturbed, rather than because they had actually done something wrong. They say that they had to watch others carefully, because they were treated erratically, that if they didn't sense the threat beforehand, they could be taken unaware. Sixes learned to hesitate, to check out danger signals, to figure out the authority's position before they made a move themselves. Afraid of being hurt or embarrassed, young Sixes had to know what others intended to do before they could take a position themselves. It is this outwardly directed focusing of attention, coupled with the feelings of children who are powerless to act in their own defense, that perpetuates the Devil's Advocate's neurotic style.

My father was the kind of man that you didn't know whether to laugh or to duck. If you laughed when you should have ducked, then you did that only once. I learned to read him when I was young; one eye on my homework, and the other eye on his mood on the other side of the door.

If it was going badly on his side of the door, then I had an escape hatch. I'd go out my window and across the fire escapes to the roof of the next apartment building. I'd wind up doing homework on the roof, wondering if he'd be asleep before I had to go home.

The common theme is that of a child who felt unprotected, without a safe place to go. The background level of apprehension that adult Sixes live with stems directly from this sense of being on a losing side, without a strong figure who would offer protection.

Both my parents were alcoholics and held themselves to be failures in life. There was a lot of sneaking around about liquor, and hidden bottles, and lying about it. The idea was to keep bad news to yourself, because it would only be a burden to them, and they couldn't help anyway.

We lived in borderline neighborhoods, and I was pretty much the new kid around, because we moved a lot. I would be going out of the house, and suddenly I'd be waylaid for my milk money, or my lunch would be taken by somebody much bigger than I was. Whenever I left the house, I was always looking for where somebody might be hiding on me. I couldn't relax on the street or in school, because of having to stay on top of whoever was around.

The Six child became mistrustful of authority figures. This resulted in either a dependency on authority "to take care of me because I feel weak and afraid," or a rebellion against authority "who is trying to take advantage of my weakness by making me afraid."

I had three sisters and was the first boy. My parents were both highly competitive, strong people with a great many expectations for their first son. I was also my mother's dearest, so when anybody did anything that did not meet expectations, a lot of fury went down her lightning rod, which was me. So I went to an Ivy League college and, needless to say, saw some of the same punitive characteristics in the U.S. government that I saw in my parents.

My family was very conservative, as (most) second-generation Jewish immigrants were, and so my mother was horrified to discover that one of the first causes that I took up was the sexual freedom league on campus. If someone had said at the time that I was just trying to get my parents uptight, I would, of course, have disagreed, but with a little maturing, I can see that some of that was true.

I've recently gone back to grad school in economics, and I have to say that I still hold my radical views, hopefully with a good deal of the kneejerk rebellion taken out of my opinions.

Authority Problems

Because Sixes have felt powerless as children, they have trouble taking action as adults. Fearful of being disadvantaged by powerful people, they tend to overvalue those who take action, and prosper, and move ahead in life. This overvaluing takes the form of looking for a strong leader to follow, or in a suspiciousness of those who take on leadership roles.

Exquisitely aware of power's abusive potential, Sixes will look for a leader's unstated intentions and be on the lookout for manipulative plans. An unusual preciseness of attention can develop around the need to "know the worst." This precision is often utilized in a biased way, however: to discover the negative qualities of powerful people, and to look for the redeeming qualities in underdogs. In other words, the haves come under close surveillance, but the have-nots, with whom Sixes identify, are assumed to have been damaged by life and are therefore scrutinized in a kinder light.

Doubtful of their own capacity to take action, Sixes project a great deal of their own power to leaders. Anyone who takes on an authority role looks unrealistically opinionated and disproportionately strong. Open anger is particularly frightening, and those who express anger easily seem far more threatening than they may actually be.

The overattribution of power to authorities is usually acted out as 1) idealizing and following a strong protector: my guru, my mentor, my führer; 2) joining with a like-minded group: us against them; 3) rebellion: questioning authority.

Following a protective leader works only as long as the leader is perceived to be fair and headed in the right direction. If the leader begins to totter on the throne, the Six disciple is cast back into an anxiety of mistrust. Six followers are likely to over-react by adopting an antiauthoritarian stance and turning on the leader.

Joining with a like-minded group circumvents the pressure of paranoia. A noncompetitive group of friends helps to dissolve a suspicious mental atmosphere for the Six, because he or she knows where everybody stands. If you are not a Six, you might capture the sense of security of an us-against-them group by imagining yourself working with others to support an under-dog cause in which you passionately believe.

The rebel's stance is obviously linked to feelings of oppres-sion. If the stance becomes compulsive, in the sense of habitu-ally looking for an external cause to explain an internal fear of taking action, then feelings of powerlessness can only increase. Many Sixes, however, believe that they gain a kind of personal power in strategically placing themselves against the odds, against the system, against the easy way.

For Sixes, there is a strength to be gained by putting them-selves up against the wall, because the situation forces them to act. Consequently, Sixes are often attracted to dangerous or highly competitive sports, because the situation demands im-mediate response. Doing has to replace thinking in a crisis of action. They are also attracted to losing causes, or turnaround businesses, where their rebellion against oppression finds a natural and constructive outlet.

I was afraid of my father, and to lessen my terror of him, I'd provoke him, make him do his worst, so that he'd look bad and so that it'd be over, and I'd feel safe for a while.

I can't remember a time when I felt that authority was on my side. My school memories are of cutting class, signing my own report cards, and leading a secret life, where I could do as I pleased. I never thought that the system was fair, so in my twenties and thirties I had no desire to enter the rat race and have to compete for status that I saw as phony and didn't respect.

Instead, I took up racing cars for a living. I got into it when I was young. Fell in love with it, actually. There is nothing in the world like coming out of a straightaway, six cars crowded into a corner, all inches apart at 170 miles an hour. You could die right there. It was great to feel that edge in my body, that my life was in my hands; it seemed hugely alive to get that close to death. I felt no fear around the races, or at certain other times when I went against the law. I used to get afraid when things got quiet.

As antiauthoritarians, Sixes are attracted to both sides of the law. Here is a statement from a Six who operates from the police side. He is a career detective who says that he was raised in Chicago in a neighborhood that was dominated by youth gangs and that he was systematically intimidated into joining the Blackstone Rangers. He has built his career around what he sees as "bringing bullies to justice," and is motivated by exactly the same preoccupations that cause many Sixes to rebel against the law.

I have always hated the misuse of power. My own experiences with lawless people has made me aware of the extent that humans will go to in order to degrade one another. I've often been afraid of retaliation when I arrest and when I testify. And even if the defendant isn't out for revenge, there's still the fact that I'm hired to go into a courtroom and testify as a witness, where I have to handle cross-examination by vicious lawyers who want to smear my credibility.

I get very scared beforehand, as if I'm the one going on trial, but the moment that I'm sworn in, there's a kind of crystal-clear moment where the shakes vanish, and then I'm on my way.

Sixes work well in a clearly defined chain of command. Accountability and delegation of responsibility lessen paranoia. They make excellent leaders in the loyal opposition position, but are likely to be self-sabotaging if efforts are accepted by the majority in power. They are loyal to the group while it is under pressure and can make heroic sacrifices for the cause. Tension can build when there is no opposition against which to mobilize, however, and paranoid attention can turn to group members when the crisis is past.

It is difficult to praise Sixes. They exert great efforts to have an underdog position acknowledged, but have trouble accepting recognition when it has been earned. Positive attention can spark doubtful thinking: This is a setup or What more do they expect? They are quick to spot ineptitude or power plays on the part of leaders and believe that they will come under the same severe scrutiny if they are placed in a high-visibility role.

On the high side of authority relationships, the same behaviors that hinder a Six—suspicion, procrastination, and the search for hidden motives—can become useful tools. Suspicion of authority can evolve into constructive critique; procrastination can lead to allowing time for the reformulation and reevaluation of ideas; imagining the worst can become believable enough to replace reality in a paranoid episode, but that same powerful imagination can generate original solutions.

On the low side of relationships with authority, Sixes can be excessively cautious, especially in winning situations, exhibiting procrastination and a search for hidden motivations in the actions of others. In addition, there are issues with follow-through and completion, even with a guaranteed win. Suspicion of others and a sense of threat intensify with success and public recognition.

An Example of an Authority Relationship: Six and One, the Devil's Advocate and the Perfectionist

If One is the boss, she or he will supervise well when the guidelines are clear and delegate and organize as long as the risk of error is low. The Six employee will respect One's fairness and feel safe with known procedures, but will secretly rebel against a One's compulsive detail overload, and will begin to cut corners, bend the rules, and encourage others to do the same. If, however, a risky decision has to be made, a One boss often becomes overwhelmed by responsibility and starts to believe that others are critical of her or his management abilities.

The Perfectionist will delegate less, spread attention to secondary tasks, and displace anger into arguments with employees over issues that have nothing to do with the decision at hand. The decision often has a tight deadline, because the One has procrastinated by spending enormous amounts of time on details.

The most stressful interaction occurs if the Devil's Advocate believes that the Perfectionist's displaced anger is, in fact, directed at herself or himself and, lacking information, assumes a worst case outcome. Six will then begin to rally allies and build a case against the One's alleged manipulations. In order to flush out the One's secret intentions, the Six is likely to make mistakes at work, which will infuriate the One and validate the Six's suspicions. Reality testing is enormously helpful for both One and Six during such a severely mistrustful period. Reality testing assumes that the Perfectionist is self-aware enough to admit to having made mistakes. By the same token, the Devil's Advocate needs to trust the fact that there may not be any hostile intent involved.

If Six is boss, the same issue of procrastination comes into play, but for different reasons. When faced with a tough decision, Six slows down and lets details slide drastically. This reads as ineptitude to the One employee, who will not cover for the Six, and will also slow down, because of the lack of structured supervision. One will judge Six's performance and perhaps feel superior to the floundering boss. When Six detects this judgment, her or his attention will shift from the decision at hand and focus upon the perceived threat from One. If Six is mature, reality testing can come into play, with Six soliciting opinions from One, rather than allowing the One's habit of judging to become the pivotal point of a paranoid fantasy that places One at the center of a conspiracy to oust the boss.

Neither One nor Six is particularly trusting of other people's good intentions: One is afraid of criticism, and Six is afraid of being ganged up on or harmed. If potential criticism can be defused, One will open; if the fear of attack is defused, Six will open. A positive interaction could begin by Six admitting to making mistakes. Having little image to defend, Sixes can be highly self-disclosing in the admission of error. Once error has been admitted, One is far less defensive and more able to disclose personal shortcomings. It would also help Six to initiate and follow through, if One could admit to anxiety and confusion. In the Six's mind, tasks would then be undertaken for someone else who is afraid. Protecting another is an easier action posture for Six than direct successful action for the self. Once the task is set in motion, the One can provide excellent follow-through and set up a schedule that will move the Six along to completion.

Habit of Assuming Worst Case Outcomes

Sixes are both blessed and cursed by a powerful imagination. The imagination is intrinsic to the paranoid worldview, because of the childhood need to predict the behavior of others and to imagine future outcomes in order to ward off harm. Sixes are sensitive to the possibility of worst case outcomes, and so tend to imagine the worst, without realizing that they have not paid equal attention to imagining the best. They so habitually scan the environment for clues to explain the inner sense of threat that many Sixes view imagining the best as a naive form of fantasy based on childish wishing.

The phobic Six reaction to fearful imaginings is easier to understand than the counterphobic Six position. The phobic type imagines danger, or thinks that danger may be near, and sensibly runs away. The counterphobic reaction would be to seek out the danger. Counterphobic types who seek out the dangerous option look like Eights (the Boss), in the sense that they can be very aggressive in what they perceive to be an up-against-the-wall situation where they have to face a threat. Counterphobics say that they have to move toward what they fear or else they find themselves imagining the issue over and over again.

This habit of attention is the inner meaning of the belief that the coward dies a thousand deaths; for example, if a menacing tiger appears on the road, a sensible phobic Six will run and climb a tree. The counterphobic type is likely to go for the tiger's throat rather than have to sit in a tree and experience a night of lurid mental imagery.

I remember in Vietnam, when I wrote home to my girl after about a month of combat, I told her that the thing that frightened me the most was the dark, at night, when they'd send me out. I was simply afraid of the dark. If somebody had jumped out and started shooting, I would have felt better. My imagination just went bananas. I saw monsters, I saw people who weren't there, and the more I saw them, the more I'd look for them, until I'd be crouching in firing position without being able to know if I was really being watched or not.

This is the soldier who shoots at shadows, the fearful one. He is a self-identified Six who has had the rare experience of watching how his own mind works under pressure. He could fire into the dark because the shadows menace him. His need to know the worst in order to prepare causes him to imagine what might be waiting in the dark, and his images can become so profoundly believable that they begin to overlay and coexist with the shapes of boulders and trees.

The war brought my paranoia into the foreground. I wasn't sure, before I went in, that I was afraid underneath. I didn't chicken out under fire, and I assumed that everybody else felt more or less the same as myself. But when I came back, I started getting anxiety attacks and I couldn't take a shower without bringing my knife with me into the stall.

The water noise made it so I couldn't hear the sounds in the house, and I'd be there with my face full of soap, and I would hear things. I would think there was someone in the bathroom, and I'd pull open the stall door and look out, and I've even, soaking wet, gotten out of the shower and gone to the front door to look out.

There was nothing specific that I was afraid of, no known enemies, and the doors were locked, but sometimes I had to have the knife in there with me for protection.

This returned vet's lifelong habit of imagining the worst is by now such an integrated part of the way that he perceives the world that in order to get through a complete shower, he would have to recognize that when he shifts his focus to hot water and soap, his habit of scanning the environment in order to protect himself is momentarily interrupted, causing him to quickly snap back and imagine the worst that may have crept up on him while he was unaware.

It is unlikely that he is aware of his imaginative habit, or the fact that he does not care to imagine the best. If this bias of attention were to be pointed out, he would probably see imagining the best as a kind of starry-eyed substitution for reality. Sixes are edgy, like children who are afraid to take their eyes off someone who is bigger than they are, because they might get jumped if they look away.

Sixes can get so preoccupied with a worst case scenario that attention gets caught up in mental images that are powerful enough to seem real. They are addicted to imagining possible outcomes, because it seems like a legitimate source of correct information. To stop imagining possibilities and consequences would make a Six apprehensive about being taken unaware. Imagination is part of a Six's attentional defense. To give it up would be to let one's guard down, to face life unprepared.

On the high side, this same habit of imagining the hidden possibilities within ordinary situations inclines Sixes to be excellent troubleshooters and effective devil's advocates.

Projection

The blind spot in the way a Six pays attention is that a point of view must have first appeared in the Six's mind in order to warrant him or her looking for supportive evidence and clues. From a Six's point of view, it is very difficult to tell the difference between the general habit of scanning the environment to make himself or herself feel secure and scanning the same environment because he or she is looking for signs that confirm a point of view. For example, if a Six believes that John likes her, then she will look for signs in John's self-presentation that this is so. John might recognize that he is being projected upon, because the Six may say that he is thinking something that he is not. She could say his affectionate feelings are appreciated when, in fact, he is not feeling affectionate. Or she could say that he is radiating anger when he is actually feeling fine.

I had been married for over ten years, and would periodically believe that my husband was hiding an affair, and that he was planning an excuse to leave. I would become convinced and accusatory, and then find out that it had no basis in fact. It made me feel crazy to have been so sure and to have been so wrong.

Then I went through a phase of my own, when I became attracted outside of the marriage. The way that I knew that I was attracted to someone was that I would become threatened that my husband was going to go and build up a whole mental story about how it was best for both of us that he should leave. I'm now fifteen years married and am quite clear that when I think I'm being left that I may have eyes for someone else.

Here is another statement about projection. It is given by a business executive who has identified the fact that he attributes his own unrecognized and unacceptable anger to other people.

My mother was a child abuser. She beat me for four years, almost daily, and the terrible memory of that still lives with me. So when I left home for college, I carried a terrible anger against women, which I did not recognize, but which was simmering just below the surface. So I came into Berkeley. Early seventies. Women's liberation movement. I was so angry all the time. Women talked about their oppression, but I felt so oppressed by women.

I would get into these collective living situations of the seventies, and always, sooner or later, got into trouble with the women. First one, and then all of them, would get down on me, call me a chauvinist, and I'd get hurt and then I could let myself feel legitimately angry at them, which had been the case all along but I hadn't recognized it. So I was afraid to feel my own anger, and put it onto others, and to prove the whole hypothesis, I would do little things to make the women mad. Like flirt with all of them at once, which, by the way, works great. And there I was, back to my mother, who I saw as basically out to beat me into obedience.

How Sixes Pay Attention

If you are not a Six, this exercise will help you understand the unconscious shifts of attention that underlie the Six's worldview. You will need a book to read as part of the exercise. When you have found a book, sit down and keep it closed on your lap.

Now remember someone who made you feel afraid when you were young. Visualize this person standing before you, the face, the body stance, the clothing, and particularly remember the way that he or she looked at you when you felt intimidated.

Now believe that you have been living with this person on a day-by-day basis for a long time in a very small house. Your intimidator has access to anything in the house and could show up at any time.

Now open the book and start to read, while at the same time remembering to stay aware of the person in the house. Split your attention between reading the lines and checking out the potential intruder's movements. You will either be able to pay attention to both tasks simultaneously, or your attention will shuttle back and forth between reading and being aware of the other's whereabouts. In either case, you have adopted the state of mind of a person who has been made to be afraid.

The next practice should be done facing a friend who is gracious enough to let you stare at his or her face while you practice shifting your attention.

Now form an idea of something that this friend might be thinking about you that he or she has never expressed. It can be either a positive or a negative opinion, but you should believe that your friend is very likely to be holding this opinion, and that you are going to look for confirming signs.

Now hold an ordinary out-loud conversation with your friend, while at the same time scanning the face for signs of the hidden point of view. All of the elements of the paranoid style are now present: an inner hypothesis (in this case fabricated), and a split of attention between the talk going on between the two of you and the need to look for confirming signs of the hidden opinion. For the true paranoid, the inner hypothesis is really a conviction. He or she *knows* that the painful opinion is true and is *looking for* corroborating evidence in the mannerisms and facial cues that the partner is bound to produce in the course of an ordinary chat.

Procrastination of Action

Sixes delay taking action because the hazards involved stand out as far more real than the promise of success. "What might go wrong" has the solid appearance of fact, whereas "Won't we be proud when we win" brings up fears of open exposure to jealousy and ill will. The cautionary habit is more obvious in the phobic types, where forward action is accompanied by currents of internal questioning. "I doubt that it will work," "Yes, but . . ." "It sounds risky; we need to wait until the evidence is in." Even the aggressive-looking counterphobic types are preoccupied with worst case imaginings and say that they procrastinate until paranoia pushes them to face their fears, rather than have to live with a mental movie of whatever has made them afraid.

Procrastination is supported by a largely unrecognized habit of intense internal questioning. Attention shifts from a good idea and the impulse to act to equally powerful counterthoughts, which doubt the correctness of the move. Thinking about doing neatly forestalls the moment when action brings the Six into the open, exposing him or her to attack by those in authority.

There is usually a history of incompletes: a degree left unfinished, a major project left undone. There is always a problem with moving directly from idea into action, which, from a Six's point of view, does not read as procrastination so much as a logical attempt to be prepared.

It took me ten years to complete my thesis. I dropped out, came back, and changed the topic several times. Each topic presented itself in terms of the unanswered questions that it raised. I could always argue it from the other side.

It peaked one night when I sat in front of the typewriter and began the opening of my argument from at least half a dozen perspectives, and each time had to return to the beginning because I had countered my own argument from the position of some authority in the field.

To a Six, these debilitating shifts of attention seem like legitimate data gathering. Each authority's point of view has to be taken seriously, and potential objections accounted for, before the thesis can move forward. That means that Sixes wind up questioning their own position more than they defend it, which guarantees that progress will be slow. The motive behind this pervasive doubt is the familiar need to counter potential objections in order to ward off harm.

Paradoxically, if the thesis were to be suddenly assured of success, with all legitimate objections honestly dismissed, its author might experience more acute performance anxiety than when the project was in doubt. Success and exposure bring on fears of being victimized by unprovoked attack; these fears are mitigated and softened by moving slowly and with doubt.

A Six's procrastination can be interpreted by others as anything from laziness to ineptitude and, particularly on work projects or when decisions have to be made, is likely to engender the very feelings of impatience and anger that Sixes spend so much time trying to avoid.

Sixes perform well when duties are clearly defined, or when placed in the devil's advocate position, with a worthy adversary to oppose. The mental habit of imagining the worst stops immediately when a real opponent appears. Paradoxically, fearful people can become clear thinking and courageous in underdog positions and under impossible odds, because their attention focuses sharply on the task when they are opposed. Fighting for survival feels very different to Sixes than competing for success. They often perform brilliantly under pressure, whereas they are less productive under optimal working conditions.

Fear of Success

My parents' expectation was that I would be a scientist, like my father, and so I aspired to be a chemist with a twist. I chose to be on staff for an environmental action group, because there I got to work for an objectively worthwhile cause, while at the same time being rebellious by critiquing big industry and big government.

My first round of success was that I wrote a popular book and really got to center stage. The end of the story came almost immediately. I had reached my ambition, I was successful in my own eyes, and, at the same time, there wasn't an opposition to push against.

My rebellion and my work had been tied together, and when I got on top, I was glad about it, but also felt that I had lost myself. There was no drive left. People were after me to come and speak, when I had no interest in those things. So I left success to its own devices and moved to another country. It felt heroic. I showed my friends, Hey, this is the way you deal with notoriety, you walk away from it. None of them could have done that.

In the end I regret. I don't regret leaving, because I came alive again in another popular cause. I do regret that I never played out whatever opportunities would have come had I stayed on.

"Up against it" defines an identity. When you are a misfit in terms of the American ideal of performance and social popularity, then you have an identity, and your task is to struggle against massive opposition in order to be heard. If you are in the underdog position, the odds are stacked against success. You are up against a worthy adversary, which liberates the energy to struggle, and to win.

If success begins to materialize, that massive resistance is removed, and real paranoia can set in. "Whom do I trust now that I'm on top?" "Where is trouble likely to creep in?" Antiauthoritarian Sixes can only believe that once they get onstage that others will see them as oppressive and doubt their good intentions. A suspiciousness of the good intentions of others increases as pleasurable goals materialize, and the old habits of procrastination and self-doubt return in force when desires are aroused.

I've taught in a number of areas throughout my life: dance, English, psychology, and, most recently, English in a foreign university. My pattern is to get to a certain level in the system, and then to start to question the political structure of where I'm working, or whether I want to be there at all. Almost simultaneously I develop a new interest, about which I really do have some passion, and then I'll leave to follow my new direction.

It is also painful to see that feelings of success don't carry over from one teaching job to another. There's an amnesia about success, so that you forget your own track record, and you can blank out on material like you're up there for the first time. I can easily forget that I've performed well just the day before, and one yawn from a student makes me so uptight about their being bored that I forget what I was starting out to say.

Sixes are clever about finding ways to circumvent success. The most common reports are that they lose interest, throw the win to someone who seems to need it more, suddenly recognize a fatal flaw in the whole procedure, get sick, or suddenly get reenergized about a previously discarded task. There is an endless list of creative solutions to delay facing the conflict surrounding success, including making genuinely creative contributions from the devil's advocate position, and becoming successful, while still feeling like a failure.

One of the hardest psychological tasks that Sixes face is to first achieve a modest degree of visible success and then to learn how to feel safe with what they have achieved.

I am a criminal attorney and worked for several years as a public defender. I loved the pressure as long as I was going up against the system for my guy and stayed excited until financial pressure pushed me into doing big-money law.

The clothes, and the socializing, and the scene, and having to turn the poorer clients down was totally obnoxious. I couldn't stand the way that I thought people were seeing me. I got the idea that I looked like a sellout and became convinced that certain people would like to cut me down. In the end the anxiety literally blew me out with an ulcer. My moment of truth came when, to save myself, I got into therapy and was advised to get a reality check from the friends that I really valued. The fact was that they were either unaware of what I had been feeling, or pretty much approved of the change that I had made.

One last way in which Sixes avoid recognizing their own success is by placing superhuman requirements on themselves. By requiring too much, it becomes impossible to move toward reasonable gains, and by demanding of themselves a contribution that will turn the tide of history, they cannot measure their own ability in a reasonable way. The megalomania of Six develops out of the desire to make a seminal contribution, to wield the powers of universal laws, to crack the code that makes the world go round. The preoccupation with power and strength covers an inner weakness. The need to make a vital and startling contribution makes it hard to honestly appreciate success.

Intimate Relationships

Sixes often have long-term marriages, because they are willing to take on "the problem in the marriage" and feel a duty to "see the problem through." Loyalty can be expressed through contingency commitments: "I'll stay until my husband/wife graduates," or "I'll stay until the kids are raised."

A committed relationship also allows trust to develop over a period of time and relieves any suspiciousness that might arise in a Six's mind about being disadvantaged if she or he appears to be too available or sexually needy. Trust is slow in building because of a Six's vulnerability to doubt. A small problem can call the whole relationship into question. The partner's basic commitment is doubted and has to be reestablished after a fight. A Six will question basic premises over and over again. Nothing is permanent. Do I really trust my partner? The question stays open.

Devil's Advocates can accept happiness and sexual pleasure more easily when the couple is seen as being in collusion against a threatening world. Sixes are loyal partners when the couple pulls together against an external stressor in an us-against-them relationship stance. It feels good to a Six to plan for a happy future, but is not as easy to accept leisure and pleasure when the opportunity arises. A pleasurable future is defined as being after the family duties are over, or when the mortgage finally gets paid.

Trust is a key issue, and Sixes often feel more loved when in the giver role. Feeling afraid, Sixes will find a place in the relationship by aiding the partner toward his or her goals, or affecting him or her sexually. The partner is seen as trustworthy because the Six knows what help to give, and because the Six can give the partner pleasure. There is no particular manipulation in a Six's giving. A Six does not give in order to get something back. The goal of affecting the partner is to feel safe, and Sixes can tolerate extremes in neurotic behavior without having to make the partner change. A different reaction will begin to surface when Sixes realize that they can be affected by the partner. It makes Sixes angry to know that they can be hurt, that what their partner does can matter terribly, and that when their pleasures are aroused that the partner has control over the satisfaction of these desires. There is an impulse to turn the pleasure off, to cave in to fears of abandonment, to leave the partnership, or to split head, heart, and belly into different relationships.

It takes Sixes a long time to develop trust. They are generally quite aware of the partner's character flaws, which gets in the way of a no-contingency commitment, and are generally suspicious of flattery, wondering if they are being set up to be rejected, or fearing that the partner expects too much of them.

Personal self-doubt can easily get projected, so that Sixes believe that the partner is doubting them. For example:

Compliments are hard. You can never quite trust them, because you're also alert to the unspoken negatives. It is a truly strange experience to watch a perfectly intelligent face start to look slightly stupid, because they've just given you a compliment that you don't believe. What has helped me most in believing that I'm doing a good job is what I call minimal intelligent opposition. That means that compliments have to be salted with constructive suggestions for improvement, so that I can really believe the integrity of what someone has to say.

It takes courage for a Six to continue to move toward pleasurable goals, because doubt and terror increase when a Six begins to trust. When loved, a Six can easily become suspicious of the partner's commitment, suspecting that the partner has committed unconsciously and doesn't really know her or his own motives. The Six may construct an elaborate hypothesis about what is really happening in the partner's unconscious and can develop an elaborate set of beliefs without any reality check. Once the hypothesis is woven, it is as believable to the Six as an operating fact; and a fight will develop in which the partner is hit with accusations that have some basis in reality, but which are largely a product of the Six's unrecognized fears of intimacy.

It is enormously helpful to the relationship if the partner reiterates a simple statement of loyalty and affection and repeats exactly the basis of her or his commitment to the Six. If possible, the partner can try to point out where fact left off and the Six's interior hypothesis took over. This can be a dangerous tack, unless the partner is able to think in a convoluted and symbolic fashion. A Six thinks abstractly and can easily dismiss a partner's honest statement because the partner is "not in touch with real motivations." A Six has a tendency to start a complicated hypothesis about the partner's real intentions when intimacy begins, and the Six begins to be threatened by being sexually moved.

The Six is faced with amnesia about success and pleasure and is saddled with the habit of doubting promises and plans. Commitments are made and then doubted. The intentions of others are always in question. "Do I trust him?" "Where is she stuck?" "Is he capable of love?" The question stays open, and commitment is acted out on a contingency basis. "We'll see what happens when the kids leave home."

Self-disclosure is always healing when relating to a Six. A Six is identified with human struggle and underdog causes and, as a consequence, is likely to understand a human error. Sixes generally believe that they can see the inner intentions of others, and if they see an unacknowledged blind spot, Sixes must feel safe enough to talk the issue through or else every action on the partner's part will be seen in the light of that single character flaw.

The partner's good example, particularly in "doing" areas, such as professionalism and creative projects, is guaranteed to generate respect. It is important that the partner's promises match with what he or she actually does.

On the high side of relationship, Sixes have many emotional facets and can be deeply moved. They are psychologically complicated and possess the potential for deep response. They are not intent upon manipulating a partner or wanting to take from them and can be extremely loyal when hard times come. They can put other people's welfare first and can feel another's successes as their own.

On the low side of intimate relating, Sixes tend to attribute their own feelings to a partner. If Sixes love, they believe that they are loved in return. If the Six is angry and attracted to another person, then the partner is quite likely to be accused of being unconsciously angry or of having an affair.

An Example of a Couple Relationship: Six and Eight, the Devil's Advocate and the Boss

Both Six and Eight are antiauthoritarian and are likely to find a common cause that draws them together. The initial relationship commonly places Six as the underdog and Eight as the protector. Sixes look to Eights for leadership, but the real agenda is, You make it happen for me because I am afraid. Six may turn on Eight if there is a disagreement about the Six's point of view. If the Six's dissatisfaction is open and Six is able to withstand several terrifying confrontations, the Eight will respect the Six's position and is likely to look to Six for counsel. If Six's disagreement is covert, Eight will feel betrayed and is likely to quit.

Both partners have trust issues in relationship. Sixes are afraid that a mate will turn on them and Eights are afraid of betrayal. If the Six is too unnerved by confrontation, there is a likelihood that he or she will "manage" the situation so that the Eight won't have anything about which to be angry. Being managed is guaranteed to infuriate an Eight. Only upfront argumentation feels honest, and any attempt to avoid anger is seen as a weak and sneaky attempt to betray trust. It is vital to the couple that the Six try to hold ground in a fight and to give an honest report even if the report makes the Eight momentarily furious. If Six can muster up the courage to tell the full truth and to fight to hold a position, Eight will become trustful and open. If the Boss can listen to the point of view of the Devil's Advocate without prematurely discrediting or abusing it, the six's feelings of trust will open.

It is also important that Six recognize that the Eight partner is relatively uncomplicated. Six wants to focus on what is really going on in the depths of a partner's unconscious, as a way of fending off potential harm; Eights, however, are relatively uncomplicated and run on simple pleasures. Six has a tendency to start a complicated hypothesis about the partner's real intentions exactly when intimacy emerges. The Six may suppress the new physical opening until she or he figures out the relationship. The Eight, however, wants to forge ahead into sexuality and does not want to discuss depth psychology. Eights are unlikely to lie or to fabricate their real intentions. This is unbelievable to a Six, precisely because it is so simple.

Both Six and Eight are relatively unattached to a polished public image, which means that their behavior toward each other is roughly the same in public and in private life. Eight is sexually comfortable, which may threaten Six's power issue with sexuality. It may be difficult for Eight to be monogamous, but Six is in the business of postponing pleasure and can be monogamous more easily. If threatened sexually, the Six is not likely to compete openly to win the partner back. The Six would be likely to leave, or to compete by matching the Eight's affair with one where she or he can feel sexually powerful again.

If a predictable routine is set, Eight is less inclined to control the relationship. There is a thin line of tolerance, however, between comfortable routine and boredom. The relationship between the Devil's Advocate and the Boss enters a severe phase when Eight has established the rules of conduct, Six has complied, and the Eight then proceeds to break all the rules. If an Eight is bored or has extra energy to burn, she or he will create trouble. This generally takes the form of breaking the rules, picking a fight, wanting to control details, or meddling in the lives of friends. Six is afraid of unfriendly people and will oppose Eight's willingness to alienate or insult those whom the Six would like to cultivate. If the Six becomes alarmed at the Eight's boredom reaction and takes the particular issues that the Eight has chosen to fight about seriously, the Six will feel abused, become fearful that the Eight will take punitive action, and may leave. Often the leaving is engineered by the Six, who semiconsciously creates an incident that makes the Eight furious. The severity of the situation is compounded by the fact that Six cannot get a reality check on Eight's actual motivation for wanting to fight, because a bored Eight will fight about anything.

The anger of an Eight's boredom reaction can be diverted by the couple getting a new interest going or pushing ahead in a personal project where they need mutual advice and support. For all of their assertiveness, Eights have a very hard time initiating their own goals. Eights fight in order to keep interest alive, but if interest is supplied externally, then the Eight will happily go into control mode to make those goals materialize. One of the best areas of partnership between Six and Eight has the Six strategizing creative options and Eight applying pressure to keep the options moving forward.

Assets

Devil's Advocates are identified with underdog causes and are capable of loyal, unrewarded effort for a cause or a creative ideal. They have capacities for great self-sacrifice in the name of duty or responsibility to others. Relatively unattached to the need for immediate success, Sixes are able to work without the reward of public recognition. They are willing to go against the odds and against the status quo for a worthwhile venture, particularly if in collaboration with allies.

Sixes bring insight into deep psychological processes. They are willing to suffer, to sacrifice, and to take up the cause again.

Attractive Environments

Hierarchical environments with clearly defined lines of authority and clearly defined problem areas are attractive to Sixes. The police force and university graduate programs. A Six, preoccupied with authority figures, will either conform rigorously to the regulations or organize against them in the antiauthoritarian stance. Self-employed positions are attractive, where there is no authority or boss.

Phobic jobs, where competition is minimized, and where the Six can work behind a strong leader. Counterphobic jobs that involve physical danger or espousing underdog causes. Bridge repairperson. The brilliant business tactician who saves the firm and then moves on.

Unattractive Environments

Unattractive environments for Six include high-pressure jobs involving spot decisions where no advance preparation is possible. High-profile, competitive jobs with ambiguous guidelines and lots of behind-the-scenes maneuvering.

Famous Sixes

Woody Allen, who plays himself as a classic phobic Six, is one well-known Devil's Advocate. Another is *Gordon Liddy*, the counterphobic Watergate plumber of the Nixon administration, who reports that he steeled himself to eat a rat because he was afraid of them. He also had to serve a fuller jail term than the other plumbers for instigating a demonstration of strength. He had become convinced that without the demonstration that he would be targeted by other prisoners.

Krishnamurti ☐ Jane Fonda ☐ Rev. Jim Jones
Sherlock Holmes ☐ Hitler (phobic) ☐ Hamlet (counterphobic)

Intuitive Style

Frightened children will develop strategies in order to survive emotionally, and a part of that survival system depends on recognizing sources of potential harm. Sixes describe a way of paying attention that they believe makes them sensitive to the unexpressed intentions of others. They say that they feel threatened by other people's unacknowledged feelings and that they trust the accuracy of what they see.

Self-aware Sixes also know that they are more than likely to attribute their own hostility to other people and that any intuitive accuracy depends upon their being able to tell the difference between a projection and an objectively accurate impression that does not depend upon physical cues.

This statement comes from a man who has been a union activist for most of his adult life and who has learned to trust his style of intuition in decision making.

I have a fine antenna for the bad intentions of people. I've had bosses who, out of their own need, have been sneaky and oppressive bosses, and I sensed it in them. Often in my organizing work, when I had dealings with them, the fear and anger jumped out of me, perhaps disproportionately, and perhaps attached to the wrong specific idea about what exactly they did. Although I may have been totally off there, in some way I had correctly sensed that they were not acting in good faith.

Other people, also authorities, would not bring that out in me at all. So I started to ask, when I'd react, Is it something in me? Some button being pushed, some old wound being pressed in me? Or is it something that the other guy does?

This man has a well-developed capacity for self-observation. If he were less aware of the need to discriminate between projection and other, more intuitive, impressions, he might well be one of those who arrives at the therapist's office complaining of being persecuted by bosses and other powerful figures in his life. The paranoid point of view usually has some basis in truth, but the objectively accurate insight that a Six might have is often washed out by an erroneous interpretation. Although the Six might be psychically accurate about the boss feeling some negativity, the Six might exaggerate the negativity drastically. The Six is then likely to defend himself or herself against the boss's bad intentions, thus making the boss angry, which looks to the Six like the verification of the fact that the boss was hostile all along.

Sixes report a second style of intuition, which seems to stem from the childhood need to adopt a watchful stance toward adults and to predict how they will act. This is a fascinating survival strategy that a fearful child is likely to adopt, which can then continue into adult life as an unrecognized factor in the way that a Six pays attention. This clinical psychologist describes her childhood watchfulness:

My specialty was in being able to figure out how people work. If I was studying a kid in a school class, I'd look closely at their face whenever anyone spoke to them. I'd see a glimmer in the eye when somebody across the room came out with something, or would believe that I saw emotions pass over the face although I also knew that the face wasn't really changing at all. I thought that if I watched a kid's face long enough, that I could figure out what they thought about everybody else in class.

If I'd want to know what they were thinking, I'd look at their face and let myself imagine what the face would look like under certain conditions. Would the face go hard or soft if I said that I liked them? If I ran for class president, would it smile or go gray all over?

I was convinced that I was totally accurate because I was making such a study of it, and I acted on what I thought I saw in the faces, although at the time I didn't check the information out, except in a secondhand way by comparing notes with special friends.

Now, in my therapy practice, I see a lot of layers in how families interact with one another. I see what I call the inner face, which shows its own emotions to me. Occasionally I let myself imagine patterns of color playing out in the air among the family members, and I try to get the impression of what the different colors and energy connections show about the ways that these people interact in their lives.

This clinician has a good grasp of her ability to shift attention from thinking about her clients to letting herself imagine their inner situation. She is also quite aware that she may be mistakenly attributing qualities to her clients that are, in fact, her own projections, but she is in a good position to check her accuracy with the clients themselves.

If what this clinician sees is based purely on the projection of her own unconscious feelings to her clients, there is no intuition at work. Her intuitive task is to be able to tell the difference between the insight that surfaces from her reverie of images and whatever images she may be projecting from her own mind.

Two important effects can result from her learning to recognize this difference. First, she can be freed from the cycle of false information that projection perpetuates; second, she can develop the ability to recognize the difference between images that are guided from herself and accurate visual impressions that appear spontaneously from a clairvoyant state of mind. Her job is to develop her inner observer to the point where she can recognize the internal shifts of attention that she is already making when she accurately sees a family's interconnections played out symbolically by colors and patterns in the air.

The Virtue of Courage

Like all people, Sixes are often unaware of the central issues that control their lives. An individual Six may believe that he or she is no more afraid than other people are and be oblivious to the fact that personal habits of thought and emotion can make one chronically apprehensive. Like people who live in a war zone and peace is suddenly declared, Devil's Advocates often recognize how scared they have been after the fear begins to lift.

Sixes will progress more quickly toward their higher abilities if they begin therapy or a meditation practice in conjunction with a physical exercise program. Fearful people are centered in the head. They scan the environment and try to think their way out of situations in which they have to act. Above all, a fearful person wants an intellectually correct stance from which to fend off possible opposition; as if a brilliant analysis will replace having to take action. Many Sixes undertake a spiritual practice that specifically builds confidence in the body's capacity for intuitive movement, such as Tantric Yoga or the martial arts.

Courage depends upon the body's ability to act appropriately from a nonthinking state of mind. It is doing before thinking, a time when the body acts before the acquired personality has time to intervene.

I took up running on a daily basis about a year ago and enjoyed it up to the point where my head had to let go. It was great with a partner, where we'd jog and talk, or alone, so long as I could still think while I ran. There was a hill on the way up to a track where we'd go, and I found that I'd be going great as long as I had enough wind to check out the people as I passed.

When the hill got steep at the top, I had just enough wind to either flick my attention to the passersby and know who was there, or just run. I'd find that if I had no running partner with me, that I'd stop every time to get my breath back so that I could still think about who was around me while I ran.

For a Six who is still in the habit of thinking before doing, even the act of running past people on the street without having the energy to check them out can be distressing. The Six runner will not make herself courageous by thinking brave thoughts or forcing herself to run blind. It would be useful for her to learn to shift her locus of attention from her head into her body and to be able to recognize the difference between when her thoughts are directing her run and when she can let her thoughts go, because she trusts that her body will act to protect her. Consider the difference between the runner who protects herself by watching the environment and this experience that was reported by a New York subway rider.

I went to City University in Manhattan and used to ride the subway to get to school. I was never uptight about the day rides, when there were crowds, and I could read assignments all the way up from the Delancey Street stop. When I had late class and had to stand alone on the empty platform, I was often apprehensive, and set it up with my boyfriend to meet me at Delancey and walk back home.

One night a crazy man got on the car. He was grimacing and clenching his fists, and you could hear him cursing all the way down the aisle. There were just a few people on the train, and no one would look him in the face.

He spotted someone in a seat behind me, pointed, cursed, and started to go for them, when I found myself blocking him in the aisle. My body had gotten up and I heard my voice talking to him, without knowing what I was supposed to say. I still can't remember what I said to him, but I do remember that when I saw a gun in his hand that I was not afraid.

It felt like going through the motions of something that had already happened. I was not surprised when I saw two arms take him from behind in a head lock, or when I knocked the gun out of his hand when he raised it to my face. When I met my boyfriend at Delancey and told him what had happened, I was so unemotional that he had a hard time believing that the story was real.

Faith as a Quality of Higher Mind

Doubt is one-half of decision making. We think up an idea, and then think out the "Yes, but . . ." qualifications that shape the idea properly, and shake out any assumptions or mistakes. Decisions are made by first proposing an idea and then countering that same idea with objections that qualify the original point of view. In the intellectual arena, healthy skepticism produces good science, testable procedures, and clearly defined rationales. Those who are overly attached to skepticism, however, can obliterate their own genuine inner life experiences by doubting them out of existence when attention shifts back to the thinking state of mind.

Christ's apostle Thomas the doubter exemplifies a Six's mental stance. Thomas believed as long as he had the physical presence of the master and the support of the like-minded disciples. When Christ died Thomas lost faith and doubted that his experiences with the master had been true.

After the Crucifixion, Christ resurrected and appeared to several of his followers. He appeared to Doubting Thomas and, recognizing that Thomas was afflicted by loss of faith, Christ offered his own crucified hand to be touched, so that Thomas's belief in his rematerialization would be strengthened. Of the twelve disciples, Thomas was given the most tangible evidence of the mysteries, yet his mind could not accept the evidence of his own senses.

For point Six, a doubt attack can call an entire structure of belief into question. One setback in a project, one argument in a relationship, can wipe out months of gradually built trust. It's as if the foundation of a well-built structure gets called into question and has to be rebuilt again if the roof is found to have a leak. There is a need to repeatedly reaffirm commitment: "Do I love him?" "Yes, I think so." There is a need to create mental structures to ensure continuity. "Until I get my degree." "Until the children are grown." Nothing is permanent. A small suspicion and doubt begins to blossom.

Buddhist practice calls this habit doubting mind. To some extent all beginning meditators are prone to countering their own experience with wondering if they have really accomplished anything at all. If the mental "Yes, but . . ." has become compulsive, however, then the shifts of attention that move a meditator closer to stabilizing awareness in a nonthinking state of mind often stimulate a barrage of highly believable doubting thoughts that act as a conduit back to the thinking state.

It requires great faith for Sixes, who are habituated to doubting mind, to continue on with their meditation practice, or with a love affair, or with a project that raises their hopes, when, for them, signs of success are so easily erased by equally believable thoughts that argue away positive experiences. From the point of view of attention practice, however, faith is not a question of believing in false promises, or using one's will to keep the faith strong. Faith can be seen as simply the ability to keep attention stabilized on truthful positive experience, rather than falling into a biased attentional habit in which questioning positive experiences seems more real.

Subtypes

These are preoccupations that developed during childhood as a way to maintain security in a life dominated by untrustworthy authority.

Strength/Beauty in the One-to-One Relationship

The preoccupation with strength stems from the need to develop personal power as a compensation for feeling afraid. This can turn into a falsely macho presentation in the counterphobic men and into a preoccupation with the power of being able to affect men sexually in counterphobic women.

Beauty is a preoccupation with aesthetics, especially in physical surroundings and physical appearance. Focusing on objective physical beauty eases the habit of scanning the environment for worst case possibilities. Both men and women have the preoccupation with beauty.

There's a real mistrust of people, so as soon as you get too close and permanent you get afraid that your partner's going to do something to you. On the one hand, you're afraid of abandonment, and on the other, you're very critical of your lover when it gets too close, so you protect yourself by being "strong" and somewhat cold.

Warmth in the Area of Self-preservation

Maintaining other people's affection is a way to disarm potential hostility. If people like you, there is no need to be afraid of them.

When I do therapy there's a big draw to aligning myself with the client against their situation. The bond is "us against them," which lasts until I have to find ways to point out the blind spots in my client's reasoning. At that stage I have to guard against becoming distant and acutely sensitive to exaggerating small signs of withdrawal on the part of my client.

Duty in the Social Area

Adhering to rules and obligations for social behavior is a way to ensure loyalty.

When I was in college, I was politically active in a Zionist youth group. We were committed to studying and taking our skills to live as kibbutzim in Israel. When my interest shifted from the idea of emigrating, I realized, with shock, that I had become so centered on our cause that I wasn't even sure that I knew the people that I had worked with for over three years.

What Helps Sixes Thrive

Sixes often enter therapy or begin a meditation practice because of a long history of incompletes. Procrastination takes on many forms, but particularly centers on the completion of projects. Typical presentations are a continuous change of jobs, problems with trusting authorities and coworkers, and finding reasons to bail out near the successful completion of a project.

Sixes seek out help because they are afraid and because they often experience sexual problems that they equate with unresolved fears about taking power.

Sixes need to have their subjective fears taken seriously although they may appear to be spreading a false alarm. A minute examination of these fears is valuable, because the Six cannot determine which fears are imaginary and which have some basis in fact. A great deal of suspicious thinking goes away when the issue is brought under close, neutral examination. Devil's Advocates need help in keeping their attention focused steadily on a positive goal without slipping into doubt. It is as hard for a Six to keep going as it is for a Three to stop.

Devil's Advocates need to make step-by-step progress toward realistic goals rather than moving into false heroics as a way of covering fear. They also need to be aware of falling into equally false ideas of defeat based on negative past experience. It is helpful for Sixes to recognize the following needs when they occur:

- Needing to check out fears against reality. Not having all the facts. Making assumptions that the odds are greater than they really are. It helps to name fears out loud to a friend who gives trustworthy feedback and to check conclusions about facts against a neutral opinion.
- Looking for hidden meaning in other people's behavior. Needing to check out own feelings of aggression when others begin to seem hostile.
- Doubting whether it is possible to be helped. Vacillation of trust in relationships. Is the other trustworthy? Mentally questioning the strength or weakness of others.
- Needing to have positions clearly stated. Needing to ask others about where they stand. Needing agreement on guidelines.

- Watching to see if others' actions match up with what they say they will do.
- Recognizing when thinking replaces feelings and impulses.
- Aligning with those who are not competent or trustworthy as a way of forestalling forward motion.
- Needing to stay in contact. Withdrawing out of fear and then projecting that others have left out of anger.
- Contracting physically and eliminating play as a way of staying tense and vigilant. Bracing physically as if under attack.
- Suspecting affection and compliments, increasingly so as the guard goes down. "The blow will come when I'm unprepared."
- Not trusting gut reactions. Wanting to have the approval of authority before making a move.
- Questioning leadership, rather than finding areas of agreement.
- Recognizing that negative memories are more available than positive memories. Remembering to recall positive memories. Sixes run on a negative memory track.
- Utilizing a vivid imagination. Imagine and talk about positive outcomes. Create cognitive dissonance between fears and positive outcomes. If attention locks on worst case outcomes, then imaginatively exaggerate possible negative outcomes in order to find a way out.

What Sixes Should Be Aware of

As attention is withdrawn from habitual preoccupations, Sixes should be aware of reactions such as

- Suspiciousness of sources of potential help, with the subsequent desire to go it alone.
- Surfacing fears of success. The fear of outdoing the parents.

· The sense of becoming passive as fears lift, of losing one's edge, of learning to meditate and never wanting to compete again.

· The habit of focusing on negative detail in a generally okay situation.

· Wanting to outthink those who are assisting forward motion. Seeing the therapist as alternately brilliant or unequal to the task.

· Nonstop talking. Letting the head take over for the heart. Talk and analysis replace acting on impressions from the gut and heart.

· A surfacing feeling of self-doubt, which easily becomes projected, so that others appear to be doubtful of one's abilities.

· Megalomania. Making the task of change too hard. Fantasy of impressive accomplishments blocks logical steps toward realistic goals.

12. Point Seven: The Epicure

	ACQUIRED PERSONALITY		ESSENCE	
HEAD	Chief Feature:	PLANNING	Higher Mind:	WORK
HEART	Passion:	GLUTTONY	Virtue:	SOBRIETY
	SUBTYPE WAYS OF BEING			
	Sexual:	SUGGESTIBLE		
	Social:	SACRIFICIAL		
	Self-preservation:	FAMILY DEFENDER		

The Dilemma

Points Five, Six, and Seven, grouped on the left side of the Enneagram, represent three different strategies for dealing with childhood fear. Sixes, at the core fear point, overprepare by vigilantly scanning the environment, and Fives withdraw from whatever makes them afraid. Sevens, looking not at all concerned, move toward people in an attempt to charm and disarm with pleasantry. Faced with a frightening early life, Seven children diffused their fear by escaping into the limitless possibilities of imagination.

Sevens do not broadcast anxiety. They do not look afraid. They tend to be lighthearted and sunny, often addicted to planning and play. Their core of paranoia (Six) does not surface as long as thinking can be channeled into visionary plans of future success.

This is the point of Peter Pan, of the Puer (and Puerella) Aeternus, the eternal child. This is also the point of Narcissus, the youth who fell in love with the image of his own face reflected in a pool. Narcissus was loved by the nymph named Echo, but because he was absorbed in the mirror of his own splendor, he could not hear her calling his name. Self-involved, he failed to respond, and her voice was reduced to an echo.

Everybody needs a little healthy narcissism. We all need to recognize our unique value and worth. Difficulty arises only when we become so convinced of our special value that we fail to hear the suggestions of those who mirror back the objective truth. Epicures are convinced of their own excellence, and they seek environments and people who will support their worth. They have sensitive tastes and want to sample the best that life can offer. Sevens like to keep up their spirits. They want adventure and to keep their expectations high. There is a chemistry for peak experience, as if champagne, not blood, were running through their veins.

The Seven worldview was sociologically prominent in the counterculture revolution of the 1960s. During the era of the flower child, the Seven ideals expanded in their purest form. Faced with going to war and the prospect of meaningless work, the flower children dropped out and turned to simplicity and to themselves, creating an idealized concept of what society could be.

As the revolution progressed, the shadow side of the Seven worldview emerged. Insisting on an idealized reality and unable to make it take form, the attitude changed from radical subjectivity, where what was unique in the individual was valued, to a narcissistic preoccupation with the self. The situation deteriorated to a level of hot-tub insight: "Oh, wow!" and "I'm glad I'm me." The inner world of drugs replaced the urge for outer change. Psychobabble and attractive escape replaced real effort and work.

Sevens are buoyed by a belief that life is unlimited. There are always interesting things to do. If life's not adventurous, why live it? Why get hung up when you can move on? The buoyancy of a belief in life's opportunities is greatly enhanced by the habit of keeping multiple options open and making commitments with backup plans.

Commitment is always buffered with backups. Agreement is "which one feels right at the time." If plan A gets rained out, go to B as the backup. If B feels sticky, we always have C. If A washs out and C gets too boring, we always have B, which may lead to D. The 1960s injunction to "go with the flow" has been reformed into an organization of attention that encourages negative options to fall through the cracks.

As a defensive strategy, planning for the future along the lines of contingency options is intended to enhance life's pleasures by eliminating the problems of boredom and pain. For example, a Seven might hold a job in a shoe store and have mentally planned the option of fitting herself or himself into the same job in a rival store located across the street. Such a plan might seem quite natural to the Seven, who would be focused on the similarity of goals and the sameness of purpose between the two jobs, rather than on how the firms might be at odds with each other.

On the positive side, this way of focusing attention lends itself to a particularly creative kind of problem solving, in which the correct fit of associations can be found between what appear to be antagonistic points of view. Sevens hold the most optimistic of all worldviews, because for them, a grand plan will develop at some point in future time where all the best possibilities fit into an ultimately satisfactory life.

Seven's habitual preoccupations include
· The need to maintain high levels of excitement. Many activities, many interesting things to do. Wanting to stay emotionally high.

- Maintenance of multiple options as a way to buffer commitment to a single course of action.
- Replacement of deep contact with pleasant mental alternatives. Talking, planning, and intellectualizing.
- Charm as a first line of defense. Fear types who move toward people. Avoid direct conflict by going through the cracks. Talk your way out of trouble.
- An attentional style of interrelating and systematizing information, such that commitments necessarily include loopholes and other backup options. This style of attention can lead to
  - Rationalized escapism from difficult or limiting tasks.
  - The ability to synthesize unusual connections and parallels between what appear to be antagonistic or unrelated points of view.

Points Three and Seven Look Alike

Sevens have a great deal of energy and will work hard as long as their interest holds. They can resemble Threes on the surface, willing to compete, interested in winning, and certainly concerned with the mirroring of their own excellence through other people's eyes. The points may look similar from an outsider's perspective, but they operate from very different internal worldviews.

Threes want power over others, because they measure themselves by the degree of other people's respect and regard. They want to pick one professional track in which they can climb to the top of the competitive ladder. The proofs of a successful climb are image, security, title, and prestige.

Sevens, sitting on the same competitive front bench, are involved in "an interesting activity; one of many that I do." They also want the high regard of others, although not in the form of power over them. They do not like to be labeled according to profession. "To call me a physician is limiting. I am far more than any one thing." The idea is to maintain an excellence in worthwhile activities. "I run, I cook, I write poems, I can do anything." Sevens are far less inclined to go to the top, particularly if there are too many demands on their time, or if they have to confront those who do not think well of them. They want to know that they were accepted to compete in the best track, but they may not want to limit their other interests in order to push forward to top rank. "I want to know I'm capable, but I do not have to prove myself." They are likely to work several days straight to earn the money to get away, rather than several days straight to buy a fancy car. The proofs of achievement are having gotten to do a lot of fascinating things in life and having risen to the top without having gotten pinned down by permanent commitment.

The psychological difference between the workaholic Three and the more truly narcissistic Seven is that for the Three, personal value rests on earned achievement. The real self may not exist, but one's credentials do. The focus of attention is on doing one thing very well, because a Three's value in the eyes of others depends on the brilliant accomplishment of a task. They work far harder than they wish to, because their reward is not in feeling good, but in the power to command other people's respect.

Sevens, equally desirous of the good opinion of others, will see their regard as an accurate mirror of personal inner worth. They need not constantly exert because "Life is good, and I'm glad I'm me." If others do not recognize their inner merit, Sevens will turn to themselves for comfort, rationalizing the rejection as no fault of their own. The self has so many dimensions, so many possible avenues of play. A bad time can be erased by a hike in the country, a good book, bright sunshine, a hot cup of tea. In a way, narcissists suffer less than Threes from the disregard of others, because they have themselves for company and because they are convinced of their own bright destiny.

Family History

Sevens have pleasant memories of their childhood years. The reports have a happy picture-book quality: a boy on his swing, a girl in her pinafore. There is usually no bitterness. "My Dad stole us from our mother. I was eight and had forgotten her by the time that I was nine." Even with an objectively bad scenario, there is little residue of hatred or blame. In scenarios that contain objectively bad memories, there is the flavor of "I decided not to be like that" and "I found things to do so I didn't get dragged down."

I've thought a lot about being a Seven and why that point speaks to me. When I first saw a panel of Sevens tell their stories, I could relate to everything except that business about being afraid. I just don't see myself that way.

But then I remembered a time when I got lost on the way home from a new school, knowing my mom was going to cream me for showing up late, and being really terrified of what would happen when she got hold of me. And then I ran into some kids playing soccer, and I just played until it got dark.

So Mom called the police when it got to be suppertime, and they came to pick me up. I remember myself riding home in the cop car, just shitting because I was so scared. And then I started looking at the lights reflected on the back window, and I remembered the soccer game, and I went right back there.

I knew that no matter what she did to me that I could just stay in my mind and play soccer until whatever it was would be over and I would have survived.

The skew of attention is toward positive memory. The boy who says he took up karate to save himself focuses on a description of his best belt tests. The girl who ran away at fifteen minimizes the reasons why and describes the excitement of her escape. Here we have the opposite skew of attention from that of Sixes: Devil's Advocates tend to remember the worst and Epicures, moving toward pleasure and away from pain, tend to remember the best.

For Sevens there are a great many recollections from childhood that are positive and objectively real. There is a tendency to favor the mother over the father, but the paranoid rebellion against male authority takes on a sweetly antiauthoritarian tone.

I loved both my parents and had a typical kind of country life. Nobody hurt me, I had a lot of love and support, and the only complaint I had was that I had to bicycle three miles to get to see my friends. I used to tell myself stories when I was alone, and I didn't much like to be told what I had to do.

I realized that I could outthink my father when I was in about sixth grade. I loved him, but I knew that I could think faster. I got him to agree to anything I wanted by first editing out the items that he'd disapprove of and then pushing for a version of what he wanted that had as many loopholes as possible.

Schedules and Plans

The day is always full of possibilities. There are mental lists of interesting things to do. Sevens are antidepressive people, for whom work is intermingled with imagination and mental play. Interspersed with your project you can be pleased by the sweep of a woman's hair in the sunlight, or fascinated by the shadows on the wall. The idea is to keep the mood up, to work just until the moment you begin to tire, and then to switch to something else before boredom or "should" sets in. Sevens can work endlessly, preferring to handle three or four jobs at a time. But projects rarely move ahead single-mindedly, and every project is sandwiched in between pleasant things to do.

I really look forward to the Sunday paper pink section. It has the listing of the week's things to do. There's a whole week of stuff laid out, a four-star movie, a ten-star meal. It's as important to me as my cookie stash. You want to know where there's something sweet to do. The cookies are hidden in the bottom drawer of my desk at work, and the pink section is in there too.

The 1960s attempt to "go with the flow" is an illustration of the intention behind a Seven's schedules and plans. There's never a reason to get depressed or hung up; all you have to do is attach yourself to a stimulating flow of worthwhile things to do.

The idea is to keep a lot of options open. You could go to volleyball, you could dress and see a movie, you could bike into the country for the day. The best part is when they're all in the same time frame. You go with the one that has the most pull, and you stay until the next one starts to call. I've gone to a movie, paid my money, gotten as far as buying popcorn, and then left for something else, just because I felt the twinge of boredom and it didn't feel right.

There is a buoyant conviction that life is unlimited, as long as options are kept in play. The idea is to not miss out on anything, so that an option can be treasured mentally, even when there's no place to work it into the schedule of the day. Casual commitments are easy, but permanent commitment is hard, because permanence closes down the sense of an unlimited future. Sevens are gluttons for experience, and they are inclined to want little tastes of the very best, rather than making a commitment to a single point of view.

I have an incredible internal schedule. It consists of time for my work, my family, and my avocations, which are music, running, and sailing on the bay. They all go on in my mind, whether I'm physically doing them or not, and I want them all. If a chance to jam with friends comes up, I have to redo the tides and charts in my head, and change my mind about when to eat, so I won't be too full if I decide to run. It all rearranges very quickly, so that I'm covered on every base.

If I'm rained out a secondary set of preferences comes into play, like restaurants to try out and which of my family is free to go, or how to squeeze a block of work time between when my friends can play music and the second seating at the restaurant.

Optional Thinking

The fitting together of options means that a Seven can never really get pinned down. There are always several mental tracks going, and because they are all interrelated in the Seven's mind, in some strange way very different courses of action can appear to be the same.

On a practical level I've always been able to make choices, although they seem arbitrary. You have to honor agreements and try to arrive on time, even though you may have changed your mind about wanting to be there. Emotional levels get tricky. I've been married now for a number of years to a man who seems forever innovative and keeps me on my toes.

Even so, at the beginning, when I was trying to make a commitment, I had parceled my problem areas out to three or four different therapies. They all seemed related to me because they were my problems, but I could see how I liked the idea of getting several different kinds of advice. Then I found myself seriously considering relationships with other men to work out certain patterns that I saw happening with my fiancé. Somehow this did not seem off the point of our agreement to monogamy. After all, I was working on a relationship, and in a very serious way.

From an outsider's perspective this Seven might seem to be scattered between too many therapies and too many directions of choice. But from the point of view of the Seven, each insight and each approach is intrinsically bound up with all the others. Consequently, she could agree wholeheartedly with one of her therapists and, at the same time, act on another one's advice. Needless to say, this habit of attention can be seen as driving in several directions at once.

You could be telling me about some new system you're studying, let's say it's Zen. So while you're going into details of the philosophy, certain points in what you say remind me of similar ideas in other systems that you know nothing about. My interest in Zen is going to be how it fits with, let's say, marathon running, the Enneagram, and golf.

What you say about Zen lights up little bulbs for me in about six or seven other interests of mine. So of course I agree with you, but I'm not committed to what you say. What I'm committed to are the points in your description of Zen that concur with my other interests, and I will fit what you say about Zen into a comprehensive system of my own. That way I can agree with you and at the same time hold my other options open.

Charm and Chicanery

Although they share a core of paranoia with both Five and Six, Sevens do not appear at all to be afraid. They are gregarious and talkative. They are engaging and they like to play. The attraction to talk and intellectualizing could also be seen as replacing action with words; and, in fact, Sevens report that they would much rather brainstorm than be limited by the drudgery of work. Both Five and Six have problems with output and completion. Both are afraid of having their projects judged. Sevens have exactly the same trouble with action, but their fear of being seen is hidden from themselves by charming talk and a pleasant style.

There is a fear of going too deeply into any one thing, which is masked by a fascination with many things. The attraction to pleasure is seen as a positive flow when, in fact, it masks a flight away from pain. Sevens have difficulty in limiting themselves to a single project, or pursuit, because with that narrowing of attention objective abilities come to light. Any inflated ideas of innate speciality disappear under close examination. Consequently, the narcissisticly inclined Seven will avoid discovery by amplifying potentials until they appear to be concrete realities. An aptitude for mathematics makes one a mathematician, because with a sufficiently graceful self-presentation and an unconscious bending of definitions, master mathematicians can be seen as those whose special insights place them above the need for academic degrees.

Sevens have also been cast as charlatans, because they are attractive and want people to adore them. They raise the expectations of others, who may not be as used to flowers, charm, and "sharing the very best of times." Sevens want to be adored by interesting people, but are easily bored by repetition, especially in the cold light of day. Their self-absorption really shows when last night's interlude is forgotten, the new friend calls, and the Seven has forgotten the lover's name.

It was very hard to find someone who wasn't boring. The trick was to try and get someone who was like me. I love my life and I love what I do, and I thought that all I wanted was someone who would come out and play. Then I found her, and to my distress I think she was another seven. Great at tennis, great in bed, and her mind everywhere but on me.

I couldn't stand it that she was so accomplished and so everywhere else, so what I did was propose, because we both wanted a family. So now we have the kids and a really good time, and I have to see this walking psychic mirror of how totally self-centered I can be.

Superiority/Inferiority

The attraction to high levels of stimulation can be used for escapist purposes, but also motivates intellectual curiosity and creative search. A pathological narcissist would simply assume his or her own mental superiority, and therefore feel entitled to recognition and support. In a Seven who is beginning to pull out of the neurotic conviction of special entitlement, we would find someone who saw that by running so quickly toward pleasure, she or he was really running away from pain.

The pain of narcissists is that they may be unveiled as less than what they believe themselves to be. There is an inner question, Where do I stand? Am I better than who I find myself with, or am I really worse? Who stands higher here? Is it me or is it my friend? In pathology the answer is always, I stand higher. For Sevens who are working on themselves, the question of comparative value is still alive in their thoughts, but can be used as a reminder to pay attention to their objective capabilities.

My clue to my own narcissism is when I start to look down on a friend. It takes on quite insidious forms. I forgive them for being stupid, or I silently scold them for being so wrong. Once the idea takes hold that I'm dealing with someone who can't keep up, I want to leave the room. I'm bored with what they're going to say, and they seem so predictable that I want to scream. Then I'll think, How small-minded, how lacking in breadth. Or I'll bury their objection with two or three arguments from an opposite point of view.

When they seem particularly stupid and hopeless, I know enough to take another look. How could a good friend suddenly look that bad? How could I be contemptuous of someone who only yesterday seemed so smart? What comes up is that if I'm not totally right, then I must be totally off; and then I'm left with seeing them as really superior and myself as nothing in my own eyes.

Self-worth can be inflated by chronic indulgence in "the best things to do." It is diagnostic of a Seven in trouble that the mind begins to race. When Sevens line up activities back to back, leaving no time in between "the components of an interesting life." When attention flits compulsively between several interesting options, a Seven is on the run.

I could never figure out how people fell into a career. How did they know what they wanted to be? The closest I could get was the prototype Renaissance man. Excellence in every way. Everything I tried suggested another great possibility, an untried approach, a brilliant idea.

I worked myself from religion to Middle Eastern studies as a major and finally graduated with over fifty more units than I could use. The dissertation spanned three disciplines and would have spread out indefinitely if my committee hadn't narrowed the topic down.

I almost dropped out when I had to submit the manuscript. The typed pages looked so insignificant in comparison to what I thought they'd be. It didn't matter one bit that I got an honors grade: the secret was out that I had needed the committee's help, that my paper hadn't rocked the academic world, and that I was a doctor of obscura, rather than the genius I believed myself to be.

Relationship to Authority

Sevens want to equalize authority, preferring an arrangement where there is no one above them and no one below them. At the outset authorities are just people, to whom the Seven feels innately superior and who often respond to the Seven's well-articulated views. But the reality is that Epicures are fear types who move forward into pleasant contact as a way of disarming authority's control. They will usually become fiercely antiauthoritarian if their freedoms are curtailed in any way. The power of a petty authority is automatically minimized. Sevens will assume that they can talk their way around anybody who happens to get in the way.

On the high side of an authority interaction, Sevens are great at raising the mood of a group. They have pleasant dispositions, know enough about everything to pretend that they know more, and speak well. They will stay with positive alternatives without shifting into doubt and are particularly good when a project is in the idea stage or in a go-ahead phase. They can align a project's purposes and goals with other theoretical positions, network with others, and promote their ideas. They are most effective at the inception of a project and in keeping the faith when the project hits a skid.

On the low side of relationship with authority, Sevens lose enthusiasm after the initial idea and planning stages. Interest phases out during the middle of a project, and endings, when the options close down, are very hard. Once an idea solidifies into a package, Sevens become unhappy with routine and the narrowing of possibilities. They would be more productive if reassigned to researching new ideas, aligning the project with a bigger picture, networking, or if they were rehired as a part-time planning consultant.

Sevens can become insistent about an interesting but impractical idea. There is a substitution of ideas and theory for the drudgery of practical hard work and a tendency to look down on those who have a "lesser vision."

A Typical Interpoint Authority Relationship: Seven and Three, the Epicure and the Performer

Both types share a high-energy approach to projects, the Three from an identification with the success of the enterprise, and the Seven motivated by interest and a chance to explore new territory. This can be an exceptional team if the Three is willing to take on the visible leadership and the Seven can have a position as adviser and partner without having to accept high-profile responsibility, deal with people's expectations about the project, or be stuck in a repetitious job. The Three will work hard regardless of whether it's fun or not, and the Seven will work equally hard as long as it holds the promise of fun.

Both types are socially skillful and can present the project to the public; both are sure that their own position is correct and want to draw others to their own point of view. If the Three is boss, she or he may assume that the employees are also personally identified with the job's successful image and expect overkill output from them. The Seven employee will skate around demands for time and energy, for example, by becoming expert at filing one report to cover two situations and learning how to be in two places at once by cutting the time for each in half. Since a Three boss will also be inclined to sacrifice quality in favor of efficiency, she or he will not be likely to question the employee's apparently compliant behavior as long as nothing breaks down. As long as the project is in a go-ahead position, the question of quality control will not occur to either Three or Seven unless a complaint brings the issue to the surface.

If the Seven employee enjoys the project, she or he is likely to be happy to work under a boss who is willing to take the public heat and the pressure of full commitment. Sevens will be most useful during the preliminary stages when they employ their skills in creative planning, innovation, and rallying other workers to the cause. As long as the Seven sticks to guidelines and doesn't innovate too freely, the Three will be pleased to have the employee on the team.

Once the project has been securely launched, the differences between a Three's and a Seven's work goals will become apparent. The Three wants recognition and money in the bank, and the Seven employee, feeling limited by those goals, will start to bend the boss's rules in order to stay interested. The Three wants machinelike production and the Seven wants out.

If the Seven is boss, she or he will not want to deal with supervision of employees, particularly in having to give and enforce direct orders. Consequently, guidelines may become too general and too cerebral, as the Seven tries to make everybody feel like an equal participant in order to eliminate the possibility of confrontation. If the Three employee is wise, she or he will solidify the boss's general directives into a workable set of procedures and will handle bad news before it reaches the boss's attention. The team will flourish if the Three can make the Seven's ideas work, particularly if the Seven extends rewards of extra salary and recognition to the employee. Threes will take on extra responsibilities as long as their efforts are respected and there are clear opportunities for advancement.

If the Seven boss introduces fascinating but conflicting options such that the leadership direction becomes vague, the Three employee is likely to spearhead a committee to redress grievances and will take advantage of any organizational structure through which the boss could be brought into line. Failing that, the employee will want to move on to a more clearly structured job with advancement potential.

Idealism and Futurism

Sevens are as antiauthoritarian as any true paranoid, but rather than becoming involved in direct confrontation, they sweetly try to equalize authority's control. "You do your thing and I'll do mine" really means that Sevens are free agents, responsible to themselves alone. It also connotes, "Get off my back; don't tell me what to do."

There is a strange incongruity between the ideals of radical subjectivity, in which each individual is respected as unique and the fact that Sevens feel superior to others. A Seven can see that each of us may have unique ability, but most of us are limited to only one ability, and Sevens believe they get to have them all. They see how mathematics and music fit together, so they need not do the work of either to accomplish having both.

An idealized self-image leads them to suppose that with a little work, and their own natural superiority of endowment, both music and mathematics could be mastered in a matter of months. A Seven's tendency toward positive imagination fills in the blanks of real information with fantasy and ideas. These embellished ideas form an idealized self that replaces a requirement for genuine substance and depth.

A great deal of a Seven's pleasure is in the planning and anticipation of events. Future events are savored mentally as sweet images that become as tangible and believable as tables and chairs. For example, the best part of a meal is often before the food is served, because all the delicious combinations can be tasted with the mind. Likewise, if an Epicure is actually eating a fine meal, the experience can be immensely expanded by imaginatively adding the best aspects of other kinds of pleasure. The memory of a magical sunrise might be briefly recreated. The sense of watching the sunrise with special friends comes into play. The best aspects of past and future options can be savored along with the actual taste of a meal. Sevens can become intoxicated by their own imagination, because within the imagination, the best aspects of every option have come together in a believable way.

Planning need not be escapist. Sevens report that they derive extreme pleasure from intellectual and mentally creative pursuits. Their natural agility of attention allows them to produce brilliant solutions to ordinary problems and to travel into realms of imagination that would seem extraordinary to those who tend to pay attention in a literal way.

The following statement was given by a Seven who works as a professional futurist. He describes his mind as his best friend and his ideas as his daily companions. His work consists of analyzing historical trends and then predicting how the better aspects of these trends might be brought into play.

My greatest lovers are ideas. There is such pleasure in getting to know them, like stroking life into a body that has no breath. It is like being in love with a woman. Each idea is lovely, and I treasure it in a certain way. I have also been in love with airplanes and with other racing machines. They put me in a place where reality falls away, and I am alone with an infinite number of directions and everything I could possibly need.

Intimate Relationships

Sevens approach relationship by sharing what is wonderful in each other, but with a special awareness of commitment constraints. They are happiest when all options are open. "What could be wrong about being in love? What could be wrong about sharing the best?" There is a definite preference for a little taste of the best adventures, rather than making a complete meal of any one of them. Being committed to a single adventure, however appealing, brings on feelings of boredom and satiation and puts a limitation on the next possible romance.

Relationships develop by doing things together and talking about what is interesting and best. This style of relating is adventurous and also buffers having to discuss the more unappealing aspects of life. If a problem surfaces, activities can be sandwiched so closely together that there is no time to talk over the issue. "Vital things to do" can be booked so closely together that a Seven will have "ten minutes to discuss our separation, before I leave to catch a plane." Confrontation and recrimination are hard for narcissists, because of the implication that they have failed. There is the desire to put serious talks on the schedule and then close the slot by switching to alternate plans.

In a sense, Sevens do not live in real life relationships, because their minds are so easily flooded with the mental associations and imaginative ideas that their relationships suggest. On the other hand, they are wonderfully able to raise the mood of a sagging partnership by moving it on to brighter things. One side effect of the fact that Sevens can so easily replace negative feelings with a pleasant option is that they often have difficulty with emotionally dependent or needy people. The fact that a partner may not be able to shift attention from a painful pattern or to let an emotional grievance go seems like a severe limitation to the optimistic Seven. They commonly report that they have to buffer a mate's depression with a schedule of things to do away from home.

Although it's hard to make a final commitment, Sevens do miss a good relationship if the couple splits. Their idealized image of love is that the mate would be added company for activities that the Seven already enjoys alone. The mate would mirror back the fact that life is good, and no limitations or restrictions would be imposed. Failing total mirroring, the next best option would be to schedule a friendship to the degree that the Seven stays interested, but never so much that the Seven gets bored, or feels required to stay.

On the high side of intimate relating, Sevens are committed to keeping feelings alive through activity, mental pursuits, sex, and play. They are able to bring in new interests to share, bury old grievances, and start again.

On the low side of intimacy, they want to bail out if the partner gets emotionally needy or depressed. Their way out is likely to be rationalization of their original commitment by introducing contingencies that change the original plan.

An Example of an Intimate Relationship: Seven and Six, the Epicure and the Devil's Advocate

Both types share an underlying paranoia. Six is openly afraid, and Seven avoids fear by adopting backup courses of action. The Seven partner can be of enormous help to the couple if she or he will take the Six's fears seriously enough to get the partner out of the house and into activities. Once in motion, a Six's fears often dissipate, and the Seven can provide the jump-start to get the Six into an activity gear. The Six will provide an unconscious service to the couple by acting out a lot of the Seven's underlying paranoia that gives the Seven an opportunity to help, and at the same time it creates distance from fearful feelings by attributing them to the mate.

Sixes feel themselves to be bound to life by duty and hard work, whereas the Seven's basic stance is one of unlimited opportunity. To the extent that each is able to lend himself or herself to the other's view of life, the Six can learn to circumvent the paralysis of fear and move into action, and the Seven can learn to focus on one thing at a time without becoming afraid.

Both types have a tendency to live in the future, the Six in order to ward off potential threats to the relationship, and the Seven in order to develop exotic plans about what the couple can experience together. Here too the couple can support each other by adopting the other's view of life. The Seven can move toward pleasurable possibilities, and the Six can stabilize plans through a realistic evaluation of obstacles. Both types are willing to work hard in the service of future goals. The Seven's enthusiasm will keep the vision alive over the Six's tendency to doubt; and the Six's ability to feel the fundamental beauty in gritty day-to-day labor will keep the couple on track long enough to make the plans happen.

Problems are likely to stem from the difference in needs about monogamy and commitment. Sixs want reassurance about commitment before they can commit; Sevens want space. The Six partner will be more vulnerable to feelings of jealousy and is likely to project the worst case outcome on the Seven's often ambiguous agreement. A Six partner is likely to read a multioption approach to life as self-indulgent or disloyal and will feel threatened by the Seven's indiscretions or time-consuming outside interests. If the Six becomes depressed or overburdened by worry about the couple's future, a self-perpetuating cycle is likely to develop in which the Six's preoccupation with future abandonment creates the kind of depressed atmosphere that makes a Seven want to leave. The Six may become angry at "having to be the one who does it all, while you go out and play," to which the Seven will reply "no one's making you do anything."

This kind of severe standoff can be averted if the Seven is willing to negotiate and agrees to keep a definite commitment to the relationship so that the Six knows where she or he stands. A great many of a Six's needless fears vanish under the clear light of agreement, which can also help dissipate a lot of the need to know with whom the Seven is spending free time. If the Seven will acknowledge the value of slowing down and focusing on the qualities of partnership that can only be gained through endurance and introspection, she or he can learn a great deal from the Six's loyalty to commitment. The couple will be greatly aided if the Six tries to remember the best aspects of the relationship and the Seven tries to focus on the negative aspects long enough to deal with them.

How Sevens Pay Attention

From an outsider's point of view, a Seven can look like a dilettante, with many scattered interests: several projects moving at the same time, three or four half-finished books on the floor. Attention moves through experience and on to more experience, in a headlong rush to the next fascinating enterprise.

From the point of view of a Seven, all these interests appear to be related. It all seems to be leading somewhere. At some point in the future it will all come together. How wonderful to find the perfect fit! In an escapist sense, attention can move fluidly between sweet memories, fascinating thoughts, and interesting future plans. The following statement was taken from a young Seven who was having trouble placing his interdisciplinary workshop material in the catalogues of California's growth centers.

I lead consciousness raising workshops and human development groups. I know at least ten systems that I can draw from; I use an eclectic approach. What I love is to go in cold, with no preparation, and just work with whoever has come. The syllabus will cover any needs the people bring. My writeup reads, "We will do meditation, martial arts, Neurolinguistics, and Reichian breathing." I always ask participants to bring a dream to work on.

This workshop leader has not developed the ability to focus seriously on a single problem area. What he wants to do is explain problems away by switching systems or by changing the scope of his plan.

The constructive side of his attentional style could come into play if he could commit himself to facing real problems rather than prematurely throwing in a new technique. If he could take the consequences of having to face up to real difficulties and stick with his clients through their very real pain, then his lifelong habit of fitting new information into multiple option systems might lead him to insights that could help his students to grow.

The next statement was given by a Seven who has organized his way of paying attention into a useful problem-solving method. His approach is different from that of the young workshop leader because he is able to focus all of his options on a single problem, rather than shifting options in order to diffuse a problem.

I work as an organizational development consultant. Our clients are corporations that are mainly in crisis or in some process of breaking down. The businesses that we advise are often multilevel companies that have severe departmental differences. Each department wants to make it at the expense of all the rest. I get reports that are totally contradictory, and I handle them like a deck of cards.

I mentally overlay the departments, until I get the points that fit. If I keep shuffling the different systems through, I'm going to find certain points about which they all agree. I see my job as brainstorming ways in which the points of agreement can be controlled so that the different departments have to cooperate with one another in order to survive.

The shuffling often causes trouble when you have to change procedures and hierarchy. Those meetings where I have to face telling people about changes give me a great deal of grief. However, my deck-of-cards technique gets the job done.

Intuitive Style

A Seven's habit of setting a new piece of information into several interdependent contexts bears a remarkable similarity to storytelling as a way to uncover intuitive ideas.

In a storytelling technique, you deal with a thorny problem by first placing it on a back burner of your attention and then starting to tell a story about something competely unrelated to the problem you're trying to approach. In the middle of the story line you begin to move your problem from the back burner by weaving it into the action. You introduce useful characters as they feel needed, and by moving the problem through different scenes and through the hands of different characters, you get insights as to how to handle the situation.

I've worked for years in a matrix career that has one foot in science, one foot in philosophy, and another couple of feet in statistics and history. It's a constant process of relating what I read about in one field to the other areas of work. I can't proceed by force of logic, like applying the mechanics of what I know from one field to another. It's more like when I come up against a wall, I want coffee and a hot croissant. I have to get my mind off on something else, like jogging or talking to a friend.

Mostly the break is just relaxing, and I do a little better when I get back to the boards. But occasionally something in the secondary activity that's totally unrelated to my problem will turn up an answer for me.

One outstanding hit was overhearing my wife explain the mechanics of a sewing machine to our youngest son. Something in the tone of her voice caught me, and while she was explaining how the needle picked up the thread, I realized that I had neglected an underlying historical tension in the article that I was writing, much like the invisible bobbin creates a tension on the sewing thread.

The Higher Mental Capacity for Work

The evasive aspect of planning is twofold. First, if the planning is imaginative and juicy enough, it is an activity preferable to really getting down to the drudgery of work. Why not live in dreams and let others pick up the tab?

The second evasion is more subtle and involves disregarding the fact that when you make a commitment, the other people involved are bound to think that you agree with the basic premises on which that commitment rests, rather than just a few of its more agreeable points. For example, if you commit yourself to monogamy, it does not then follow that because monogamy is a result of mutual love and you have fallen in love with someone else with whom you want to live, that you are still monogamous because you love both people involved.

Most Sevens, of course, would see through this argument, but they would be inclined to minimize the fact of a broken commitment and empasize the line, "But what could be wrong with love? Love is an equalizer; isn't all love the same?" This has the effect of putting those who are dutiful in the position of being less sophisticated people, who cannot go with the flow.

Work implies a complete commitment to a single course of action, rather than circulating between many courses of action because you don't want to miss out on something good. Work does imply a certain degree of voluntary limitation. You have to limit your other options and commit yourself to a single plan. You are not going to change the plan when it hits a bad spot, and you are not going to quit if you get criticized, or other people are less than enthusiastic about your good ideas.

From the point of view of attention practice, work means the commitment to keeping attention stabilized in the exact present moment and being able to accept exactly what comes up, whether it is joyous or saddening, whether it makes you feel great or it makes you feel bad. When you work you stay focused on one thing at a time until the project gets done.

For the meditator with narcissistic traits, the task of keeping attention single-pointedly focused on an inner object of contemplation is boring work. Attention is attracted to fascinating ideas and dreams, and it is very hard to slow the mind down in order to focus on a single point.

The task is made even more difficult when the material that starts to emerge in meditation reveals us as less evolved than what our ego leads us to believe. It takes fortitude and courage for narcissistically inclined meditators, who may be sincerely convinced that they have already evolved past any personal shortcomings, to pay attention to the aspects of themselves that are really not okay.

I was in residency training before I hit the wall of medicine that I was unwilling to do. I had been unconsciously motivated by the idea that medicine was antideath, that somehow I would always be able to do something. So then I got on oncology rotation, and every day I was informing families of the seriously ill that there was nothing I could do.

At first my mind just wouldn't accept the truth. There had to be ways out for my patients. A different strategy, some kind of multiapproach treatment plan. Eventually I had to accept the fact of death and realize that I had held myself above that fact. I didn't believe I was going to die. So I got into cancer in a serious way. I got into really looking at it, and it became fascinating to me.

I had what I would call a spiritual experience with a microscope. I was looking down the barrel, having a battle with my mind. I would try to concentrate on the cancer cell plate, and keep my breath down low, and all I could think of was a book I was into and my date for later that night. It felt like being on the edge between life and death. There was death in those cells on the slide, and life was calling to me.

What happened was the cells started to open. They were stained on the slide, but they started to pulse like little suns. All I did was watch them pulse and open, knowing they were very much alive. As soon as I came back to myself, I was convinced that I had been in some kind of altered state; and that by holding my mind steady, I had gotten a glimpse of some reality that was between life and death.

It didn't change anything about the fact of cancer as a serious killer, but it did make me more available to my own mortality and limitations.

Gluttony

The gluttony of Sevens is characterized by a bodily hunger for excitement and experience. Sevens say that they are addicted to their own adrenaline. They love the rush of physical energy, the excitement of adventure, and mental stimulation. They are also often attracted to psychedelics and any other substance that will serve to keep them high. Gluttony is a bodily hunger for stimulation and experience rather than a hunger for platefuls of food. In fact they would rather leave an experience before they become satiated, in order to be sure that their interest remains alive. Sevens have a gourmet taste for experience, little tastes of the very best, rather than an overdose of a single-experience meal.

Mental gluttony has been described as monkey mind in spiritual practice. The teaching uses the image of a monkey who agilely leaps through the forest trees.

The problem with monkey mind is that a sharp attentional focus flits through associations, fantasies, and mental plans with such agility that the meditator cannot penetrate deeply into a contemplative state. The meditator's task is to get attention to sit quietly with a single point of contemplation when the habit of attention is to welcome the seduction of fantasy and plans.

The bodily version of monkey mind is described by Sevens as the desire to have every possible experience. They say that they feel most alive when they are moving between several fascinating activities and that they have infinite resources of physical energy available to them as long as their interest stays alive. Their secret is to leave one activity just at the moment that they begin to tire or begin to sense the edge of boredom. They also say that they would rather do without sleep than give up something interesting to do.

The Virtue of Sobriety

Sobriety simply means being able to continue in a course of action without having to introduce diversions or exciting secondary plans. Sevens say that they fear slowing down and committing themselves to a single course of action because commitments always entail boredom and pain.

On a mental level, Sevens have a skew toward positive imagination that is exactly opposite to a Six's habit of imagining the worst in order to be prepared. Epicures can become intoxicated by the power of their own imaginations, and they also experience a physical high that is close to intoxication when they can fully indulge their desire to cram in as much excitement as possible.

Sevens are buoyed up by a grand plan for the future, which generally contains a vision of an integrated way of life in which chief interests and special comforts are synthesized into a whole; no hassles, everything running smoothly, lots of stimulation, and no hard questions asked.

On a practical level, sobriety means that each moment has to be taken for whatever experience it honestly provides. Both the good and the bad need to be treated with equal interest, rather than selectively paying attention to positive experiences. A sober Seven is able to take one thing at a time and appreciate its real value and worth, rather than juicing it up by imagining it as more than it is.

Assets

Seven's assets include enthusiasm for creative possibilities and a real ability to reach out to people and to bring in new ideas. Excellent networker and brainstormer, particularly at the beginning or inception of a job. They are willing to experiment and to relate their own principles to new concepts, to see the overlapping points of agreement between opposites; to see the best in everything. Able to raise the emotional tone during the dark phases of a project or a relationship. Genuine interest and energy for adventuresome projects. Willing to work hard for good times, interesting projects, and a worthwhile cause, in the same way that others will work for salary and personal gain.

Attractive Environments

Sevens are often editors, writers, or storytellers. They are theoreticians of a new paradigm. They are planners and synthesizers and idea gatherers. They seek out natural ways to stay high.

They are eternally young, and to stay healthy and active they inhabit fitness centers and health food stores. They appear in the pages of New Age journals. They are idealists, futurists, and world-class travelers. "Soon I'll be on the airplane, so I'm not all here today." They seek the very best as food and wine enthusiasts. The ultimate sip, the quintessential view. They appear on university faculties as people who push for interdisciplinary studies.

Unattractive Environments

Sevens are usually not found in routine work that does not carry the spirit of adventure. Lab technician. Accountant. Close-ended job with predictable routine. Job underneath a critical boss.

Famous Sevens

Doonesbury's character *Zonker* is a Seven who has slipped in and out of Yale, a medical education, and the British peerage through good fortune, charm, and the assumption that being true to oneself is better than a lot of hard work.

Ram Dass □ Thoreau □ Peter Pan □ Kurt Vonnegut
Groucho Marx □ Rajneesh □ Tom Robbins

Subtypes

The subtypes name preoccupations that Epicures develop as ways to maintain an idealized self-image. The words identify three issues that are central to narcissism—mirroring, futurism, and idealization.

Suggestibility (Fascination) in One-to-One Relationships

For Sevens, new experiences and ideas become heightened by positive imagination to the extent that they take on the force of accomplished facts.

I think of myself as a Don Juaness in my love life. My attractions are immediate and riviting; I want to share all the wonders that I've discovered, and have him with me while I go on to accumulate more.

Sacrifice (Martyr) in the Social Arena

Sevens can accept the limitation of options imposed by obligations to others, because they couple it with the belief that all limitations are temporary, and move toward positive future goals.

Sacrifice was so built in that I never thought I was making sacrifices. We were an immigrant family, and landed in a tough Italian-speaking ghetto neighborhood scene. I got out of the local parochial school into another district, and was made quite aware of the differences between my family and what the other kids had.

At some level I knew my folks would never get past the language barrier, but at another level I could see how we were all moving toward a totally transformed life.

Family (Like-minded Defenders) as a Self-preservation Tactic

A Seven likes the security of belonging to a group of like-thinking people, who mirror back the Seven's beliefs.

I used to think of myself as a circuit rider, with a kind of compulsion to make the rounds of my friends, and not miss out on the interesting things that each of them did. I kept imagining that if we could collectivize our talent that we'd brainstorm the perfect lifestyle. I rode the circuit for years until I realized that none of us would get along under close quarters. I still have the idea that we're mentally connected, although the dream of living together has gone away.

What Helps Sevens Thrive

Sevens often enter therapy or begin a meditation practice because they want to "get more out of life." Another common entry comes during midlife crisis, a time that highlights the discrepancy between imagined expectations and what has really gotten done. Typical presentations are the conviction that others in the family have problems, the inability to commit to a relationship, and trouble with sweating out a tedious or obstructed project at work. They may experience difficulties with jobs, drugs, and finances resulting from the flight into pleasure as a psychological defense.

Epicurians need to recognize when attention shifts from real pain to a positive mental reverie or a pleasurable activity substitute. Sevens can learn to help themselves by

- Recognizing an attachment to youth and energy. Allowing oneself to see the value in maturity and age.
- Learning to stay with a painful issue long enough to see that a problem exists. "I must be defective if I need help."
- Noting the times when mental evasions occur: overscheduling, multiple projects, new options, future plans. When thinking and activity move into hyperdrive Seven is on the run.
- Recognizing the habit of substituting an idea of what pain is like for the tension of living through the real thing.
- Noting that superficial pleasure and lack of depth in commitment leads to a compulsive desire for more pleasure and fun.
- Noting that one is missing out on depth of experience and pleasure by staying on the surface.
- Noting that superficial or premature discharging of emotion replaces deep reactions. The fear of committing deeply to oneself.
- Recognizing the assumption of being entitled to special treatment.

· Seeing the scope of real responsibility, which is usually a
lot more than a Seven wishes to do.
· Holding ground when the underlying paranoia arises. This
can be overwhelming. The fear that life will turn completely
bad.
· Trying to see the difference between criticism and realistic
self-evaluation. Noting feelings of fear when ideas about
self-worth are challenged and the desire to promote oneself
in order to feel superior again.
· Being willing to work through episodes of fury when inflated ideas of self-worth are questioned. When wounded,
noting the tendency to split the perceptions of loved ones
such that they look all good or all bad. Holding ground
when things look bad.
· Recognizing efforts to charm the situation. To make things
interesting, to make things nice. Needing to be okay.
· Seeing the tendency to make up a story in order to avoid
pain. Producing entertaining stories that are only tangentially related to the truth. Using analogies to intellectualize
painful emotions. Shifting attention to a mental image in
order to block the experience of pain.
· Recognizing the escape into fantasy, mood elevators, sen-
sory overload. Developing the ability to stay with the present moment rather than escape.
· Letting unfulfilling options go. Noting the sense of limitation and fear that arises when an option goes.

What Sevens Should Be Aware of

Epicures should be aware that some of the following issues
are likely to surface during change:

· Feeling bored with therapy, which can manifest itself as
bringing gifts, charming the therapist, deflecting attention
to interesting intellectual pursuits.
· Feelings of superiority. Looking down on the mildly ridiculous therapist. Looking down on the pedestrian life.

- Associating a difficult situation with so many mental parallels that the incident loses force.
- Wanting to speed activities up when commitment issues arise. Anxiety when other options disappear.
- Feeling stuck and bored with commitment. "I want my options back again."
- A concern with inner hierarchies. "Where do I stand? What's my place? What are the others seeing in me?"
- Authority issues. Not wanting to be the boss. Not wanting to be under a boss. Equalize authority to avoid the pain of being told what to do.
- Guilt at having gotten away with so much, at the success of charm.
- Wanting to leave therapy as soon as the presenting issue feels better. Flight into health.
- Wanting to get to altered states, to apply higher meanings to problematic issues. Flight into light.
- Faulty memory about negative past experiences.
- Expressing anger by making fun of the problem. Seeing it as ridiculous. Trivializing and being amused by other people's concerns.

13. Point Eight: The Boss

	ACQUIRED PERSONALITY		ESSENCE	
HEAD	Chief Feature:	VENGEANCE	Higher Mind:	TRUTH
HEART	Passion:	LUST	Virtue:	INNOCENCE
	SUBTYPE WAYS OF BEING			
	Sexual:	POSSESSIVE/SURRENDERING		
	Social:	SEEKING FRIENDSHIP		
	Self-preservation:	SATISFACTORY SURVIVAL		

The Dilemma

Eights describe a combative childhood, where the strong were respected and the weak were not. Expecting to be disadvantaged, Eights learned to protect themselves, becoming exquisitely sensitized to the negative intentions of others. Eights see themselves as protectors. They see themselves as shielding friends and innocents by placing them behind their own protective bodies while continuing to struggle against unjust odds.

Rather than being cowed by conflict, Eights find their identity as enforcers of justice, taking great pride in their willingness to defend the weak. Love is more often expressed through protection than through demonstrations of tender feelings. Commitment means taking the beloved under the wing and making the way safe.

The central issue is control. Who has the power and will that person be fair? The preferred position is to take charge, to exert one's own power over the situation, and to maintain control over other strong contenders. There is a need to test the fairness and capability of authority. "Will I fall into the hands of wrong-minded people? Are they a bunch of fools? How will they react under pressure? Let's test them out."

If Eights are in a subordinate position, they will minimize the fact that authority has real power over their behavior and will push the limits and interpretation of rules until penalties are made clear. If placed in a leadership position, an Eight will want to secure the borders of a personal empire. The strategy will be a full-out takeover, rather than seeking out alliances that depend upon delicate negotiation or diplomacy.

The usual test of power is to press people's vulnerable spots and watch to see how they'll react. Will they retaliate? Will they buckle and be weak, or stick to a principle at whatever cost? Will their story change when they're up against the wall? Will they lie, will they manipulate, or will they spit out the truth?

The Boss is checking out motivations during a fight with a friend. It is a request for deeper intimacy, because Eights believe that the truth comes out in a fight. The fact that fighting can be a way to achieve intimacy is shocking to those who are intimidated by open anger, or who are unnerved by the fact that intimacy and anger can be closely linked together.

An Eight's tough exterior protects the heart of a dependent child who was prematurely exposed to adverse circumstances. Many Eights live out their lives without looking within themselves to rediscover the tender feelings that they have hidden since the loss of childhood innocence. The unfortunate result of a lifetime habit of looking outward for who's to blame is that when attention finally does turn inward, the realization that we all play a part in our own undoing can hit an Eight with suicidal force. Eights say that however much they may blame others, that it could never carry the punishing force of the self-blame that they direct against themselves. Blame and the desire to punish wrongdoing are key preoccupations because by defining a point of blame, one can legitimately act to sieze control as a protector of the innocent and enforcer of justice. Anger and action can be mobilized against an outside threat, and anger makes an Eight feel powerful, by instantly replacing the underlying fear of being made vulnerable to others, or of being betrayed by someone whom you trust.

Stemming from a worldview in which the strong survive and the weak do not, Eights carry a deep suspiciousness of ambiguous presentation, mixed messages, or unclear chains of command. Security means knowing who you have to go up against and who is going to cover your back. Under pressure, attention narrows to a measuring of one's own power against the strength or weakness of an opponent. Is the opponent innocent or guilty, friend or foe, warrior or wimp? Bosses rarely question their own opinion. Waffling on the merits of an opinion or probing one's own psychological motivations would only serve to erode a strong personal stand.

Eights want predictability and control of their lives, but they quickly become irritable and bored without the challenge of a position to defend. Once the rules of conduct are laid down, Eights will often proceed to break the guidelines upon which they themselves may have insisted. If Eights are bored, or have extra energy to burn, they will create trouble. This often takes the form of picking a fight, meddling in the lives of friends, or ventilating an enormous amount of energy on a secondary issue—"Who stole my potato peeler? Who's to blame?"

Excess is another way to blow off extra energy and a common Eight solution to the problem of boredom. Too much of whatever feels good in the way of sex and substances. All-night binges. Heavy entertainment. Working so exhaustively that you drop like a felled tree. Liking the taste of the dinner so well that you finish three plates in a very short time. Once attention locks on pleasure, it is hard to divert it. One good thing leads to another and another, until the Eight is the last one left at the party.

As with each of the nine Enneagram types, maturity and self-observation will lead the Boss to recognize the limitations of a narrow point of view. Each type is ultimately led back to a recovery of a valuable aspect of essence by the path of its own preoccupations, which, for an Eight, means the recovery of that

original childhood innocence that was sacrificed in order to survive in a frightening world.

Eight's habitual preoccupations include
- Control of personal possessions and space and control of people who are likely to influence the Eight's life.
- Aggression and the open expression of anger.
- Concern with justice and the protection of others.
- Fighting and sex as a way of making contact. Trusting people who can hold their own in a fight.
- Excess as an antidote to boredom. Late hours, heavy entertainment, bingeing. Too much, too loud, too many.
- Difficulty in recognizing the dependent aspects of the self. When affected by others, can deny real feelings by withdrawal, by claiming boredom, or by internally blaming the self for past misdeeds.
- An all-or-nothing style of attention, which tends to see things in extremes. Other people appear to be either strong or weak, either fair or unfair, with no middle ground. This style of attention can lead to
  - Not recognizing one's own weakness and the automatic denial of other points of view in favor of the single "legitimate" opinion that is going to make the Eight feel secure, or
  - The exercise of appropriate force in the service of others.

Family History

Eights survived their childhood by taking a tough personal stand. Their world felt dominated by bigger, stronger people who wanted to control their lives. The child struggled against a sense of unfair odds and survived by any form of confrontation that would make enemies back down. Reports range from beaten children who fought back to inner city children who gained respect from peers for not crying, for not showing weakness, and for winning fights. Where there was no physical abuse in the family, Eights report that they were respected for being strong and rejected when they looked weak.

When I was young, fighting was a way of life. Tough school, tough neighborhood. You had to get on top and hold on tight. People listened if you yelled, and left you alone if you pushed them back. I had a reconstruction recently, when I went back for the holidays. Conversations had a tone of having to take sides. Politics, opinions, everything felt shaded with antagonism.

Every time I would try to move out of the way of a direct challenge, my mother would look repelled. She finally walked away from the conversation, saying that I was a wimp who had no opinions. I had to realize that she liked me as a fighter and dropped me when I started to look weak. As an adult, the feeling is, "don't hit me," when I try to put my guard down, or when I become open to another person, because I've been so humiliated for looking weak.

Eights commonly describe themselves as having tried to be good when they were young. They say that they initially wanted to please others, but that their innocence was taken advantage of, and that they were hurt when they showed their vulnerable side. They believe that they began to push back in self-defense and quickly found that it was more fun to break the rules than it was to try to keep them.

My parents are fundamentalist Baptists; and we were raised with the idea that anything done in the name of the children's salvation was justified. My father was violent with us, and for about four years I got beaten with a strap every two or three weeks. One time when I was about fifteen, I knew I was big enough, and I got it away from him and told him next time it was going to be bare fists.

My mother's concern about the state of my soul seemed somehow more insidious. I got saved at about eleven and for months took the vows at face value. It was impossible. One small sin and you went down in flames; it was either heaven or hell, with no salvation in between. The reality that my parents outlined for me just wasn't acceptable. If this was life, then why not end it then and there? So I went against it and was always getting warnings like, "If you do that you're over the line, there's no redemption, no turning back." So I'd always just do it and push the limit.

When I was in high school, I burglarized the church that we attended. My father was a deacon in this church, so we had to leave in shame. Before that I had been forced to go to church a lot—Sunday mornings, Sunday nights, Wednesday nights, prayer meetings—and it was just agony for me. Looking back, I think it woke them up to what was happening to me, but at the time I just thought that I needed the money.

Denial

Young Eights flourish in an atmosphere of open competition, using whatever natural endowments they have as leverage to win. A small, intelligent child will manipulate another or offer an insulting opinion; a bigger child may lash out physically or shout down the opposition. Small warriors in combat cannot afford to think about their weaknesses; they rely upon themselves and learn to press ahead against the enemy's defense.

These are children who have learned to deny their personal limitations in order to appear strong. Once an Eight's attention becomes locked into an argumentative stance, the field of perception narrows to a fixed focus on the weak points of the opponent's defense. The Eight is unlikely to understand the opponent's counterarguments, because internal attention will no longer fluctuate to reconsider the question. Once an Eight's attention moves into battle stance, most contradictory evidence will be denied, because the Eight cannot afford to shift attention long enough to think the evidence through.

All through school I was the one who was going to take on the teacher for my friends. I thought I was looking for the truth, which came out as questioning authorities. Did they know what they claimed to know? Where did their information come from? I never thought anybody liked the "good" kids, I thought they liked me better.

I wasn't going against authority because I was trying to alienate anybody, it was that I wanted the attention of the other students through a challenge, through a struggle, and I thought that teachers were going to respect my spirit and my strength of mind. I rarely considered the possibility that my opinions could be wrong. In a way it didn't matter anyway, because it was the active confrontation that excited me and made me feel alive.

As an adult I've taken on projects without any consideration that I haven't the background and really can't perform. Lately I took on an article for a national magazine on the new gene technology, without having taken even an elementary course in biology. I just assumed that I could do it. Work captivates me. It's all work and no play, and then play as hard as I can and don't work at all. Whatever it is, it's all or nothing.

The preferred state of existence is highly amped, fully energized forward motion. Bosses have learned to follow their own impulses, and to go toward what gives them pleasure, without being overly concerned about their motivations. Consequently, they are relatively uninhibited and have a good deal of physical energy at their disposal that might otherwise be tied up in introspection and self-questioning. Once a desire takes hold, they move quickly into action before frustration develops. The time lag between impulse and action is short; and once a desirable goal is fixed in mind, a Boss moves into the kind of inflexible attention that underlies a battle stance.

I've always generated a myth of invincibility about myself. I remember wanting a piece of pie late one night, a few minutes before the pie shop's closing time. The shop was across town, so I took the motorcycle and cut across Telegraph Avenue at top speed. The cycle hit a hole in the road at a construction site where the warning light was down. I made it up on my feet, with blood all over my pants, and all I could think of was kicking the bike into gear.

I remember fending off a couple of people who were trying to help, with the thought in mind that I had to get to the pie before it was too late. It had nothing to do with heroics or pie. It had to do with the enormous rush of having made it through again.

It is incredibly painful to me to feel as vulnerable as I do when all that power is gone. So I keep the myth alive, with high speed as a kind of metaphor for the fast lane where I go full out, because without that, it feels like nothing's happening.

The denial of personal limitations often leads to a parallel habit of denying one's own physical and emotional pain. Eights often tell stories about how they finished the big high school football game with a bandage on a damaged knee and passed out from the pain after they got back home. They can also tell revealing stories about their denial of emotional pain, such as the fall from innocence of young Bosses who realize that they have been played for a fool by a sweetheart or a trusted friend and instantly find a way to block out the feeling.

The alteration of awareness that is necessary to deny a painful experience is a fundamental asset to a good fighter, but can become a source of terrible suffering when that fighter begins to be affected by what other people think or begins to fall in love. At the beginning of love, Eights find themselves torn between the reopening of the tender feelings of the heart and the habit of denying softer emotions.

In *Our Inner Conflicts*, Karen Horney offers a moving description of the Enneagram's Eight–Two line, which depicts the dilemma of the individual whose primary habit of defense is to move against others, but who at heart remains attached to their approval and love. She devotes one chapter to describing the individual whose primary defense is to move against others (Eight), one chapter to those who protect themselves by moving toward others (Two), and one chapter on those who move away from others (Five). According to the Enneagram's threefold view of human character, these three apparently distinct categories of behavior show up within an individual Eight's primary point, security and stress.

Control

Bosses try to maintain territorial control over anything that can influence their lives. They develop an acute sensitivity to the justice of other people's actions and are habitually preoccupied with the potential that others have to manipulate power or to assert control. The internal slant of attention could be described as, "Who's in charge here?" and "Will that person be fair?"

In a way, my life has been a search for just what the rules really are. Not just somebody's idea of how to bully me, but the real rules of conduct. My sense of the world is that there's real evil out there and people who are wanting to keep me down so they can keep themselves up at my expense. I'm as entitled to what I need as they are, and to get that, I have to evade those people who want to disadvantage me, while at the same time trying to behave with honor in my own way.

Eights feel secure when they can control a situation by calling the shots and making other people obey. They also feel powerful when they can go against the rules of conduct to which others submit. They are sensitive to any attempts to regulate their behavior and will become irritated and rebellious until they are free of outside interference. Because they want the power both to set limits and to break limits, their behavior often appears to fluctuate between imposing puritanical demands for righteous behavior on themselves and others and the opposite extreme of blowing out on all the things that they have forbidden themselves to do.

An example of a Boss taking control would be for him or her to set up a backbreaking list of requirements and then go fishing for a week. The week would be guilt-free and deliciously flavored with troublemaking. Another example would be the boss personally harassing employees to get to work early in the name of efficiency and then keeping the same employees seated at a general meeting for an hour before he arrives.

Eights are concerned with being able to limit, or at least being able to predict, the degree of influence that others can have over their lives. Trust is established by getting full self-disclosure and eliminating as many unknowns as possible, which can come out as pressuring other people into taking a position, or taking a controversial stand in order to see how others will react. Bad taste ethnic jokes, homosexual innuendos, and past life regression stories are the kinds of conversational ploys that can polarize almost any social situation into friend and foe factions and can push people into presenting the kind of underbelly reactions that satisfy an Eight's preoccupation with control.

As soon as I start to get interested in a friendship, I want to get straight about how we're going to deal with each other. I want us both to play by the rules, which comes out as watching my friends for signs that they might break their end of the bargain. Once I let my guard down, if I'm blindsided by someone I trust, I feel totally betrayed.

If they hurt me innocently, or through stupidity, I make sure it doesn't happen again, but if it was deliberate, then I have to even the score. I want them to admit it, and I want them punished. To allow myself to be taken advantage of would so weaken my idea of being fundamentally right that I would feel I must be totally wrong and would have to submit myself to them.

A Boss's perceptions are anchored in a view of the world where small oversights and badly handled details hold the potential for escalating beyond control. Small errors upset Eights and will cause them to react loudly, because they have been unpredictably blindsided. Large scale errors are paradoxically appealing, especially if they are catastrophic enough to call for a full-out confrontation.

In any unpredictable situation the Eight attentional habit of focusing in on the weak spots of the case will come into play. The Eight will want to flush out potential difficulty before it has a chance to escalate, and if something surprising or out of order does occur, attention can become so narrowly focused on a small mistake that the Boss becomes oblivious to other people's reactions and to obvious ways to fix the mistake. This can have embarrassing social consequences, as the Boss becomes dogmatic and insistent in an attempt to reestablish control.

I have an investment in taking charge, so that I'm sure everything will get done right. So I tend to get into detail control about how everything should go. Last week we had dinner out with another couple, and the soup came out cold from the kitchen. To me it seemed like I was trying to deal with the waiter and the cold soup situation, and only afterward I realized that the others had been embarrassed. What I wanted was hot soup on the table, and getting it there loomed large in my mind, because if we let it get by, then the entrée might be bad. You have to intervene immediately to save yourself, or an anxiety starts to rise that everything's going to get out of control.

Revenge

Thoughts of revenge buffer a resurgence of the anxiety that the child experienced at feeling powerless. Planning how to get back serves to block out feelings of humiliation or of endangerment that stem from having lost out to an adversary. A grudge has a way of keeping the game going. We haven't lost yet, we are merely waiting it out until we meet again. An Eight's habit of blaming others as the source of difficulty and of mentally dismissing contradictory opinions as stupid or dumb, without thinking them through, are other lines of defense against feeling controlled by outside influence.

To just sit there and take abuse is enraging. The fact that you've been done in stays in your mind and waits for the proper moment where you can take action. Revenge is not a hatchet job, it's more like you want it to be a teaching tool, exactly right and proper for the degree of the crime. I imagine how to bring it about in the appropriate way, so that at the moment that it occurs, my enemy has to realize just what a shit they've been.

Eights commonly confuse their desire to even the score with the idea of justice. They have been hurt, in what feels like an unfair way, so consequently retaliation feels like balancing the scales of justice, rather than simply taking revenge.

This last week I went out to breakfast with a friend. The owner of the place was totally rude when he took the order, and for the whole rest of the breakfast I couldn't get this out of my mind. Should I just tip the table over when I leave? Should I create a scene with this guy? What could I do so that my day wouldn't be too humiliated and that would make me feel better? I couldn't stop thinking about what I could do to him. So I didn't do anything and left. But I've still got juice on it. When I drive past the restaurant, I think, "What if I could just break a window?" It doesn't leave you alone until you do something.

Justice

The need to maintain control plays a part in Eight's preoccupation with justice. "Can others be trusted? Are their actions fair?" The preoccupation is fueled by the unfulfilled childhood desire to find an authority so trustworthy that control could be given over without fear of being tricked or dominated. The sensitivity to justice makes Bosses pay particular attention to any signs of unfair intentions.

I have the tendency to look for signs of unconscious or malevolent behavior; to try to get a handle on how somebody's mean, or in what way they would be mean if pushed. Whether they're manipulative, and do they have a taste for it? Do they enjoy it?

It's wanting to see the worst that they're capable of, so there's no nasty surprise. Not taking a hearts-and-flowers view of someone and then being surprised at some more base motivation. Looking for the bottom line. What does this person want, and what can I count on from them?

There's a lot of watching how people interact. Where are they blind to themselves? What's the underbelly like and watching for the Achilles' heel reaction. I realize that once somebody has scored on the "don't trust" barometer, it's very hard for me to change my opinion. I want the predictability that once I've made up my mind, it stays that way. If I want to test out the way someone really is underneath a smooth presentation, I'll put the pressure on them and irritate them to see what they'll do when they're pushed.

The Boss applies pressure in order to discover people's real motivations, especially whether they are fair. The Eight's self-concept is that of a defender of the weak, who would naturally wish to enter and take charge of an unfair situation. The unfortunate boomerang effect of the defender position is that Eights are often so confrontational in their defense of a worthwhile cause that they can be perceived as troublemakers rather than as useful allies.

Eights are also vulnerable to being manipulated into fighting other people's battles. They are superb examples of committed leadership in defense of justice, or when oppression needs to be confronted, and are consequently much in demand as a heavy ally. A typical scenario is reported by Eight children who are approached with a story of injustice and find themselves set up as the front runner for other children's interests. An example would be a classroom situation where students feel that the teacher is giving them too much homework. The likely spokesperson would be an Eight child, whose security depends upon taking direct action against injustice, and who could be easily maneuvered into taking the blame for other children.

In troubled families it is often the Eight child who senses and acts against the unacknowledged anger of adults. In this scenario other family members are likely to point to the Eight as the troublemaker, without realizing how clearly their own internal aggressions broadcast to the child.

Truth as a Quality of Higher Mind

The preoccupation with fair play focuses attention on other people's hidden intentions. Bosses want to test out the truthfulness of what people say and to actively confront them on sensitive issues to see how the truth might alter under pressure. Looking for the truth does not feel combative from an Eight's point of view; it feels like sensing when a partial opinion is being stated, or when information is being withheld, and following a natural impulse to shake up all parties involved to the point where they'll blurt out their real feelings. Fighting is felt to be fundamental to friendship, because people do reveal their hidden agendas under pressure.

Eights respect a fair fight. Their idealized concept of themselves as personally powerful is projected outward as admiration for people who will back up a strong opinion. There is an identification with those who hold their ground under fire and disrespect for any who attempt to avoid confrontation.

From an outsider's point of view, the Boss's "fair fight" can look like two uncompromising opponents squared off in a boxing ring. Those of us who are out of touch with our own aggressions often scheme to stay out of an Eight's way, to withhold bad news, or to doctor information, as a way to avoid annoying a potentially explosive person. From the Eight's point of view, fighting is a source of excitement, and it is a lot more fun to work out against a worthy opponent than to score an easy win.

If the opponent is worthy, a sustained emotional rush takes place as the Eight mobilizes to meet a powerful force that threatens to get out of control. The anger that rises to meet the situation is experienced as coursing, focused power. It feels exciting, rather than being experienced as a negative emotion. An angry Eight can sense the energetic power of the emotion as a force to get to the truth of the matter, as a tool to get the job done, as excitement that is an antidote to boredom and self-forgetting. A fair fight is, in fact, a win–win situation for an Eight. Winning out over an opponent gives the satisfaction of asserting control, and losing to a worthy opponent, who has been tested and found to be fair, eases the mistrust surrounding those who have power over one's life.

When Eights act from their ego, they mentally focus on a version of the truth that gives them maximum benefit and insist that their version is the one objectively truthful course of action. Once convinced that their version of the truth is correct, they lose sight of the fact that it may be objectively self-serving, or represent only a partial view of the facts. Mentally geared to roll over any opposition, their attention moves into battle stance, which targets the negatives of the opposition's case, and the positives of their own. Alternate opinions are mentally labeled stupid, and can automatically drop out of mind without being thought through, because the Eight's attention is narrowly focused upon achieving the goal that supports his or her security.

Once in battle stance, Eights lose the flexibility of attention with which they might be able to reflect upon their own course of action, or consider new information that could weaken a firm personal stand. Eights can remind themselves that battle stance attention is going into effect by cultivating an awareness of the times when another person's idea sounds utterly stupid and appears to be so beneath consideration that it is mentally discarded without mention.

One Eight exemplar described the battle stance mental state as "being the quarterback, running with the ball under your arm. You never turn back to question your own defense, and all you look for are the holes in the other team's line." Like a verbal quarterback, a highly fixated Eight operates from a state of mind that gets so riveted to one "truthful" course of action that she or he may be unable to switch attention to an alternative point of view.

With maturity, and some life experiences with fair authorities and safe friendships, an Eight's perceptual defenses soften and, when not threatened by a takeover, she or he will begin to be aware of compromise solutions.

In a mature Eight the neurotic need to create conflict as a way to discover buried truth is a habit of the past; and what has evolved from that point of neurotic suffering is a rare capacity to recognize each individual's real truth. No longer threatened by the possibility of being unfairly controlled by others, an Eight moves naturally toward an objective perception of each person's real wishes. Wanting only to get to the truth of the matter, Eights can learn to recognize those small fluctuations of attention that convey the degree of sincerity surrounding a statement of opinion.

How Eights Pay Attention

Eights have several ways to not perceive threatening information. Their psychological defenses revolve around an idea of themselves as more powerful than any potential opposition, so consequently their perceptions tend to maximize their own strengths and minimize an opponent's real advantages. One exemplar described himself as "not really brave, because I rarely see anything to be afraid of. I would believe myself to be brave if I felt fear and went ahead in spite of it. As it is, when I get into an argument, people look like pushovers to me." One classical way to not perceive a threat is to bury it by shifting attention to something else. For Eights, excesses like bingeing and overspending easily serve to block out the surfacing of a painful insight, or an awareness that could threaten a sense of personal power. A self-aware Boss can actually use the urgent desire for immediate satisfaction as a reminder to look within and find out what real needs are being subverted by excess.

A second way in which Eights can block unwanted insight from awareness is to so forcefully deny a painful issue that for them it ceases to exist. This way is not a matter of burying something you don't want to think about by diverting your attention to pleasurable excess. This way enables you to stare straight at something and not perceive that it is there. An extreme example of the attention style that supports denial was reported by a recovering alcoholic, who, at the time that she was drinking, confronted her husband from behind a mound of whiskey empties piled in their basement. She believed that she had convinced him that she did not drink, because in her mind the bottles didn't exist.

Another example of our capacity to deny what we cannot accept is illustrated by the common request that physicians make when a severe diagnosis has to be given. The request is that a relative or friend accompany the patient, on the assumption that people tend to deny or rationalize threatening information. Eights are particularly prone to the specific shift of attention that includes only safe information and blocks out the rest. They are prone to this attentional style because of the childhood circumstance of having to oppose superior force.

A skillful adversary necessarily overlooks a great deal of information that is incidental to the task of laying waste to the opposition. In combat, perception takes on a black or white coloration, with a minimum of nebulous grays. In the kind of altered state of mind that anger can generate, attention narrows to a measuring of the opponent: "How do I take him?" "Where's the hole in her character?" "What will make him back down?" The internal assumption of one's own position as fundamentally right is essential; it guarantees immediate, unwavering action. The unfortunate side effect of a full-out confrontation is that the ability to accommodate new information is lost.

I still don't want to listen to other points of view. I was so angry at adults who "couldn't help it," and kept messing up, that I just want to know exactly what to expect and to ensure that it's going to happen. The idea that there are multiple correct positions for different people is okay as a mental construct, but put into practice it so weakens my idea of being fundamentally right that I feel I must be totally wrong. It's a question of being all right or all wrong.

Outsiders may see an Eight as being stubborn in the face of rational alternative arguments. The Eight's perceptual ground tends to take on either/or reference points. "Are you friend or foe? Leader or follower? Strong or weak? Against me or for me?" The insight that a middle ground of compromise exists is generally accompanied by a feeling of extreme vulnerability. Compromise leaves an Eight psychologically open to attack from any side, because the situation, being no longer black or white, is no longer predictable.

The following statement comes from an eighteen-year-old Boss. He is describing his predicament in becoming aware of threatening information that he has previously denied. He is also giving a voice to the attentional dilemma that we all face when our prejudices are aroused, when our racism is tested, when our politics come under question. In any situation where people become polarized into "me against you," attention quickly fixates upon the weakness of the enemy's position, with a consequent denial of the enemy's better qualities, or the weaknesses of one's own. The opponent starts to look like a nonperson, and his or her better qualities cease to exist, because one cannot afford to keep them in mind.

I got my full growth by the time I was in my second year of high school, so by the time football season came around, I was 6'3" and about 240 pounds. Prime meat for the line. During an early season game, someone on the other team baited me, so I took him out. I got mad, and got my head down, and hit him as hard as I could, which cracked his ribs and three vertebrae. He was hospitalized for a long time, and then gradually recovered movement. For all that time I'd hear about it, but it wasn't true to me that it was serious, and it wasn't true that I had done it. The idea would come into my mind and it wasn't true, so I'd forget about it. I got the nickname Killer, which was fine because it backed guys off on the field, and because it didn't apply to me.

Around midseason it happened again. Same setup, a hard hit, an injury, and the guy was out cold. It was stunning. The whole first incident came back to me while I was lying on the ground. It was like taking blows. His pain, the weeks in bed, and I believed I felt the hatred of the guys who had been calling me Killer. It all came at once and kept coming up for the next few days. The end of the story was that the second guy I hit had a clean fracture that wasn't much; and that I quit playing. I took a lot of badmouthing from the team, who liked having a hulk on their side, but I didn't trust what could happen if I got into a blind rage again.

From the point of view of meditation practice, denial could be illustrated by the notion Don't let yourself think. This is a *false* practice, a mistake that beginning meditators commonly fall into when they first attempt to clear the mind of thoughts. In this *false* practice, the meditator does not really withdraw attention from preoccupying thoughts as they come and go, but instead attempts to block out thoughts with a forced concentration on an interior blank space. The rigid focusing of attention on interior blankness has the side effect of blocking out the normal awareness of thoughts and other impressions. As soon as the meditator relaxes concentration on the mental blank space, thoughts rush in again, and it becomes clear that awareness has never really shifted away from the thinking state.

Bosses will recognize the "don't let yourself think" state of mind as a kind of controlled wall staring, which they are likely to find themselves doing when something painful needs to be buried. An Eight can wake up in the middle of having been staring at a blank wall or an empty tabletop for God knows how long and find that he or she has a hard time thinking. The Eight is perceptually blanked out. If the mental blankout had a voice, it would say, "nothing painful gets past the tabletop blockade."

One Eight described the lifting of denial as "like opening the curtain on a stage. Everything you've been fighting against is staring straight at you with the force of total truth. You're totally wrong. You're an idiot, you've made an unforgivable error, and you want to punish yourself for what you've done." The special problem with denied material is that it can emerge into awareness suddenly, and with great force, which, given the Boss's preoccupation with justice, precipitates a barrage of self-hatred and self-blame. In the case of the young athlete, he was either a hero or a killer, with no apparent middle ground between the two extremes.

Eights also report that the lifting of denial with respect to one incident can act as an interior wick that allows other examples of the incident to emerge, in a kind of chain reaction of memory. Eights say that once they perceive something bad about themselves, they also remember many other examples of that bad thing that they've done in the past.

Eights say that insight can act like a jack-in-the-box with a shocking punch. They open the box of an opinion where they believe themselves to be totally right, and the fact that they have been wrong is so startling that they move into battle stance attention and cannot think of any compromise to cushion the insight. What was totally right has become totally wrong; and the need to punish wrongdoings is immediately turned against the self.

Intuitive Style

The intuitive style most common to each of the types develops from the way in which the type pays attention to information that supported childhood concerns. Eights were concerned about power and control, and so the child learned to register impressions about the degree of force that others generated within their bodies. Eights say that they are attracted to energy; that they can sense the quality of energy in people and in situations because an Eight's sense of self pervades the open space of a room. They produce statements like: "When I'm angry I feel that I get larger," and "people think of me as being six feet tall when in fact I am quite small." The following statement, taken from a University of California student, illustrates the typical placement of attention described by Eights who have made it a habit to observe themselves.

My partner says he can feel my presence as soon as I get in the front door. He says he feels like he has to take account of me even when he's in his study with the door shut. My sense is that I, and the other Eights that I know, take up an excessive amount of space, that I extend myself out into the space that I'm in and fill up the whole house with myself.

This student's understanding of the placement of her attention is that it resides in an enlarged sense of herself that pervades physical space. This is typical of reports from Eights. They uniformly describe a body-based impression of space rather than reporting that they are flooded with other people's feelings or that they habitually channel attention to mental imagination. Consider the similarity between the student's statement and the following description of an intuitive impression reported by a research physicist who works at the same university. He is a self-identified Eight.

I take my measurements from machines that are very delicate and break down easily. Everything in the experiment depends on the minute adjustments of a set of probes that go out of balance with the slightest excuse. The biggest headache of the whole operation is the fact that it can take up to three days to find the break in the equipment once the apparatus fails.

Last year I had a report deadline to meet for our grant agency, and the machine went down. I was frantic, but after staying up all night I knew I wasn't going to make it. In desperation I remember starting to curse the whole project and having to stop myself from smashing the machine. I felt like I hated it so much that some part of me struck out at the table where I had components out for electrical testing, and as I went out I felt the dead spot in the machine.

Open Anger

The open, uninhibited expression of anger is central to the Eight psyche and is a point of great pride and great suffering to them. There is pride in the fact that if something needs to be said, then an Eight will speak out, and great self-blame for those same words that, spoken in anger, can lead to the loss of friendship. Bosses have been rewarded for being powerful in the past, and it can be shocking to them to realize that winning an argument can lead to rejection, rather than respect.

Eights report that when they get into an argument, they become so focused on winning that they are oblivious to the fact that the other people involved are becoming alienated by a display of force. The physical high of arguing full-out in a worthwhile cause does not feel at all negative to an Eight; in fact, open anger feels essential to building a trustworthy relationship.

I'm most comfortable when I see my friend's anger. To me, anger is the road to deeper feelings, like deep sadness and repressed desire. It's exciting to me as long as someone stays angry and can stick with it. If they start to cry, then it's terrible. I feel bad and believe that they've taken on the victim role to manipulate me into being an aggressor, and they aren't telling me the truth about what they've got against me.

For a long time anger was the feeling of choice. You learn to move so quickly when you have to that any fear is minimized before the anger rush comes on. I was in Hawaii on vacation recently, and I got myself into one of the few fear situations that I can remember. I got down an abandoned trail to a wonderful natural pool surrounded by sheer cliff face and thought I'd climb up to dive. Somehow I maneuvered myself into an amazing cliffhanger, where the rock face crumbled behind me on the way up, and I got stuck into an indentation that was too far away from the pool to dive and hit the water. It was a set of reactions that I barely recognized: belly tight, knees weak. It was kind of marvelous. "So this is the real fear." Once I wormed my way out and down, I realized that I am not really brave. It's that I so minimize the possibility of danger that I have no reaction to it.

Anger, on the other hand, can be instantaneous, and it's very physical. It serves to ward off the worst fear, which is the fear of falling into the hands of mean people. Anger is discharging; it makes you feel strong and has an energy to it that is enjoyable. It's best for me when others are openly angry. If they're holding it in, that's scary, and that's what most people seem to do. "Hi there" on the outside, and they're vibing it underneath. That's very unpleasant to me. You want to get it out in the open and see what it is, because it's scary. Open anger is better, and as long as it stays on the open, civilized plane, and I know that nobody's going to jump me, I'm good at it.

I've taken on a roomful, and I feel like a karate champ. I'm not inclined to give in if the issue's right. I think that a lot of the time that people think I'm being argumentative or, quite correctly, that I'm not going to give them negotiating room once I'm launched into what I have to say. That's because I often hear that people are not talking to me neutrally. There's an extra something behind the issues that isn't being admitted—some irritation, some unadmitted hostility on their part—and then I just won't listen. I won't allow it in, because to me it's contaminated. It's not just a conversation, it's not the truth. It's hard for me to then draw out all the hidden extras and try to deal with them. It seems more honest to just shut the door on the whole contaminated conversation and be done with it.

I actually have much more respect for people who won't submit to me. If they submit it's probably a sign that they're holding back something. If they don't agree and are open about it, that's okay, but if they agree and can't hold eye contact, or can't match my intensity, then I get the idea I'm dealing with a wimp.

The Virtue of Innocence

Innocents walk into new situations without prior ideas or expectations about what they are going to find. They are open to whatever the situation presents, which allows them to naturally accommodate to a correct course of action. An Eight's innocence is overshadowed when he or she selectively focuses attention in order to take control, or to impose a point of view. Consider the difference between an unaware Eight, who automatically tries to dominate a situation, and a more self-aware Eight, who would have the confidence to accommodate to changing courses of action.

Like all of the higher impulses, innocence is felt as an energy in the body that moves an individual appropriately, but without direction from the thinking self.

This particular bodily awareness would be natural to a fully functioning human being and would depend upon an accurate sensing of the degree and quality of power present in any given situation. An unaware Eight would be likely to expect opposition as a matter of habit and would unconsciously exert as much force as necessary in order to take control. That behavior would be marked by an inflexibility of opinion, an insistence on a partial truth, and an inability to shift attention to other points of view. The energies used to take control would be physical force and anger.

An Eight who has moved beyond that automatic response would be able to modify her or his own degree and quality of energy in order to accurately sense the the fluctuations of power that ebb and flow in any given situation.

Lust

Eights are inclined to follow their impulses. In childhood the ability to move quickly from impulse into action was part of a survival system that depended on acting first and thinking second. Bosses are inclined to believe that whatever makes you feel good and powerful must be a correct course of action, and because they are relatively free of the guilt and internal questioning that most of us associate with our own bodily excitement, they find it natural to follow through on sexual attraction. They are not embarrassed about expressing their anger, or by acting on sexual feelings.

I want that intensity in intimate relationships. Somebody who draws out the life in me, where there can be excitement. I've been in a relationship for seven and a half years, and there are moments that are very dull. I'm having to learn not to provoke fights just for the excitement of it. The intensity is still the draw. Let's have a project and go for it together.

I count on sex as the major attraction. It's really what I look for. In all of my thinking about love, how I know that I'm loved is if somebody's hot for me. I really don't believe in much else. There's a lot of psychobabble around about love when people are really just looking to get their expectations met and their egos pumped up; and it seems to me that if you pay too much attention to that stuff; then you stay confused all your life.

Eights have a low toleration for frustration. It is hard to hold back anger, to refrain from acting on a sexual attraction, or to not go back for a third plateful at the Sunday brunch. Unsatisfied wishes will surface in their minds over and over again, in the same way that an unresolved dispute captures their attention, making them anxious and irritable until they can take action to resolve the situation. "I have to get it settled in person, or else I write letters in my head for weeks."

Bosses say that getting angry with people is often a positive contact for them. A good fight makes them trustful about another person's real intentions, which allows them to feel more confident in the relationship. They also report that a kind of intimacy can arise during a fight, such that anger turns to sexual feelings, and a fight winds up in making love.

I've been married to an Eight for almost twenty years and have had to learn to be totally upfront with whatever crosses my mind, or else he's on me to find out what I'm holding back. When we first married I thought that anger was the last resort. I saw it as an animal emotion that civilized people should rise above. You had to have your bags packed and a lawyer on call if it got to the shouting stage.

About three years into the marriage, I got pushed to the wall. I had no idea that he was looking for intimacy by being such a pain. All I knew was that he was insulting me in public. I got so resentful that I had to fight back, which meant the end for me.

I still don't think I would have done it if I hadn't been absolutely sure that he wasn't going to hit me. I remember getting two steps up on the stairway so that I could see him eye to eye, and I told him off right in his face. I repeated his position back to him point for point, and then told him that I did not agree. I could see from his face that it didn't compute. If I could say his position back to him, then I had to agree.

When I screamed off my own points, it was amazing. It turned him on. He got smiley, and affectionate, and lost his anger with me. I'd never seen anybody change so quickly; the combination of me two steps up the stairwell and screaming made him love me.

Excess

Getting more of whatever feels good is an Eight's solution to the core issue of indecision about real personal goals (core point Nine). Overstimulation has the effect of deadening the awareness of other feelings and replaces the need to examine real emotional goals. Although Eights can mobilize energy for the satisfaction of their needs, and appear to be uninhibited in their desire for gratification, they can, in fact, be as far removed from their own real wishes as the self-forgetful Nine.

An Eight's capacity to act stems from an intense focusing of attention on pleasure, and the excitement of conflict, as a way of getting up steam, rather than energy being mobilized from deep psychological priorities, or from an awareness of soft emotions. By seeking out stimulation, Eights eliminate boredom, and also manage to deny their personal vulnerability.

Pushing the limit into pleasurable extravagance offers a magnified sense of life. Once attention is attracted, there is very

little ambivalent wavering or self-questioning. The goal becomes desirable, and whether it is a psychologically genuine
goal doesn't matter anymore. The party starts and the party
keeps going, with an Eight carried away on enjoying a little
more of whatever's going around.

I've felt worse since I started looking at myself. Being aware of what I
do brings up the embarrassing fact that I'm laughing the most, arguing
the loudest, and dying to get some action going. Living by your instincts and being unconscious is great. It carries the sense of wanting
to get away from the improverishment of life by living in an expanded
way.

There's always a vague dissatisfaction with having to hold myself
back. Like I have to qualify what I do because nobody else wants to
keep up. So I want peak experience, and then a string of them, one
after the other, so that there's no letdown in between. Once you get a
taste for something, it spreads like wildfire. Like one good meal and
you want another one; or if you buy one dress, it means you're likely
to go for the whole rack next time around.

Once you get involved, it's like a suction cup, it takes an enormous
amount of effort to disengage and go on to something else. There's no
flair for moderation. You're either obsessively interested or flat-out bored. You want to stay in bed and make love all day, or you're basically
not interested. You're in your lover's lap or staring out the window,
with not much flair for in between.

The desire to step up intensity in order to feel alive stems
from the feeling of living in an all-or-nothing world. *Nothing* is
a dead halt, a deep desire to stare at the wall for a long time.
All is described as wanting to push the limit as a way to get the
juices flowing.

If I'm driving and following the speed limit and obeying the laws, my
attention's not there. I go somewhere else. I get bored and I actually
make mistakes. But if I'm going really fast and I have to watch out for
everything, and I have to watch for cops, then I'm awake. I almost
never make mistakes that way. In fact, the way that I get tickets is that
I'm asleep, going down the freeway at sixty-five. If I'm going eighty-
five, nobody sneaks up on me. I'm alert when the intensity is there.

Intimate Relationships

In a way, Eights are predisposed to be loners rather than intimates. A loner has only one person to look out for and one territory to defend. At the beginning of an Eight's interest in relationship, sexuality and love are approached on a conditional basis. "We sleep together, but spend a lot of time apart." "We're great in bed together, but we're not the greatest of friends." Intimacy and friendship start out along the lines of coalition politics: "I know in exactly what ways I can trust him." "I know exactly where she stands." Views are exchanged, positions are made clear, and relationship is based on adventure, good sex, and activities that you enjoy doing together.

As friendship moves to intimacy, Eights step into the uncustomary position of having to consult with someone else. A partner's opinions are supposed to be taken seriously, and Eights find themselves affected by someone else's moods. Bosses look to themselves as a source of power, and dependency upon others does not fit into a power system that is geared to self-gratification.

Eights become vulnerable very slowly and with great trepidation. They are likely to create a safe turf where they can begin to let down their guard by taking charge of the mechanics of the relationship. They will want to know all about what goes on in their partner's life and will have strong opinions about who the partner sees, as well as when, where, and how he or she spends time. When Eights realize that they are becoming dependent upon a partner's love, they will be spurred into a counterreaction of relating as a powerful ally and protector. They will want to take charge, which can easily shift to controlling the mechanics of the partner's life, as a way of feeling less vulnerable.

If the partner submits, an interesting conflict will arise. The Eight will want to dominate, but will be far more attracted if the partner resists domination. The key to the apparent contradiction lies in the Eight's preoccupation with power. Bosses can predict, and therefore trust, people who are willing to submit and give up the control of their lives. They are, however, easily bored by people who submit too readily and quickly lose interest in anybody who cannot take a worthy opponent's stand. Consequently, the route to intimacy lies through tests of power, because Eights also trust people whose use of power has been tested and found to be fair. Those who fight back will be given a rough time, and if they continue to stick by their position, will be treated with the same degree of respect that Bosses accord themselves.

Eights describe their great loves as taking the mate under their own skin. They surrender control of the relationship by gradually trusting the mate in the same way that they trust themselves. The Boss may still feel like a loner with respect to the rest of the world, but feels that the mate has become a trustworthy part of a single organism.

I feel that people are attracted to my strength, my self-confidence, my anger, and the stimulation that I give them. What they don't want is my sadness or my hurt. I feel that when people see that, they run. I lead with my strengths, and I feel that people are going to disrespect me and leave if I'm not strong. If "going against" is my first choice, then needing to be alone is my next favorite.

I've always been a loner; even in intimacy I feel alone. Once I get attached to someone to the point where I'll miss them, it gets frightening to me in the sense that I am alone with the part of them that's under my skin. They become familiar, safe, and I can't imagine not having them around. I both want to withdraw and isolate and to possess their soul. My instinct is to protect them in the same way that I'm always aware of covering my own back, because we have become one person, and I'm just as hard and demanding on them as I am on myself.

Even in restaurants I want my back to the wall, so I can see who's coming in the door; and when I'm with someone whom I love, then I'm looking out for both of us, which can get really draining. I can stay extended to another person for just so long, and then there's a reaction of stay back, stay away.

Even when I know what I want and am planning to ask for something personal, I know that I won't. The underlying assumption is that you can only count on yourself, so the idea is to take what you need without consultation. I can ask for sex, I can take control of the mechanics of my life. What's really hard to go after is what counts to me, especially if I have to admit it to somebody else, or make it public. It looks like I'm an advocate, a tough-minded person, because for me it's not hard to stand up for an idea or a principle.

But to go after my heart's desire is very hard, and it seems easier to not take the risk, to stick with whatever you're good at, or to get somebody under your skin who cares desperately about something, and help them get theirs.

An Example of an Intimate Couple Relationship: Eight and Four, the Boss and the Tragic Romantic

Both types share an attraction to edge-of-life experiences. They are both amoral, believing at some level that the usual rules to not apply to themselves. The Four is above the law and the Eight is stronger than the law. The couple can appreciate each other's desire for adventure and need to push the limits of what is permissible and will support each other's inclination to ignore social constraint. Both are easily bored by repetition, and if the outer climate is not adventurous enough, each will intensify the emotional climate in their own way: the Eight by fight and the Four by dramatic acts and suffering.

The Eight partner will appreciate the Four's personal style and want to be included in matters of taste and presentation. The Four will be attracted to the Boss's blunt emotional approach as being in touch with "real" feelings. Fours will also appreciate the fact that Eights hold ground under attack and go toward a fight rather than away from one. Eights are unlikely to become unstabilized by a partner's depression, and they will be able to maintain a consistent emotional tone during those times when a Four's mood fluctuates between wanting to push the partner away or trying to pull the partner back into relationship.

There are several natural meshings of habit between Eight and Four. For example, an Eight will prefer a Four's company if she or he is "up" but will withdraw if the Four becomes depressed. Eight may even counter the Four's depression by going off to have a good time somewhere else. The failure to get attention will either make the Four very angry, which will break the depression, or will make the Four afraid of losing contact, which also breaks a depression. Another example of the natural meshing of habit is that Eight will become impatient with any glorification of personal emotionality and try to break through the Four's dramatized feeling stance for underlying real feelings. Not treating moods and feelings seriously infuriates Fours, who, when angry enough, bring real feelings to the surface.

A serious interaction can develop if the Four becomes too emotionally dependent, too inclined to masochistically enjoy being victimized by an Eight's punitive side, or too inclined to the dramatic push–pull pattern of relationship. The predictable Eight will either become outrageously vindictive as a way of cutting the relationship off or will want to cut and leave without comment. Conversely, if the Eight begins to indulge in feelings of power over the Four—wanting to demean or to control—the Four will either spiral into a deep depression or will become caustic and embittered.

A severe situation can be alleviated if the Four will shift focus from wanting the Eight's attention to a personal project that the Eight can help to support. One of the best configurations of a Tragic Romantic–Boss combination has the creative Four developing a project and the powerful Eight as providing the appropriate pressure that makes the project happen. Another excellent configuration appears when Eights begin to see the value of the complexity and drama of a Four's interior life. If Eights can tolerate the initial anxiety that attends deep emotionality and deep experiences in meditation, they will find that they have unusual resources of stability in shifting awareness to the inner states.

Authority Relationships

The major issue is control. Eights assume that they know the correct approach and that they are in charge whether or not they actually are. They prefer to assume leadership and to maintain strict supervisory control of all aspects of an operation. There is also a desire to protect the innocents of the organization from poor treatment and to mobilize those who are subject to unjust hierarchical controls. Most of all there is a strong desire to test the fairness and capability of other authorities.

An Eight's interest will likely be directed toward competition with other leaders, motivated by the goal of securing the borders of a personal empire. Eights are more interested in power than in reward. They therefore heavily focus on matters of security, especially in the trustworthiness of allies and subordinates. They particularly need reliable information, because once they move into a go-ahead position, they can become blind to new information. Once in action, attention becomes focused in a dead-ahead, single-tack direction that targets the weak spots in an enemy's defense. Consequently, they have a poor perception of diplomatic opportunity or proper timing and prefer a full-out takeover to the subtle changes of position that are required in negotiation.

The key to working with Bosses is to keep them fully informed. People often try to hide bad news from Eights out of fear that they will they get angry and aggressive when bad news comes. While this may occur, Eights will be more angered if they feel that they are being kept in the dark. In addition, if the bearer of bad news is out of touch with his or her own aggression, the Eight's anger will appear to be personally directed and potentially violent. From the Eight's point of view, being blindsided is one of the few real threats to oneself; full information is the guarantee of security making an accurate reporter a trustworthy ally.

On the high side, bosses have immense capacities for continuous pressure and follow-through on a project. If made to feel secure in leadership, they commit completely to a go-ahead position. They extend protection to "our people." They make the way safe for allies and willingly take on aggressive competitors.

On the low side, they are interfering and meddlesome when bored. They look for someone to blame and punish when things slow down or go wrong and are unwilling to give the other guy an opportunity to save face or to regroup. They have a marked tendency to become aggressive toward other people who display a negative trait that is similar to one that is being unconsciously denied by the Eight.

A Typical Interpoint Authority Relationship: Eight and Nine, the Boss and the Mediator

If the Eight is the employer, she or he will often develop a complicated and comprehensive set of guidelines that attempt to cover every possible contingency. The guidelines will then be erratically enforced, depending on the Boss's frame of mind. If the Boss is feeling expansive, all rules are off. If the Boss senses that rules are being bent without explicit permission, there can be a spate of enforcement, such as spot inspections and impossible deadline requirements. Eights enjoy the control of both making the rules that others are required to obey and having the power to go against the rules without having to suffer the consequences.

A good relationship will develop between the Nine worker and an Eight employer as long as the Boss's attention is directed away from the employee and toward the project. The Nine will appreciate firm leadership in either a defensive or a go-ahead posture and will cooperate fully for the good of the group. If the organization is threatened from the outside, the Boss will line up an excellent defense, rally the workers, and serve as an example of leadership in the defensive posture. Not one inch of territory will be surrendered without concessions or a fight. Merged with the group spirit, the Nine will work tirelessly for the common cause.

A more difficult interaction may arise if the Boss attempts to push the Nine employee into greater production or into responsibilities that the Nine is unwilling to take on. The Boss will expect obedience and the Nine will evade. The Boss will perceive any slowing down or passive-aggressive activity as a direct assault and will retaliate publicly. Looking for someone to blame, the Eight is likely to deeply humiliate the employee without actually meaning to and will publicly focus upon the errors made without remembering to mention the Nine's past efforts and success.

If pushed, the Nine employee will seem to comply but in reality will evade and will cover up any errors. The Nine is unlikely to move into a direct combat stance, becomes internally furious and unwilling to speak. Most Eights are oblivious to emotional dynamics, and if not directly informed they will not understand what is happening to the Nine, and will continue to punish passive-aggressive activity. The situation can become explosive, resulting in either the Eight firing the employee or the Nine quitting after "the last straw."

This kind of a severe situation can be eased if the Eight boss can demonstrate a willingness to draw out the Nine's complaints, can be generous with rewards and praise for the parts of the job that have been well done. A Nine will open if rewarded, recognized, or made to feel needed. If the Eight boss is self-aware, she or he could also point out that a Nine's habit of digressing to secondary tasks or getting distracted on the job is terrifying to the Boss, because the employee appears to be out of control. An Eight's heavy-handed attempts to gain control are often fueled by a terror of losing control.

If the Nine can confront the Eight's inevitable anger, is willing to face up to open arguments, and does not withhold information or attempt to shift blame, the Boss is likely to respect the employee's strong stand. Eights are made furious by a Nine's stubborn refusal to speak but are comforted by direct confrontation, and they will open if they can understand the motives of the people involved.

If the Eight is the employee, there will be periodic tests of authority. The more definite and unambiguous the leadership, the less the Eight will need to test. Any ambiguous or vague request on the part of the Nine boss will be questioned, or tested out by disobedience. The staff is likely to feel polarized, as the Eight pushes them into taking sides, even about minor policy, in an effort to determine who is friend and who is foe.

The Eight is likely to be cooperative if inspired by honest leadership or somebody else's good idea. The best use of Eight employees is to put them in charge of implementing an interesting point of view. The Eight will be far more useful to the organization if sectioned off into a small sphere of influence and given complete control.

Assets

Bosses are preoccupied with power and control. They can be hounded by their need to take charge and to be looked to for leadership, or learn to use their slant of attention to benefit themselves and others. Fixated Eights will find security in making others submit to their point of view; but that same commitment to power can be developed into a talent for exerting just the right amount of pressure to move a massive undertaking forward. Eights are examples of committed leadership in confronting obstacles and taking direct action.

For all of their assertiveness and extravagant behavior, Eights have a hard time exposing their deepest wishes and initiating their real goals. An Eight makes trouble and fights, in order to keep interest alive, but if interest is supplied externally, then an Eight will happily go into control mode to make goals materialize.

Eights let others know exactly where they stand. When they attempt to manipulate, it is usually so heavy-handed that it is immediately obvious and therefore ineffective. They want the bottom line truth in relationships and, having little public image to defend, will go after exactly what they want. They are generous with their time and energy toward friends and have an immense stamina for partying.

Attractive Environments

Bosses are often power brokers, or back room politicians. The robber barons who seized control of the American financial empires. Mafia mentality: "my turf, our people." Hell's Angels, trade union leaders, backwoods survivalists, "Don't mess with me." Tenderhearted, tough-minded people. The corporate head who controls with one hand and enforces justice with the other. The developer who makes a fortune in condos and spearheads a program for homeless shelters.

Unattractive Environments

Bosses are usually not found in jobs that depend upon good behavior and following orders. They do not like situations that are susceptible to unpredictable power maneuvers or takeover. They mistrust jobs that rely on the goodwill of superiors, without the power of redress of grievances.

Famous Eights

Famous Eights include *Henry VIII*, who began his own religion, under heavy opposition, in part to legitimize his lust.

Fritz Perls □ Gurdjieff □ Madame Blavatsky □ Pablo Picasso
Sean Penn □ Nietzsche □ Eldridge Cleaver
Garfield the Cat

Subtypes

The psychological subtypes represent preoccupations that the Eight child developed as a way to minimize vulnerability. The control of one's own feelings and the control of the people who affect one's life buffer a resurgence of anxiety about being unfairly used.

Possession/Surrender in One-to-One Relationships

Eights want to possess the heart and mind of the mate. They desire access to the partner's soul. Surrender is the desire to give up obsessive needs for control to a partner who is completely trustworthy.

I went through a million therapists before I found the right one. He would call me on my bullshit and let me know exactly where he stood. I wound up able to see that what he pointed out to me was true, even though at first I disagreed with his position.

Friendship in Social Relationships

For Eights, friendship is the trust extended to those whom you protect and by whom you are protected.

It takes years for a friendship to develop. I get into agonizing as the tension builds up to fight, wondering if we'll make it through. Once I believe that they'll hold their ground and not go away, I trust them more, because I know that people spit out the truth in a fight and then there's nothing unspoken standing between us.

Satisfactory Survival in the Area of Self-preservation

Eights focus on control of the mechanics of personal survival and space. A preoccupation with the control of survival needs replaces the search for essential needs.

There's a kind of panic about anybody getting control of your life. Who gets in and out of your house? Has someone else used your hairbrush? You feel violated if someone hasn't left enough milk for the morning coffee. If the little things in life get out of control, it feels like opening the door to chaos.

What Helps Eights Thrive

Eights often resist entering therapy or beginning a meditation practice, because the prospect of allowing softer emotions to surface or accommodating to the wishes of others stimulates the fear of being controlled. Eights often come to therapy at the behest of their family, or by court referral. Typical presentations include problems with coworkers, depression, and excessive substance use.

Eights need to recognize when attention shifts from real wishes to a tough cover that denies those wishes. They can help themselves by

- Asking for clear definitions of a relationship. Seeing that fighting is a way to develop trust.
- Asking for a clear set of rules in relationship or in therapy. Recognizing the desire to break rules once they are made.
- Trying to see the buildup of circumstances that creates adversary relationships. Sensing when there is a desire to control or to stir up trouble as a way of seeing who is friend and who is foe. Letting others initiate action.
- Noting that feelings of boredom are a mask for other emotions.
- Trying to see the equally valid logic of other people's behavior. Noting that others are consistent within a different point of view.
- Noting that real feelings often begin with depression. Reframing depression as a sign of progress.
- Recognizing when real wishes are replaced by excessive socializing, substance abuse, and the desire to control people.
- Seeing how the preoccupation with justice and the protection of others can polarize people into friends or foes.
- Trying to shift attention from "my way versus your way" to recognize the many shades of opinion in between.
- Remembering to write down insights as they occur. Trying to work against pervasive forgetting. Remembering to review insights mentally as a way to combat denial.
- Learning to delay the expression of feelings. Learning to count to ten before letting anger out.

- Recognizing the habit of seeing the source of trouble as outside of oneself rather than recognizing one's own participation.
- Recognizing how hard it is to admit that one has been wrong.

What Eights Should Be Aware of

Intervention must account for an Eight's need to forget and deny feelings of vulnerability and dependency. Eights need to support any signs of emerging softer feeling or the ability to empathize with other points of view. As change occurs, Eights should be aware of reactions such as

- Misinterpreting sympathy from others as patronizing.
- Detail control. Premature overcontrol of the details of an interaction. "The whole party's off until I find my favorite saucepan."
- Alienating potential sources of help. The need to say the worst to someone for his or her own good. Intuitive tactlessness. Pressing other people's sore spots without recognizing the damage.
- Forgetting goals. Excessive entertainment, food, sex, drugs. More is better. Wanting the next mouthful before you've swallowed the one you have.
- Displaced aggression toward others who display a negative trait that is similar to one that is being unconsciously denied by the Boss.
- Difficulty with compromise. Wanting to either control or withdraw. No awareness of a middle ground.
- Fighting awareness of dependency. Experiencing small oversights as a betrayal of trust.
- Shut-down feelings. Periods when everything closes down. Not caring at all.
- Blame and the need to find fault as a way of countering vulnerability.

- Making rules and trying to assert control over others.
- An exuberant desire to break one's own rules as a way of feeling powerful and uncontrollable.
- Black despair, in the form of an overwhelming all-at-once awareness of negative past actions.

14. Point Nine: The Mediator

	ACQUIRED PERSONALITY		ESSENCE	
HEAD	Chief Feature:	INDOLENCE	Higher Mind:	LOVE
HEART	Passion:	SLOTH	Virtue:	RIGHT ACTION
	SUBTYPE WAYS OF BEING			
	Sexual:	SEEKING UNION		
	Social:	PARTICIPATION		
	Self-preservation:	APPETITE		

The Dilemma

Nines are the children who felt overlooked when they were young. They remember that their point of view was seldom heard and that other people's needs were more important than their own. Eventually Nines fell asleep, in the sense that their attention turned from real wishes and they became preoccupied with small comforts and substitutes for love. Realizing that their own priorities were likely to be discounted, they learned to numb themselves, to divert their energy from priorities, and to forget themselves.

When a personal priority does develop, it can be easily sidetracked. Errands can become as pressing as an important deadline; it appears that the entire desk must be cleaned before an overdue bill is paid. The closer a Nine gets to having the time and energy available for a priority, the more attention can get diverted into secondary pursuits. When time becomes available, less gets done, because the Nine may have difficulty telling the difference between a critical matter and less important things. One student of the Enneagram realized that she was a Nine when she was working to meet the deadline for a term paper and "woke up" to find that she had spent an entire morning of precious time trying to find matching lids for the storage jars in her kitchen.

Nines report that they lose contact with what they want by merging with the wishes of others, by diverting energy to secondary tasks, and by spacing out with a TV set, a predictable routine, and too much food or beer.

Nines tend to go along with other people's agendas. Believing that their own position will be discounted, but still wanting to maintain connection, they have learned to incorporate other people's enthusiasms as their own. The initial phases of a relationship or a new project often feel to Nines like they are being carried along with the excitement that other people are experiencing, rather than having made a clear decision to join. Nines can wake up in the middle phase of a commitment, feeling dragged along by the wishes of others, wondering how they got there, and having a hard time saying No.

Saying No is particularly difficult for people who are prone to taking on the feelings of others. Saying No to another person can feel as disappointing to Nines as being denied something in their own lives. It is far less threatening to appear to say Yes, to seem to agree because you haven't said No, and to go along, rather than run the risk of open anger, which could lead to separation.

The thread of connection between the Nine child and others depended on keeping the peace, on being able to sense out others' wishes and to go along with them. A Mediator's apparent agreeability, however, should not be mistaken for real commitment. Nines can go along with a situation for a long time while still trying to decide. It is so easy for them to identify with another person's point of view that they can see the rightness on all sides of a question. Why take a position, when every side has merit? Why have a personal priority, when it's so easy to feel the rightness of all parties concerned? Nines say that it is for easier to know the inner condition of others than it is to find a viewpoint of their own.

When a decision has to be made, a Nine still looks agreeable and may still be going along, but the outer placidity covers an internal turmoil. "Do I agree or do I disagree with my friend? Am I in this group or do I want to leave? Should I buy this house or look for another?" The list of obsessions is endless, and attention shifts back and forth between the sides of the question. It is less threatening to obsessively think about a decision than to make a choice and risk having one's efforts discounted, or having to defend a point of view against others. Nines have taken refuge in the safety of not knowing what they want, in not having a position to defend, and in staying in an uncommitted limbo where decisions are still pending.

Paradoxically, Nine is the most stubborn point on the Enneagram. Because Nines obsess over a decision does not mean that they can be hurried into resolving it. Those who try to help Nines along with a decision, or pressure them to take a side, find they dig in their heels and refuse to move. Nines do not necessarily see holding out as a No response. They are more likely to see holding out as resisting being pushed into a premature commitment, because they haven't yet made up their mind. Their deep anger at being unheard is contained by not making a choice. They are angry about having to go along with others and angry about being overlooked if they don't go along. A Nine's decision is to make no decision, to stay angry but to hold it in, and to seem to go along while internally remaining divided.

Once a position has been established, Nines can be just as stubborn about holding onto it as they were against having to choose it. The most natural state of mind is to be on the fence, both committed and still not sure, but once a position is adopted it feels so fragile to Nines that they tune out any compromise, lest they find themselves back up on the fence. Nines are called Mediators and keepers of the peace precisely because their natural ambivalence allows them to both agree and yet not fully commit to any one point of view.

Decision making is also slowed, because a Nine's mind is already stuffed with unresolved prior questions. Memories of events that happened years ago can surface with the force of something that happened just last week and need to be thought through yet one more time. Decisions mean that one has to finish up, let go, change, and move on, all of which restimulate fears of separation. Nines tend to take on more, while letting little go, and to want to continue a known course of action rather than risking a sudden shift.

Because other people's wishes seem more pressing than their own, Nines are faced with the choice of merging with others' agendas or of tuning others out so as not to be influenced. If pushed, they are likely to control by passive means, by slowing down, by sitting down in the middle of a conflict and waiting it out, by not responding and hoping that the problem goes away.

Mediators' difficulties with decisions, anger, and finding a personal position stem from the fact that they have forgotten themselves and made others the active agent in their lives. Their neurotic obsession about whether to agree or disagree with other people is both a burden and a blessing to them. Their burden is that they suffer from not knowing what they want, and their blessing is that by having lost a personal position, they are often able to intuitively incorporate with other people's inner experience. If you identify with each of the Enneagram types you are very likely a Nine.

Nine's habitual preoccupations include
- Replacement of essential needs with inessential substitutes. The most important things are left to the end of the day.
- Trouble with decisions. "Do I agree or disagree?" "Do I want to be here or don't I?"
- Acting through habit and by repeating familiar solutions. Ritualism.

- Difficulty in saying "No."
- Containment of physical energy and anger.
- Control through stubbornness and passive aggression.
- A way of paying attention that reflects other people's positions, which can lead to
  - Difficulty in maintaining a personal position, but also the development of a marked ability to sense others' inner experience. Similar to point Two, the Giver.

Family History

Nines felt overlooked as children and as a consequence formed the habit of discounting their own essential needs. They describe family situations that range from neglect to being overshadowed by siblings to being ignored or attacked when they stood up for their own ideas.

What is common to all of these childhood prototypes is the sense of not being listened to when an opinion was put forward and realizing that showing anger directly did not help their opinion to be heard.

I had very loving parents, but watched my older brother, who was the rebel in the family, not getting a lot of goodies because of his behavior. So it was clear to me that if I did it their way that I could get love by giving in to what they wanted. I recall one instance, when I was probably three or four years old, of being held so tightly by my mother that I was suffocating against her coat.

It felt like I could either struggle and be dropped or go limp in her arms. I essentially held my breath and gave in, and eventually became so attuned to taking on what my parents wanted that if I said No to them, I would feel their disappointment inside myself.

A Mediator's desire to keep the peace is often the result of having been caught between opposing factions. Why take sides when you can see the value in everyone else's opinion? Why add an opinion of your own when nobody will listen anyway?

It was damned if you do and damned if you don't. I was the youngest of four boys, and if I did what my parents approved of, then my brothers would get on me, and if I went with the brothers, then I was looked down upon by my parents. The easiest way was to stay hidden, to not take either side, and to stand there and space out until everybody went away. I remember once being punished by having to sit in a chair facing the corner. I was still there a few hours later when my mom remembered me, and by that time I was so far inside myself that I could have sat there all day.

Nine children become resigned to the fact that they cannot change the family situation. They learn to space out, to buffer their feelings with small physical comforts, to hang out until someone else takes the initiative.

My father was energetic and clever and related best when he was being adored. Mom had a lot of problems of her own and very little energy for the kids. It felt like safety was in sliding between the cracks without a ripple or a bump, and keeping everybody comfortable so that I would be included. There was always the feeling of getting along with the others, not because I really wanted to, but because their views felt louder to me than my own.

Do I Agree or Disagree?

The Mediator's point of view is best explained by its position at the apex of the Enneagram's inner triangle. With one leg grounded in image and conformity (Three), and the other leg rooted in antiauthoritarianism (Six), point Nine is caught in a conflict between wanting approval from others and wanting to disobey. The wing point One, which is the position of the good girl/good boy of the Enneagram, and the wing point Eight, which stands for the bad girl/bad boy, amplify the issue of wanting to be correct and wanting to go against the rules. Nines are said to have fallen asleep to themselves because their habit of attention focuses on whether to agree or disagree with other people's views, rather than looking to a position of their own. If a Nine commits to a position, it stimulates internal concern about either alienating others and therefore being abandoned, or about having to submit to others and therefore be controlled.

The Nine child attempted to resolve the dilemma of whether to comply or rebel by not choosing either option. Nines tend to sit down in the middle of a choice, rather than fighting, or withdrawing, or trying to influence the decision in a direct way. They seem to agree, because they haven't said "No" directly, but internally they may still be trying to decide. Saying "No" directly means having taken a side, and Nines are committed to seeing all sides of a question, so as not to have to choose. They may seem to agree, but are actually simply waiting to see how others work the situation out. "I wonder how each of them will work out their position?" Meanwhile, the Nine will wait and see. There is always time, there is always tomorrow. Without a strong motive, there is no driving force to make decisions tip in one direction or another. Without a firm position, there is always time for problems to work themselves out. Nines can hold up their end of a discussion while at the same time spacing out and not being there at all. In that way a Mediator can agree with everyone, while not running the risk of taking a side. The anxiety that Nines experience over personal choices is softened by setting up routines. Once they set a schedule, Nines can wake up in the morning and know exactly what they have to do without being faced with a choice. They can move from task to task by sectioning off just enough attention to get the job done, without having to think about it. When acting out of habit, Nines say that they "go on automatic," like sleepwalkers who go through life without volitional choice. There is no problem with having to choose, because the next thing to do is already scheduled and accounted for, but while complying with the task, Nines may be so internally preoccupied with other thoughts that they become oblivious to the environment. They are asleep at the wheel in the sense that while they are working, they are either so spaced out or so extremely preoccupied in thinking about unresolved personal material that an extreme effort is required to shift their attention to anything that is not within the routine.

Habit

The deadly sin of sloth is attributed to Nines because their habits are designed to drain energy and attention away from what is essential to them in life. The easiest way for a Nine to forget herself or himself is by surrendering attention to an addictive habit, which can range from craving narcotics or alcohol to numbing out on TV, gossip, and the small comforts of life. Nines can forget what's most precious to them in life if their existence is defined by a habit that has become so strong that they cannot think beyond it.

Most Nines have an elaborate repertoire of ways in which they can forget their real priorities, and they can be fiercely defensive about giving them up. For a Nine to give up an inessential substitute, such as a food habit or an addiction to TV, means giving up a predictable and comfortable way of diverting attention away from having to remember what she or he really wants out of life.

Many Nines develop high-level replacements for real priorities. For example, a pediatrician who is a Nine has for years had the dream of initiating a drop-in clinic for sick-child care. He says that he allowed himself to be diverted for year after year by sidetracking himself into the constant care of children within the existing hospital structure. His diversions were sometimes lifesaving, but at the end of each day for all those years he would remember his dream and realize how many times he had allowed himself to get drawn away from the pile of papers on his desk that involved his real priority.

A creative sidetrack takes years to play itself out and can have rewarding benefits of its own. Nines are energetic and productive within a structure that makes them feel secure, but if an activity is inessential, in that it is secondary to a deeply felt need, then it inevitably leads to the sense of having lost what is most important in life.

Nines say that they go "on automatic," that they learn a routine and then divert their extra energy to trivial pastimes. Secondary interests often get as much attention as those that are at the center of emotional or professional life; and what is most important is either left out or crowded in at the end of a busy day.

Once a habit is set, a Nine can look energetic and mentally present, but may, in fact, have sectioned off just enough attention to get the job done. For Nines it seems as if habit does the work and they need to wake up—by having to pay full attention—only when something spectacular intrudes upon them or they realize that a mistake has been made.

I've worked as a printer for years, and I'm able to operate high-speed presses with literally a fraction of my mind. At the same time that a huge operation is rolling and I'm checking out all the details on the paper run for a four-color job, I'm carrying out an interior monologue that can get as compelling as a face-to-face conversation with the people who are talking in my head. I'm in and out of memories that the interior conversation brings up, following the whereabouts of people passing through the shop, and remembering the fifteen other things that I have to do that day.

In the end it's as if the paper printed itself rather than me being aware of what I was doing. It can get crowded inside; the sense of being too full of too many things to do, all of which seem equally important at the same time. You're carrying the weight of them all, and because you feel responsible to get it all done, you get stuck and can't start on any of them. I can be shopping, and at the same time rerunning a memory that has enough charge in it that I miss the can of tomatoes that I need, when it's sitting on the grocery shelf in plain sight. Then there's the checkout line, where I can space out to the point where I, and the very loud thoughts in my head, bag the groceries, pay, and leave, but the bag gets left behind. Then I might find myself driving the long route home because it's the way that I used to drive from the store to my old apartment. It's fifteen minutes longer, but I've made the turn onto my old freeway entrance, and settled in with whatever I have to think about.

Structure can be a lifesaver to a Nine who is caught in the ambivalence of having to make an important choice. With a well-thought-out structure, a Nine can keep going because choices are directed from the outside. A good graduate program or the needs of a friend will pull a Nine's attention away from obsessive thinking and help the Nine refocus, because the pressure of constant choice has been eliminated.

Essential/Inessential

Real priorities will surface if there is enough time and energy available. Consequently, when a Nine needs to forget herself or himself, more commitments get taken on, while fewer original commitments get finished, giving an outward appearance of laziness. From the point of view of the Nine, there is so much to do that priorities get lost because of other commitments that have gotten in the way. Priorities often get buried because the Nine does not recognize the difference between essential and inessential tasks. The so-called lazy Nines are perpetually overburdened and therefore unable to complete what is most important to herself or himself.

I'm chopping carrots for lunch at noon, people are coming over, and I'm quite clear about what I've decided to make. I'm not sure whether I'm really up for company, but I start on the carrots. Pretty soon my mind wanders off on several trains of thought that seem equally real and relevant at the time. Laundry has to be done by tomorrow and so does the telephoning for next week. My mind moves into an unresolved conversation with one of the phone people, which brings up a memory of another conversation. I'm also seeing the drift of the curtains in the currents of the room, which brings another memory to the surface. I'm still in motion but have likely shifted to sorting laundry. It gets to be like a dream, the real room with the chopping board, and the piles of clothes, and the phone list half-completed, and the reveries, all of which seem just as important as the fact of guests arriving soon.

The essential noon deadline was never really forgotten, but it did get pushed to the periphery of other things to do. The personal decision, in this case whether to have guests for lunch in the first place, got buried by the shifting of attention to less important things. Eventually the decision was made by waiting too long to call the lunch date off.

Accumulation

Nines take on more without letting anything go. Extra space gets filled with clutter, extra time gets filled with errands. The mind gets filled with unfinished business, and a Nine's many circulating trains of thought effectively block out what is central and correct. As long as any question remains alive, no final decision is made. As long as the closet hasn't been totally cleared out, nothing has to be thrown away.

Mediators hold onto memories with a tenacity that gives them a charged existence. By holding on so firmly to the past, Nines make less of a commitment to their own present. Memories do not drop away easily, and can be turned to, and relived, with the vigor of having happened just last week.

A Nine's accumulation can be literal, like the hobbyist whose extra space is full of materials, collected and stored in case of need. Accumulation also extends to making collections of anything from teacups to vintage comic books. Specialty collecting lends a pleasurable structure to accumulation and allows a Nine to fill up free time in a useful way. One highly constructive version of accumulation is a Mediator's ability to absorb volumes of information about a favorite subject from every conceivable point of view and to reconcile the differences among them all. The following statement was given by an inveterate collector who specializes in first editions and butterflies.

There's an appetite to collecting, which is very much like getting the munchies late at night, and wanting to drive all over town to get whatever you're hungry for. The feeling takes over that you've got to have that particular kind of cookie or that exact brand of peanut butter, and you're willing to go twenty miles to get it. Whenever I'm most confused in my life, I know exactly what I want to eat, and exactly which book I want for my collection. There's also a kind of shopping appetite, where everything you see seems really useful at the time.

I recently cleared out our closets and took several bags to a flea market sale for my kid's Girl Scout troop, and realized, after I got home, that I had brought back one bag more of everybody else's kitsch than I had taken away.

Containment of Energy

Anger serves the function of clarifying a personal position. We know exactly what we don't want when we are angry, which brings us a little closer to becoming aware of what we do want. Likewise, if we have a lot of physical energy, it's harder to block out the awareness of what we want to do with that energy. If Mediators become energetic enough to become angry, then a clear position would have to emerge, at least by a process of elimination. Not that Nines have to eventually eliminate everything but a first choice. In fact, Nines are more able to make a decision if offered a series of choices. The one that isn't rejected is the preferred option. Nines often manage to siphon off their energy before it gets to the critical point of getting angry or having to make a choice.

I've had on ongoing weight problem for all of my life, with fluctuations of over fifty pounds. I finally got on a regimented exercise program to get mobilized for a thesis that I had to write, which turned out to be highly successful. I started to sleep less and got mobilized during the day. The difficulty for me was that the more awake I got, the more projects started to materialize.

I wound up doing a house renovation, because the resale possibility was too good to lose, and began two new relationships, which also seemed too good to miss out on. I had the real sensation of my physical energy being sucked away from the thesis and spreading out into everything else I had to do.

Nine is the core position for the three anger types, Eight–Nine–One, situated at the top of the Enneagram, and is the point of passive aggression, where anger fell asleep. By keeping available energy siphoned off into inessential tasks, a kind of holding action develops, in which there is never enough energy in the system to face the conflict that surrounds going after personal desires.

Nines commonly report these reactions to feeling surplus physical energy: They can spread it to secondary interests. They can absorb the extra energy by overeating or overindulging in some other way. They can paradoxically feel exhausted and want to sleep while not being physically tired. Or they can use the energy to face the task of knowing what they want.

I literally fell asleep on the mat for the first year that I studied martial arts. I'd look forward to the class, I was fine during warm-ups, and by the time we'd get to falls and throws, I'd be zinging with energy. A couple of times I remember checking my backrolls in the practice mirror that ran the length of the hall. My complexion was high, I felt great, and the next thing I remember, we sat to watch the teacher demonstrate, and the guy next to me had to nudge me awake, because I had spaced out and fallen asleep as soon as I sat down.

The idea of operating with all that energy in the real world is terrifying. It's exhilarating for a moment, and then I get scared, and then I get caught up in the old obsessions, almost with a feeling of relief.

Inertia and Depression

The containment of energy guarantees a state of equilibrium, where there is always just enough energy to maintain the inessentials and leave the essential task for the end of the day. In this way there is no time for depression, which might creep in if there was nothing to do, and certainly no time for raised expectations or the setting of real priorities. By sticking with familiar, known activities, Nines maintain a holding pattern that forestalls having to face a dead halt, or having to set priorities for a new phase of action.

I feel that if I stop that I'll never start up again. I once spent the better part of two years hanging out between the couch, the refrigerator, and the TV set. I was responsible to no one, and in between naps would take long walks by myself, feeling totally free. When I finally realized that I was depressed, it felt like I could die without ever having known what I was supposed to do with my life. I will do anything to avoid that place of no energy and no hope.

Inertia is one of the laws of physics. It states that a body at rest tends to stay at rest and that a body in motion tends to stay in motion. The body-at-rest phase of the law applies to a Nine's quality of "armchair" depression, in which nothing much is expressed in words, but life comes to a dead halt in the slouched, unhappy contours of a comfortable living room chair. When a Nine is in dead halt, she or he usually needs help from the outside. A new relationship, or a new opportunity, or a clearly defined schedule can help the Nine get going again. Nines can rally more easily if they can attach themselves to another's enthusiasm or respond to another person's need.

I can find myself having done something for ten years, but it doesn't seem to me that I have chosen it. It never felt like a choice or an aspiration. I went to law school and joined a partnership in that way, feeling like I had backed into it, that it was simply there to do. If I had to admit that I made my own decision, then I would have to get mobilized behind really being a lawyer, which makes me wonder who is being a lawyer, because I'm not identified with the profession. I always seemed led to my position, or I got there through a back door or a chain of circumstances that I never initiated. I could, of course, describe the course of action that my life seems to have taken on, but I could not say that I decided to arrive where I am.

Once energy is mobilized in an activity, the Nine is out of depression, but may still remain oblivious to real needs. The second phase of the law of inertia states that a body in motion tends to stay in motion, which means that an active Nine has a choice between the old habit of sectioning off enough attention to perform the activity mechanically or paying close attention to themselves until a real priority can emerge.

Anger That Went to Sleep

Nines express their anger indirectly. The hope is that leaking anger off through indirect actions will forestall that open confrontation that seems to lead either to abandonment or to having to defend a position against other people.

Having to make a choice can be so traumatic that decisions are often made by letting the situation deteriorate to the point that it falls apart. Because Nines know what they don't want, rather than what they do want, there is also a tendency to store up complaints internally until a critical level is reached and a volcanic outburst occurs. A choice is often made because the current situation has become impossible.

I worked as a teacher in a music school for a long time, and the treatment of the teachers was just awful, but I could never get myself together to go to the office and say, "This has to be reorganized, it's no good." I just let it go on until a terrible scene happened in front of a student, where I stormed out and then wrote a letter where I hit them with all the negative things that I'd known about them all along and stored up while I was still trying to see things from their side.

It was an avalanche letter with a lot of unpleasant repercussions, which wouldn't have gotten played out if I hadn't had to wait until they became an intolerable bad guy for me to pit myself against.

There is a tendency to hold onto unexpressed anger until a critical level of irritation is reached that forces a Nine into action. Holding onto unexpressed resentment is a way of internally not complying with others, while appearing to agree, and that resentment provides the fuel for passive aggressive tactics.

Nines report that they express their anger in several indirect ways. The first is by going stubborn, which means planting oneself down in the middle of a discussion and controlling the action by refusing to make a move. Another way is to simply tune other people out and head for other things to do; or by acting in such a way that others will have to show their anger first.

Mediators always know what other people want, and so they can make others angry by simply not doing what is expected.

They could, for example, perform poorly on the details of an important job, or begin to slow down when others are in a rush, or play dumb while knowing that others are highly invested in a certain course of action. One way or another, an angry Nine will see to it that the other person does not get what she or he is expecting.

The direct expression of anger is a great relief to Nines. An argument is the culmination of a great deal of holding back and internalizing of the positions of all the parties involved, and it is simply a relief to have the argument over and done with.

Anger takes a long time to surface, because at first other people's opinions seem correct to a Nine. Next comes a long period of delay, while the matter gets examined from all sides involved. Finally the conviction emerges that it's all right to be angry, and last of all anger is expressed, and often with such volcanic force that it can be shocking to those who have become used to a Mediator's agreeable side. There is often a long period of sullen slowdown before an outburst, but when sleepy Nines wake up to the fact that they are actually angry, they are said to resemble hibernating bears: furious because they have waited so long for the satisfaction of essential needs.

It is difficult to recognize my own position, but often enough I'm angry about what other people are doing, but don't show it. In those few times in the course of a year that I explode, it feels terrific. It's exhilarating. My whole body is alive and it's pounding. That bodily rush feels like the reward for having found my position and put it out.

The trick now is to be able to get going without having to build a case against somebody, so that I can find myself by opposing them. It's also a revelation to me that the world isn't going to fall at my feet just because I've put my position out. It takes so much to even say what I want that I feel terrible when I then have to go out and do all the work to make it happen.

Intimate Relationships

Mediators take on their partner's interests and priorities as their own. The partner becomes the reference point for decisions, with the Nine either animated by the other's wishes or stoically holding out against the partner's will. Nines describe this centering of attention on the partner as merging with the other. They say that merger is implicit in relationships where there is love and that with merger the sense of separation between people disappears. Nines are often more able to describe the other's feelings than they are able to recognize their own. They also report an uncomfortable feeling of possessiveness and the need to blame if decisions do not turn out well, precisely because they have made the other the active agent in determining a personal point of view.

When Nines love, it is often with the wish to totally merge with a partner, to take on the other's life as their own, rather than with the desire to manipulate, to profit, or to dominate the partnership.

Mediators typically have greater capacity to generate energy for a partner's needs than for themselves, so that relationship is a key way for Nines to get going. They identify so strongly with the desires of others that, on the positive side, there is a real ability to know another person in depth and, on the negative side, there is the possibility of losing a personal point of view.

I can become so aware of what my husband wants that when he questions me about what I want, I flounder. I can lose myself totally in what I feel as our connection, so that it's a question of Whose face is whose? Whose emotions are whose? It's the feeling of completely blending, that there's one person between two, and it can happen suddenly, so that I'm standing on the other side of the room, feeling that I've left myself and become him. If he prods me for a position, especially when I feel merged, it feels like he wants me to say something that will separate me from him, and I don't want to break the connection.

Because Nines are able to sense a partner as a part of themselves, there is the desire to merge completely with an ideal mate, who will then become the motive for life. There is also great difficulty in letting a relationship go, because it feels like cutting off a part of one's own existence. Consequently, relationships often continue on long after the juice has run out, with both partners relating out of habit rather than from real choice. Without a partner to relate to, Nines experience their own inner numbness and a feeling of What's the use? Numbness can also be masked by indiscriminate attraction to multiple partners or by putting energy into inessential activities that artfully disguise the neglect of real needs.

Nines want to be consulted, to have their opinions drawn out, and to be helped toward their own position. Their wish to merge, however, is coupled with an equally powerful wish to be autonomous, to fight the desire to dissolve into another, and to struggle against what the partner might demand. Outer compliance is often matched by an inner defiance that is acted out by an unwillingness to make the final gesture, a digging in against complete commitment, a holding onto the inner question Am I making the proper choice?

The fact that I can get so merged with a woman makes me feel controlled. If my expectations are aroused, and then the rug gets pulled out, I can hold the grudge, literally, for ten years, and the memory can come up with the same feelings of jealousy that I had back then.

If I'm the one who wants out, I get on the fence of not wanting to go and not wanting to stay either, which is so familiar to me that I feel stuck in a kind of ambivalence that can go on, literally, for years. Meanwhile, I've indicated very little to the woman that I'm with.

I'd be likely to find some indirect way of dealing with her, by going for support to other people, or somehow reporting my feelings from a distance. If I start to obsess too much on whether to go or to stay, I'd also be likely to start up a lot of relationships, without being able to make up my mind about which one I preferred.

On the high side of relationship, Nines can offer unconditional regard to others. Having little image or position to defend, a Nine can listen nonjudgmentally. Nines can identify with other people's emotional needs, often feeling another's dilemma within themselves. They can hold a solid and productive schedule in the midst of emotional difficulty.

On the low side Nines can fall asleep to real motivations and love out of habit rather than because the feeling is alive. The highs and lows of emotional life can be reduced to a safe middle ground of predictable relating.

An Example of a Couple Relationship: Nine and Two, the Mediator and the Giver

The Nine is often confused about personal purpose, which draws the Two forward with the desire to help. To the extent that this is a mature effort, the Nine will be pleased to be singled out to receive attention. Nines flourish with support and affection and are more likely to develop their own potentials if they are pleasing to someone else. The Two will be particularly helpful if the Nine does, in fact, have the potential to excel in an area in which the Two can take pride.

Both partners merge emotionally. Nines want to find a motive for living through a mate, and Twos want to find out which of their many selves is authentic. As a consequence, each can be deeply affected by the other at a nonthinking level. The Two tends to alter along the lines of "what my partner would like," a maneuver that the Nine is often able to detect because a Nine also merges. The Nine is in a position to help the Two tell the difference between the authentic self and the adjusted self, and the Two is in a position to alter into an image that will move the Nine erotically.

Each will focus attention on the other, and each will wish to meet the other's needs. Nines can use sex as a way to wake up to real contact, and Twos like sexual attention. Although Twos may prefer attention to actual sex, both partners will have a natural understanding of nonverbal contact that can become a cornerstone of the relationship. The sexual encounter could stand as a metaphor for the best support that a Nine–Two couple can offer each other. The Two is asking, What do you want? and the Nine is responding, I want you as you really are, which is the self for which a Two is in search.

A Two is conscious of physical image and social charisma and will boost the Nine's confidence in personal style and presentation. The Two will draw the Nine's potentials out in the safe environment the couple has created. To the extent that a Nine remains uncertain of a personal direction in life, she or he will merge with the Two's agenda and become what the partner wants. If this happens, then the Nine will mold herself or himself into whatever will make the Two proud. The Nine is likely to wake up in the middle of the relationship and realize that choices of job, friends, personal style, and time commitments have all been influenced by the partner's will.

A crisis emerges when the Two has become indispensable and the Nine starts to feel controlled. The Nine suspects that she or he is really working to fulfill the Two's unrecognized needs and responds by stubbornly refusing to cooperate. Nine holds her or his own potential back as a way of getting even and spreads attention to other things. Two gets bored if Nine fails to potentiate and furious if attention is withdrawn.

The boredom reaction leads a Two toward demanding freedom. The demand for freedom wakes a Nine up, but makes the Nine possessive, which adds fuel to the Two's freedom demands. If Nine chooses to withdraw attention, the Two partner becomes furious and competitive about getting attention back. Nine exerts maximum power in the relationship by not giving attention when it is expected. This kind of severe standoff can be eased by the Two supporting the real aspirations of the Nine, rather than using the Nine to meet personal needs, and by the Nine taking responsibility for finding out what is really essential in life.

Authority Relationships

Nines are good leaders if the situation presents a clear course of action, but they are not comfortable if leadership demands a continuing set of decisions. Decisions are difficult because the pros and cons can appear to have equal merit, which, when coupled with the Nine's tendency to polarize against new or risky procedures, can lead to a holding action in leadership. Nines prefer known procedures and predictable outcomes, rather than the uncertainty of raised hopes, which could lead to disappointment.

As employees, Nines relate to authority through organizational structure. Relationships are best when there are clear procedures for advancement and reward. Nines may or may not actively compete for the rewards, but want to know that the opportunity is there. The Nine habit of merging into the lives of others manifests as taking on the coloration and opinions of coworkers. Nines will blend with the situation, not with the authority. They may be ambivalent toward those who are in power, both wanting to be directed and sullen about being told what to do. Anger toward authority is likely to be expressed indirectly, through slipshod job performance or passive aggressive behavior.

On the high side of authority relationships, Nines are excellent mediators because they can identify with all opinions involved. They are especially effective if they are brought in before the stage of open hostilities. They want friendly and cooperative feelings and are interested in hearing out other people's points of view. They work well if given public credit and positive regard, but will not actively seek out recognition. They flourish in a situation that offers a fair and regular return for efforts.

On the low side, Nines can internalize the tensions of a group without being able to articulate constructive change. The sense of a personal position is weak and objections are often unvoiced even if they are recognized: "They wouldn't listen anyway." Nines tune out the problem rather than taking action, hoping it will go away.

Nines can indirectly control by shifting responsibility or spacing out on duties. Unexpressed anger can lead to a stubborn resistance to being supervised. There is a pattern of inertia in job performance: hard to begin, mobilizing near the deadline, and a high-speed completion crisis. Once in gear it is hard to stop, and the surplus energy may spread to trivial activities.

An Example of an Authority Relationship: Nine and Seven, the Mediator and the Epicure

A Nine leads by setting up schedules, appointing enthusiastic helpers, and moving along methodically. These habits are diametrically opposed to a Seven's desires for experimentation and cooperative leadership. An unhappy relationship can develop if the Nine goes mute and does not clarify or defend a position, and the Seven rebels by redefining the procedures for self-advantage and by taking on several projects simultaneously. The Seven will see the Nine as ponderous and uncompromising, and the Nine will see the Seven as flighty and uncommitted.

The Nine boss will have trouble supervising the Seven if this requires confrontation. The tendency is to let things slide to a crisis point, with the hope that the employee will get back on track without having to be personally informed. Once blame has set in, a Nine boss can be unforgiving and unwilling to negotiate, while at the same time withdrawing leadership. Eventually a confrontation will occur, with the Nine dug into a no-compromise position and the Seven employee still uninformed about the severity of the situation.

If both are mature, a rearrangement of responsibility can resolve this difficulty. For example, Sevens are talented at meeting and greeting and are not overly interested in co-opting leadership. The Seven can handle promotional efforts without the Nine feeling undermined by an employee's professional ambition. The Nine must be willing to direct the Seven and to clearly state how projects are to be represented, as the Nine will want a conservative image, whereas the Seven will gravitate toward a more innovative presentation. The Seven, in turn, has to accept the Nine's need for accountability and document all follow-through.

If the Seven is boss, procedures can become muddled or even contradictory. A Seven's thinking process can alter what sounds like a definite promise into one of many possible options. Leadership will seem capricious to the Nine, who then becomes uncertain of a position. If Nine feels unappreciated a passive sabotage will ensue. The Nine will lose interest and slow down to the bare requirements of the project's needs, leaving loose ends that will attract the boss's attention. There will be a stubborn resistance against any supervisory efforts, an insistence upon working at her or his own pace and timing, and an estranged silence that broadcasts unexpressed anger.

This predicament can be avoided if the Nine employee's opinion is sought out and a place is made for grievances to be ventilated. If a Nine feels heard, then the passive aggressive stance can be averted. If the Nine is not drawn out, then she or he may stoically accept the situation, harbor resentment, and fall asleep at the wheel. If the Seven boss is wise, the Nine employee will be put in charge of scheduling, guidelines, and the kind of detail work that Sevens dislike. If the project is in trouble, the Nine can offer steadfast support over long periods of time. If the project can be salvaged, a Nine can mobilize enormous reserves of energy for a last-minute save.

Assets

Nines can offer unwavering support. The quality of support is special, because Nines have less investment in having things go their way than they do in mediating, in keeping the peace.

Nines are deeply affected by the lives of other people. They can listen and accept another, without having to exert power over the relationship, or insert themselves into a troubled person's life. They are able to listen and to understand. More important, they are able to sense what is essential in other people's lives. Precisely because they have systematically submerged their own position in favor of reflecting the wishes of others, they are gifted in their ability to identify what is crucial to other people's well-being.

Attractive Environments

Attractive environments for Nines include jobs that depend on routine, protocol, and recognized procedures. Bureaucracy, jobs that depend upon keeping track of detail.

Unattractive Environments

It's rare to find Nines in high-image jobs that require continuous self-promotion. They are not happy in jobs that require rapid turnover in procedures, or where structure and detail is sacrificed in favor of theory.

Famous Nines

The U.S. Postal Service is a famous Nine. It's great on organization and detail. The rules are implemented by the workers slowing down when it's important to speed up and politely putting up the Closed sign on the door at 2:59 p.m., while you are running up the walk with your package.

Julia Child □ Luciano Pavarotti □ Buckminster Fuller Oblamov □ Eisenhower □ Alfred Hitchcock □ Ringo Starr

How Nines Pay Attention

When Nines "go on automatic," they can complete complicated tasks without paying conscious attention to what their hands and bodies are doing. We all have the ability to learn skills and to perform them mechanically. For example, there is the common experience of "waking up" upon arriving home, with no recollection of having made the drive. There is also the example of speed typists, who report that they can fantasize or think about a problem, while turning out reams of accurate copy at 90 wpm.

The trick for the typists is to type without reading the material. They section off just enough attention to get the mechanics of the job done, while simultaneously ruminating about other things. This style of attention can be called coprocessing, a way of doing more than one mental operation at the same time.

Nines report that they dip in and out of conversations. A sector of their attention is mechanically focused on what is being said, but they can simultaneously coprocess another train of thought or feel themselves merging into what they suppose other people are feeling. Most Nines describe coprocessing as sliding from one object of attention to another. For example, a word in a conversation may trigger a memory, trigger an inner monologue about the memory, trigger feelings about how the present conversation is similar to the past.

These interior diversions go on while the Nine is still aware of how the conversation is developing. Like the motorist who arrived at home without a memory of having driven there, Nines can wake up to hear themselves give a passable reply, having forgotten the topic of conversation. Nines say that they tune their mental radio to two or three stations, slipping between classical, country, and rock 'n' roll.

A profound version of the ability to coprocess is described by some Mediators as having a mind full of pinwheels. In this version attention is simultaneously focused on several things at once, perhaps the carpet pattern, the buttons on a sleeve, a profound emotion, and a couple of trains of thought. A Nine who looks blanked out and inattentive to others may internally be laboring under the burden of too much to do.

Because Nines are asleep with respect to their own position, they do not habitually look for information that supports a strategic course of action. New situations can be perceived globally, where all the elements are recognized and can be described, but no one thing stands out as particularly important or worthy of mention. This is in contrast to the perception of point Three, which is focused on the elements in new situations that support particular tasks. It is also distinct from the perception of type Six, which is skewed toward the hidden interactions between people.

Nine is aware of all the surface elements and all the interactions under the surface, but finds it hard to pick out what is important and significant from the inessential details. Nines are aware of everything, but they find it difficult to identify the correct starting point or discriminate between the critical issues and the background noise. Attention circulates freely between what is essential in a situation and what is irrelevant to the central task. It is this habit of attention that perpetuates the loss of a personal position. How can one decide upon a meaningful position when everything seems to have equal importance? There is no sense of conflict, because nothing stands out as more important than anything else.

Intuitive Style

As children, Nines felt overlooked, and eventually they learned to maintain connection by sensing the qualities of others within their own bodies. When their global style of paying attention is focused on other people, Nines may find themselves "being" another person who has had a strong influence on them. Nines sometimes have the feeling that they are being taken over. For example, they may lose their own position so completely in a conversation that they start to pick up the mannerisms, the energetic quality, and even the opinions of someone who has captured their attention. Nines seem to perceive others as a whole, taking in whatever they sense is going on within a friend.

When I am close to somebody, it's like one person is sitting in the room instead of two. There's no separation: I forget myself but am full of impressions in my body, which I have learned may be because I am being my friend for a while. Once I feel connected there's no desire to separate or pull back. The deepest intimacy that I know is being so merged with whatever my friend is going through that it's happening to me at the same time.

Nines relate to the word *merger*. They report that they can describe another person's point of view far better than their own. They describe their merger as becoming another person, and their self-descriptions of how they blend sound remarkably like the sensing practices that underlie the disciplines of martial arts. The blend of a martial arts training is organized to accomplish exactly that sense of inseparableness that the Nine child felt driven to achieve.

I am driving across the Golden Gate Bridge, and my attention is attracted to someone in a car in the next lane. All of a sudden I'm starting to feel how that guy is sitting in the driver's seat and how he's driving his car. And then I'm driving like he's driving, and I'm taking on his body shape and handling the car his way, although by now he's fifty feet away.

Consider the similarity between the Nine driver's experience of merging and this statement taken from a third-degree Aikido black belt, who is a Six.

The blend happens from the belly. You learn to extend your perceptions to include the space around your body and to sense whatever comes into your field as if it's within yourself. You can feel the force and quality of people's movement, and you learn to join with it and make it your own.

Mediators say that they can sometimes feel whatever is in other people's bodies, that when they are "being" another person that there can be a physical sensing of their illnesses or their health and an awareness of the discrepancies between feelings and thoughts or between conflicting desires. Nines seem to take in others as a whole and often have difficulty sorting out the source of their information while they are in the physical presence of someone who affects them strongly. Is this your reaction, or my own? Am I enthusiastic about a project, or am

I picking up your excitement? Do I want to go to the movies, or am I merged with what you would like to do? Do I feel good about what I have done, or do I sense that you are pleased with me? When the other physically leaves, a Nine's attention tends to return to the self, and she or he remembers a personal position again. Nines can merge with many people in the course of a single day, but feel particularly drawn to merging when they love or when they are drawn into union by someone else's need.

Intuitively inclined Nines are also able to merge with decisions that have many diverse components. The following statement comes from a San Francisco businessman.

I've been a manager for over twenty years, and I make my decisions both by analyzing the problem completely and also by getting a literal body reading of the way that the factors in the organization feel inside myself. I install the feel of one of the organization's units inside my body, then start to sense other components against it. Sometimes there's a feeling of fit, but often I can get quite involved readings from the sense of how different elements interact inside me.

The Virtue of Action

Laziness for a Nine is not necessarily laziness of body, in the sense of not holding a job, or sleeping late in the morning. Nines often hold two jobs and pride themselves on having a lot of physical energy. They do a lot, but are blocked in the ability to perceive a correct course of action and to stay on track without becoming diverted by inessentials.

There's always a mass of things in the way between me and what I really want to do. My mind looks like a cluttered room full of boxes stuffed with memos. I'm scurrying between the piles, trying to get a little bit of each thing done before one of the piles topples over on me. It looks like nothing is getting done from the outside, but that's because I'm running between piles of too many things to do on the inside.

I have always known that I had tremendous reserves available to me, because every now and then I have a day when there's no tie-up between knowing what I have to do and being able to get directly to it.

I had one fabulous experience of being directly merged with an action during a freak accident where a boulder fell on the highway just after we had passed the spot. I knew that a car would be swerving around that same bend and would smash into it, and without thinking about what I was going to do, I got out, ran full speed back up the highway, and shoved it off.

There was no way that I could have moved that much weight, and yet there it had happened. That incident is one of the benchmarks of my life, because in my desperation the rock and I were one thing, and all I had to do was move myself.

Love as a Quality of Higher Mind

Nines tend to absorb the identity of the group, the environment, or the significant people to whom they relate. On a psychological level, there is a need to identify with the wishes of others as a way of being included and as a compensation for forgetting to pay attention to the self. Without a group or partner to relate to, Nines experience their own internal numbness and report a sense of "What's the use? If it's for myself, alone, then life is meaningless."

If a Nine forms a relationship out of the desire to merge attention with an ideal partner who then becomes the reason for existence, then, in fact, the higher mental quality of love is not present in that relationship. Nines can merge and take on the partner's life as their own, but the real agenda is, Please don't separate from me, and I will not oppose you. Because Nines can merge so totally in love, they are also vulnerable to terrible feelings of jealousy and despair, as if their very being is threatened by the loss of someone who is perceived as part of themselves.

In its higher aspect, love has less to do with an emotional response than with a specific placement of attention that requires a reference point within the self from which the beloved can be included. The task is to learn to tell the difference between losing a personal reference point, and therefore being taken over by the wishes and feelings of others, and being able to sense the condition of others while still being aware of the self. Nines have the potential of loving unconditionally in that they have a lifelong habit of perceiving others through their own bodies. Their habit is to sense others within themselves without the desire to control or to make other people change.

Subtypes

Psychological subtypes represent preoccupations that Mediators developed during childhood as a way to replace real wishes with compensatory substitutes. Replacement buffers a resurgence of the anxiety that the child experienced when personal wishes were overlooked by adults whose priorities lay elsewhere.

Union in the One-to-One Relationship

For Nines, union is the desire to completely merge oneself with a mate. The preoccupation can also extend to an absorbing wish to unite with the divine.

When I meet someone there's the sense of recognizing several inputs at the same time. I get so drawn into all the levels of what they're saying, and all the ways that the different parts of them are reacting, that the actual words seem almost irrelevant.

In intimate relationships the feeling of connection with my husband has gotten intense enough that I feel the rewards for my own accomplishments through him. For myself alone, I am deadened to the pleasure of what I do, yet I can feel his reactions inside of myself, and when he feels good about me, I can identify my own pleasure through him.

Participation in Social Groups

Nines are either totally aversive to joining groups, or they like to hang out with social groups, such as special activity clubs, and with friends. There is an attraction to the energy of people doing something together, which provides a pleasant distraction but also provides a constant background of energy that the Nine can dip in and out of. Here's a statement from a Nine who likes to participate.

When I was a kid, I was a champion bowler. I set up leagues for most nights and stayed continuously active with them. Interestingly, although I'd practice hours a week to perfect my style, I had less juice for the win than I had for the camaraderie and the feeling of being carried away on the enthusiasm of the teams.

Appetite in the Area of Self-preservation

Nines have a habit of replacing essential wishes with inessential substitutes, such as too much food, too much TV, too many novels, or elaborate hobby interests. Appetite also extends to collecting voluminous amounts of information about a secondary pursuit.

I was writing an article for publication, which mattered a great deal to me. The typewriter faced out on our back yard, which started off an out-of-control chain of events. When I sat down to work, I'd be attracted to the need for a view to center me, so I bought gardening books, I drew detailed seasonal maps, so there'd be a constant rotation of color, I organized a block committee to buy plants and shrubs collectively. I spaded up and planted the entire backyard, and I lost three months on my article.

What Helps Nines Thrive

Mediators need to recognize when they are starting to fall asleep. In this context *sleep* means shifting attention from a genuine personal priority to obsessional thinking or an inessential activity. Nines often enter therapy or begin a meditation practice because they have gotten off track with an important commitment, or have engaged in a bout of substance abuse. Typical presentations are depression, as inessential activities come to a standstill, or the surfacing of rage. Nines must be aware of their ability to act through force of habit while "asleep." An asleep Nine can section off just enough attention to appear to be perfectly present in a conversation or in the therapy hour, while at the same time cushioning what they hear.

As creatures of habit, Nines tend to take on the coloration of the environment in which they find themselves. Change can come about more easily with a change of environment and paced, methodical efforts toward building new habits. Eager for identity, Nines respond well to structured support, such as a schedule that is reinforced by tangible evidence of success and the enthusiasm of friends. Support should be offered unconditionally in order to avoid the question of complying with, or rebelling against, others. Nines can help themselves by

- Finding a way to get positive regard from others for a personal position and to set a structure to get the position accomplished.
- Noticing when another person becomes the referent for decisions. "Do I agree or disagree with him?"
- Noticing when an obsession with the pros and cons of a decision has replaced real feelings and real desire.
- The strategic use of deadlines, structuring of projects as a way to stay focused on goals.
- Recognizing when personal opinions are being withheld.
- Voicing own opinions.
- Learning to finish projects without becoming diverted to other things.
- Focusing on the feelings that precede the shift of attention to inessential substitutes, such as food or TV. Observe the feelings as they come up, rather than going for replacements.
- Asking for choices. Nines know more easily what they don't want, and by process of elimination get to preferences.
- The exercise of acting out other people's positions, then acting out their own position, as if they were somebody else.

- Learning to set limits on time and commitments when attention spreads to inessentials.
- Focusing on immediate next step, rather than final goal. The final goal will seem too voluminous to handle.
- Being aware of going stubborn when pushed.
- Expressing anger through the imagination. Imagine saying or doing the worst, until the charge of anger lessens.

What Nines Should Be Aware of

As attention is withdrawn from the inessential, Nines report reactions such as those in the following list. Rather than viewing these as merely neurotic, they can be seen as signs of progress during change. As priorities materialize, anger that has been expressed in passive aggressive ways, such as going stubborn or slowing down, will come to the surface. Anger is the energy of change and can be cultivated to make a personal position clear.

- Becoming dependent upon sources of help and not wanting to separate.
- Blame. Having been so merged with the wishes of others that "it's their fault" when things go wrong.
- Going stubborn. Feeling pushed by others. Unwillingness to bring up loaded issues. Holding out, which forces others to move first.
- Eagerness for new commitments that suck up time and energy.
- Tuning out. Dipping in and out of conversations, thinking of several things at once.
- Having to discriminate between real decisions and the tendency to let small issues occupy attention obsessively.
- Having to discriminate between real goals and the habit of setting routines and acting mechanically.

- Numbing out. Waiting other people out until they go away. Waiting out difficult conversations rather than voicing a position. Wanting the unstated negatives to remain unsaid.
- Not wanting to put all the pieces together that would demand a definitive position. Needing more information, waiting for an explanation, looking for a holding action, hoping it will go away.
- The idea that the job is already done once a mental priority has been reached. Judging self by potentials and others by what they actually do.
- Leaving loose ends on the job. Feeling irritated and not wanting to be careful. Minimum output.
- The feeling that simple tasks are overwhelming burdens, that it is hard to begin. There is too much to do. Where will the energy come from? Tasks require too much effort, which leads to
  - Extreme sensitivity to having efforts overlooked, criticized, discounted.
  - Fearing risk and fearing change. Believing that change will lead to further suffering.
  - Diverting attention away from the self by introducing sidetracks in conversation, telling lengthy sagas about oneself and repeating old material.

Appendix: Empirical Research on the Enneagram

Empirical study of the Enneagram typology has recently begun, based on published descriptions of the Enneagram theory.[1-3] Studies in this area are useful to the degree that research findings integrate Enneagram theory with Western concepts of personality. Current research focuses on the stability of the individual person's Enneagram point over time and the relation of Enneagram type to other theories of personality. Also, researchers are developing personality assessment instruments that may reliably and validly predict Enneagram type.

Initial Research on the Enneagram

A first research program, reported by Wagner and Walker,[4, 5] examined 390 adults who knew the Enneagram system. Most of the subjects were members of various Roman Catholic religious congregations in the Midwest.

To assess the stability of Enneagram type over time, subjects were contacted and asked to report their original and current self-determined Enneagram point. The time lapse from initial learning of the Enneagram until the survey was conducted ranged from three months to nine years. The respondents averaged 85 percent agreement about their type in the past and present.

These subjects also completed the Myers-Briggs Type Indicator (MBTI), Millon-Illinois Self-Report Scale, and an experimental Enneagram inventory at varying times before, during, and after learning the Enneagram. The MBTI, based on Jungian personality types, is designed to assess patterns of attitudes, assumptions, and actions on the personality dimensions of introversion–extraversion, thought–feeling, sensing–intuition, and judgment–perception.[6] The Millon-Illinois Self-Report Scale [7] is designed to assess personality patterns that are organized into eight personality styles. Wagner notes that Millon's formulation of the development of personality patterns "parallels the conception of the development of ego-fixations" in the Enneagram typology.[8]

Wagner found significant differences among Enneagram point groups on the Myers-Briggs and Millon scales, with patterns of descriptors summarized by him as follows:

Table 1. Comparison of Positive Correlations Among Enneagram Styles, Millon Personality Patterns, and Myers-Briggs Preferences (from Wagner and Walker, 1983)

Enneagram types	Millon Scales	Myers-Briggs Scales
Point One	Disciplined	Judging
Point Two	Cooperative, sociable	Extravert, feeling
Point Three	Self-assured, disciplined sociable, assertive	Extravert, sensate, judging
Point Four	Cooperative, sensitive	Intuitive, feeling, perceiving
Point Five	Apathetic, sensitive	Introvert, thinking
Point Six	Cooperative, sensitive, apathetic	Introvert
Point Seven	Sociable, self-assured, assertive	Extravert, intuitive
Point Eight	Self-assured, sociable, assertive	Extravert, intuitive, thinking, perceiving
Point Nine	Apathetic, sensitive, cooperative	Intuitive, perceiving

Also administered to subjects was Wagner's Enneagram Personality Inventory, consisting of 135 items (15 for each type). Subjects indicated a degree of agreement or disagreement. In two administrations of the inventory, before and after training, Wagner found that Enneagram type was significantly associated with scores on the inventory. Wagner's findings suggest that the objective test can predict type with a greater-than-chance accuracy and that learning the Enneagram theory increased the predictive validity of the test.

Wagner's study contributes to the delineation of Enneagram theory by evaluating the typology against two other typological approaches in a relatively large sample. Also, his efforts to develop an objective assessment of Enneagram type should promote study leading to the determination of the reliability and generalizability of type, description and distinction of types, and prediction of type in a simplified, valid manner.

Our Current Research Program

We have also conducted research on 172 volunteer subjects who are adult students of the Center for the Investigation and Training of Intuition.[9] At the time of the assessment, all subjects had determined their Enneagram type from one month to several years prior to testing, with 47 percent being aware of their type for one year or less. Enneagram group size ranged from ten subjects identified as point Three to thirty-five subjects identified as point Nine. Cross-tabulations indicated that there were no significant associations in our sample between knowledge of the Enneagram, sex, professional status, and Enneagram type.

To assess personality differences among Enneagram types, we selected the MBTI (as had Wagner) and the Minnesota Multiphasic Personality Inventory (MMPI). The MMPI is the most widely researched personality index, but has not been previously studied in relation to the Enneagram. The ten clinical scales of the MMPI assess major categories of abnormal behavior, including hypochondriasis, depression, hysteria, psychopathic deviation, gender identification, paranoia, obsessiveness and compulsivity, schizophrenia, hypomania, and social introversion. Further, the MMPI provides for an assessment of test-taking attitudes, such as consistency, social desirability, and faking pathology.

We also developed an inventory of the Enneagram typology for this research program, the Cohen-Palmer Enneagram Inventory (CPEI). The CPEI is a compilation of statements of behavioral tendencies for each Enneagram point group. The CPEI totals 108 items, with twelve items in each of nine imbedded scales. Dichotomized responses to the descriptive statements are demanded, i.e., "like me" or "not like me." We hypothesized that the highest scale score would predict the Enneagram type of the subject (which had been determined prior to administration of the inventory).

Results: MMPI

Using one-way analyses of variance and post hoc comparisons, we found significant differences among Enneagram groups on four of the clinical scales of the MMPI: depression, psychopathic deviation, psychasthenia (obsession-compulsion), and social introversion. The average group scores for each group are presented in Figure 1.

As can be noted on the depression scale, Group Four demonstrated the highest average score and was significantly higher than group Seven or Group Three (p<.002). Group Three demonstrated the lowest average score, with groups Four, Five, Six, Nine, Two, One, and Eight scoring significantly higher than Group Three. This finding is reasonable, given the tendency of point Three to deny emotional responses and the tendency of point Four toward behavior descriptive to their title, Tragic Romantic.

The significant differences among groups on the scale of psychopathic deviation (p<.006) were found between Group Eight, with the highest mean score, and Groups Seven, Nine, and One. Group Seven had the lowest mean score, significantly lower than groups Two, Six, and Four. The underlying dimension of this scale is thought to be assertion, with "energetic, enterprising, venturesome, and social" as positive counterpart behaviors, and "hostile, manipulative, impulsive, and antisocial" as negative counterpart behaviors.[10] This finding is

Figure 1. Average MMPI T-Scores of Enneagram Point Groups

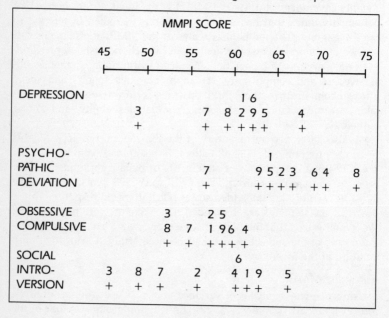

plausible, given the tendency of point Eight to be highly assertive and the tendency of point Seven to maintain social acceptability.

Significant group differences (p<.03) were also found on the psychasthenia (obsessive-compulsive) scale. This scale is thought to reflect anxiety, usually of a long-term nature[11] and to assess a "person's inability to resist specific actions or thoughts regardless of their maladaptive nature . . . taps abnormal fears, self-criticism, difficulties in concentration, and guilt feelings."[12] Group Four demonstrated the highest mean score and differed significantly from Groups Three and Eight. Group Three had the lowest mean score and differed significantly from Groups Four, Five, and Six. These findings might suggest a relative tendency toward ritualistic behavior among point Four types and a greater tendency among point Three types to be flexible in behavior. Both concepts are coincident with chief features of these Enneagram points.

Highly significant differences were found on the scale of social introversion (p<.0000), with Group Five demonstrating the highest average score and differing significantly from Groups Three, Eight, Seven, Two, and Six. Group Three scored the lowest average score and was significantly lower than Groups Two, Six, Four, One, Nine, and Five. The items of this scale are concerned with uneasiness in social situations, insecurities, worries, and lack of social participation. The higher the scale, the more the person prefers solitude; the lower the scale, the more the individual seeks social contact. The underlying normal dimension assessed on the social introversion scale is posited to be autonomy.

Results: MBTI

Using one-way analyses of variance, we also found significant differences among Enneagram groups on the scales of extraversion–introversion, sensation–intuition, and feeling–thinking. Figure 2 illustrates the average scores of the nine Enneagram groups. It should be noted that, for individuals, a score of 100 is interpreted as "no clear preference" on a dimension.

On the extraversion–introversion scale, the different Enneagram points were well separated. As one would predict from a knowledge of the Enneagram, points Three, Seven, Eight, and Two were most distributed toward extraversion, and points Five, Nine, One, and Six toward introversion. Statistically, there were significant differences between point Five and all other points; point Nine and points Three, Seven, Eight, and Four; point One and points Three and Seven; point Six and points Three and Seven; and point Four and point One. The

Figure 2. ENNEAGRAM GROUP PEFORMANCE: AVERAGE MBTI SCORES

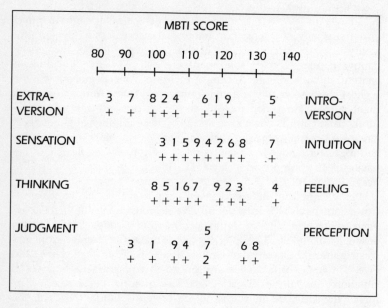

clinical interpretation by test authors suggests that extraverts "relate more easily to the outer world of people and things than to the inner world of ideas." In contrast, introverts "relate more easily to the inner world of ideas than to the outer world of people and things."[13] Findings on the extraversion–introversion scale are convergent with findings from the social introversion scale of the MMPI, on which Group Five had the highest mean score and Group Three, the lowest.

On the sensation–intuition scale, the different Enneagram point groups scored closer together, and all were distributed toward the intuition side of the scale. This preference toward intuition in the whole sample is plausible, and may be specific to this sample, given that subjects had previously displayed their interest in intuition through involvement with the Center for the Investigation and Training of Intuition. Points Seven, Eight, and Six were most distributed toward the intuition side of the scale. The clinical interpretation of preferences by MBTI authors suggests that subjects scoring in the direction of sensation "would rather work with known facts than look for possibilities and relationships" and those scoring toward intuition "would rather look for possibilities and relationships than work with known facts."[14]

On the thinking–feeling scale, Groups Eight, Five, One, Six, and Seven were most distributed toward the thinking end of the scale, and group Four toward the feeling end. This finding is plausible, given the description of point Four as deeply and aesthetically emotional. MBTI test authors interpret the preference toward feeling on this dimension as indicative that judgments are made "more on personal values than on impersonal analysis and logic."[15] There were no significant differences among Enneagram groups on the perception–judgment scale in this study.

The Cohen-Palmer Enneagram Inventory

We attempted to predict each subject's point group based on their test performance on the CPEI; calculated subjects' scores on each of the nine imbedded scales; selected the score that was the highest; and used it to predict their point group. There was a significant association between our prediction and subject's actual Enneagram point group. Successful predictions ranged from 26 percent for Group Two to 72 percent for Group Eight. Though these associations were significantly better than chance ($p<.0000$), we sought further analyses to improve our ability to predict Enneagram group.

Using discriminant analysis, we assessed the contribution of the CPEI test items to the distinction of groups. Discriminant analysis is a maximization technique in which items are weighted and then linearly combined in such a way that groups are forced to be as statistically distinct as possible. Weights or standardized discriminant function coefficients are calculated for each item, indicating the strength of the item to separate groups. Using these weighted items we were able to reclassify 97 percent of the subjects into their correct Enneagram group. Further research with the CPEI is needed to evaluate the validity of the weights assigned to the test items in this discriminant analysis. By assessing new samples using the CPEI and scoring their tests with weighted scores, we can determine the ability of items of the CPEI to discriminate among Enneagram types and to predict type. We plan to test multiple groups in this evaluation process.

Discussion

Our study program partially confirms findings by Wagner that Enneagram types differ significantly on the dimensions assessed by the MBTI. Our findings were similar to Wagner's four, with some major exceptions. First, though we found similar trends using analysis of variance approach, we found no significant differences among groups

Figure 3. PREDICTION OF ENNEAGRAM GROUP BASED ON DISCRIMINANT ANALYSIS

ACTUAL GROUP	*NO. OF CASES	PREDICATED GROUP								
		1	2	3	4	5	6	7	8	9
1	16	16 100%	0	0	0	0	0	0	0	0
2	15	0	15 100%	0	0	0	0	0	0	0
3	9	0	0	9 100%	0	0	0	0	0	0
4	11	1 9%	0	0	10 91%	0	0	0	0	0
5	15	0	0	0	0	15 100%	0	0	0	0
6	24	0	1 4%	0	0	0	22 92%	0	1 4%	0
7	10	1 10%	0	0	0	0	0	9 90%	0	0
8	11	0	0	0	0	0	0	0	11 100%	0
9	27	0	0	0	0	0	0	0	0	27 100%

*N = 132. Cases with missing values are deleted as a part of the analysis.

on the judgment–perception scale. Wagner, using a correlational approach, found a significant correlation for points One and Three with judgment, and points Eight and Nine with perception. Also, Wagner's subjects identified as points Two and Eight exhibited a preference for extraversion, the point Two and point Eight subjects in our sample, as groups, indicated a slight preference for introversion. Finally, in Wagner's study, membership in the point Five group was significantly correlated with a preference for thinking, but the subjects in our sample indicated no clear preference for thinking or feeling.

These discrepant findings suggest that point Two and point Eight behavior may tend toward introversion or extraversion; and that point Five may tend toward thinking or feeling. These findings may be unique to Wagner's and our samples, or may be influenced by the types of statistical analysis used. As such, further research is needed to replicate findings and clarify the differences.

Our examination of the MMPI yielded new findings that are plausible, given the existing descriptions of Enneagram point characteristics. Enneagram Group Four was high and Group Three low on the depression scale; Group Eight was high and Group Three low on the psychopathic deviation scale; Group Four was high on obsession-compulsion; and Group Five was high and Group Three low on social introversion.

Last, our test development activities are most encouraging when considered together with those of Wagner. The development of a reliable and valid Enneagram assessment instrument appears possible and useful. Our future research will include the validation of the CPEI in new samples.

Notes for Appendix

1. J. Lilly, "The Arica Training," in C. Tart, ed., *Transpersonal Psychologies* (New York: Harper & Row, 1975).
2. J. G. Bennett, *Enneagram Studies* (York Beach, Maine: Samuel Weiser, Inc., 1983).
3. J. P. Wagner, "A Descriptive, Reliability and Validity Study of the Enneagram Personality Typology" (Ph.D. diss., Loyola University of Chicago, 1981). *Dissertation Abstracts International*, 41, 1981, 4664A. University Microfilms no. 8109973.
4. J. P. Wagner and R. E. Walker, "Reliability and Validity Study of a Sufi Personality Typology: The Enneagram," *Journal of Clinical Psychology* 39(5) (Sept. 1983).
5. I. Myers and K. Briggs, *Manual: A Guide to the Development and Use of the Myers-Briggs Type Indicator* (Palo Alto, Calif.: Consulting Psychologists Press, 1985).
6. T. Millon, *The Millon Self-Report Inventory* (Philadelphia: Saunders, 1974).
7. Marlene Cresci Cohen, Helen Palmer, and Martin Stuart Cohen, *Empirical Comparison of the Enneagram Personality Types*. In preparation, 1987.
8. Wagner, "Enneagram Personality Typology," 145.
9. J. Kunce and W. Anderson, "Normalizing the MMPI," *Journal of Clinical Psychology* 32 (1976): 776–80.
10. R. L. Greene, *The MMPI: An Interpretive Manual* (New York: Grune and Stratton, 1980).
11. J. Duckworth and W. Anderson, *MMPI Interpretation Manual for Counselors and Clinicians* (3rd ed.) (Muncie, Ind.: Accelerated Development Press, 1986), 189.
12. Greene, *The MMPI: An Interpretive Manual*, 99.
13. Myers and Briggs, *Manual: A Guide to the Development and Use of the Myers— Briggs Type Indicator*, (Palo Alto, Calif.: Consulting Psychologists Press, 1985).
14. Ibid., 54.
15. Ibid., 54.

Notes

Chapter 1

1. We think of ourselves as the cohesive structuring of our thoughts, feelings, bodily memories, and other identifications that were laid down in early years. These identifications together form a self-concept that in spiritual teachings is sometimes referred to as the false personality, and more often as the ego. Once formed, ego becomes what we think of as the self, because we have no access to other, nonegoic states of consciousness.

   A contemporary Sufi teacher, A. H. Almaas, makes this distinction between the Freudian concept of the ego and the ego of spiritual tradition.

   The Freudian ego has the functions of perception, motility, reality testing and so on. These functions are not included in the term ego as used in spiritual and [Gurdjieff] work literature. This latter ego denotes mainly the identification of the individual that gives him the sense of self or identity.

   Psychoanalytic ego psychology, and specifically its object relations theory, has formulated in a very useful way how this sense of self or ego-identity develops. Basically, what is called a self-representation develops through the organization of the early experiences of the individual from smaller units into larger, more comprehensive ones. This happens concurrently with the development of object representation.

   A. H. Almaas, *Essence, The Diamond Approach to Inner Realization* (York Beach, ME: Samuel Weiser, 1986), 43.

2. *Diagnostic and Statistical Manual (Third Edition-Revised)*, (Washington, DC: American Psychiatric Association, 1987). This detailed ordering of disturbed mental functioning is a standard reference for the health professional. It is used nationally for health insurance purposes.

3. Correlations between the Enneagram and the cabala's Tree of Life are recorded in James Webb, "Sources of the System," *The Harmonious Circle* (New York: G. P. Putnam's Sons, 1980).

4. Webster defines consciousness as an awareness that something was or is happening or existing. The Enneagram system implies that there are different orders of consciousness in which one can be aware of nonhistorical and nonpresent events. The classic work on defining states of consciousness is Charles Tart, *States of Consciousness* (El Cerrito, CA: *Psychological Processes*, 1983), originally published in 1975. Another good treatment of levels of consciousness from the Gurdjieff point of view can be found in Charles Tart, *Waking Up* (Boston: Shambhala, 1986).

5. The practices of self-observation and self-remembering are described in Charles Tart, *Waking Up* (Boston: Shambhala, 1986).

6. P. D. Ouspensky, *In Search of the Miraculous* (New York: Harcourt, Brace & World, Inc., 1949), 294.

7. The usual objects of attention in ordinary consciousness are physical sensations, emotions, and thoughts, memories, plans, and fantasies (also called guided images or daydreams).

8. G. I. Gurdjieff, *Life Is Real Only Then, When "I Am"* (New York: E. P. Dutton, 1975), 51.

9. Kenneth Walker, *Venture with Ideas* (New York: Pellegrini and Cudahy, 1952), 152.

10. Kenneth Walker, *Venture with Ideas: Meetings with Gurdjieff and Ouspensky* (New York: Pellegrini & Cudahy, 1952), 183.

11. Ouspensky, *In Search of the Miraculous*, 155.

12. Kenneth Walker, *Gurdjieff, A Study of His Teaching* (London: Unwin Paperbacks, 1979), 96.

13. Walker, *Venture With Ideas*, 114.

14. See note 1 to chapter 1. It might be added that the practices that develop the remembrance of essential qualities can have a disintegrating effect upon the personality. Therefore it is important to take care that personality remains aligned with the emerging access to essence. This integrative function is best handled through appropriate therapy.

15. A. H. Almaas makes good distinctions between ways of engaging the relationship between personality and essence. In *Essence, The Diamond Approach to Inner Realization*, (York Beach, ME: Samuel Weiser, Inc., 1986), 78, he says:

Some of these systems base their method on the contrast between essence and personality, and the work is then to free essence as a whole from the personality as a whole. . . . Some systems do not pay attention to essence at all; they look at the personality, see it as the barrier to freedom and the cause of suffering, and work on dissolving its narrowness. . . . Some systems are based on only one aspect of essence, which is emphasized and seen as the real truth or the only reality, ignoring other aspects.

16. Jan Cox, *Dialogues of Gurdjieff: Vol. 1* (Stone Mountain, GA: Chan Shal Imi Society Press, 1976), 169.

17. Ouspensky, *In Search of the Miraculous*, 267.

18. P. D. Ouspensky, *A Further Record: Extracts from Meetings, 1928–1945* (London: Arkana Paperbacks, 1986), 246.

19. C. S. Nott, *Journey Through This World: The Second Journal of a Pupil* (New York: Samuel Weiser, Inc., 1969), 87.

Chapter 2

1. See note 7 to chapter 1.

2. Attention can be seen as organized in both a conscious and unconscious way. When attention can be voluntarily shifted and focused, it is under

conscious control. Attention can also be unconsciously organized to include safe information and to exclude unsafe information.

3. *Hara* is the Japanese word for belly center, located between the navel and the pubic bone. The same center is identified in all mystical trainings, regardless of the culture in which the trainings originate. The Sufi equivalent of *Hara* was called the *Kath* point by Oscar Ichazo.

4. Open sensing practice entails a specific shift of attention in which the sense of *Hara* is extended to include the qualities of energy in the environment and in others.

5. This shift of attention involves the merger of the inner observer with a visualized representation of nonpresent events.

6. The veils could be seen as resulting from the shift of attention from the child's at-one connection with the environment and with others to an identification with the preoccupations of personality. The lifting of the veils would therefore imply remembering the ways in which attention can be mobilized to regain the lost connections.

Chapter 3

1. There are several more detailed summaries of the way in which the law of three and the law of seven interact. They can be found in John Bennett, *The Enneagram* (Gloucestershire, England: Coombe Springs Press, 1974); Kathleen Riordan Speeth, chapter 7 in *Transpersonal Psychologies*, ed. Charles Tart (New York: Harper & Row, 1975), reprinted by Psychological Processes, Inc., 1983; Kathleen Riordan Speeth, *The Gurdjieff Work* (Berkeley, CA: And/Or Press, 1976), reprinted by Simon & Schuster (New York: 1978); and Michael Waldberg, *Gurdjieff, An Approach to His Ideas* (London: Routledge and Kegan Paul, 1981) (reprinted from the 1973 French edition).

There are also two books that apply the change of sign between active, receptive, and reconciling forces to a process analysis of business management procedures. These books indicate a renewed interest in applying the governing laws of mysticism, which specifically apply to the process of an event in the material world, to areas other than psychological process. The books are Saul Kuchinsky, *Systematics* (Charles Town, WV: Claymont Communications, 1985) and Robert Campbell, *Fisherman's Guide* (Boston: Shambhala, 1985).

2. The idea that energy can be transferred from one internal system to another is basic to all spiritual systems. To transform consciousness one needs a continuous supply of energy and a degree of restraint upon the usual outlets for that energy. Energy can be raised in many ways, including meditation, breath exercises, physical exercise, and the controlled summoning of emotional passions. The restraints are attention shifts that prevent energy from discharging into habitual thoughts, feelings, and bodily movement.

3. Walter Otto, *The Homeric Gods: The Spiritual Significance of Greek Religion* (New York: Octagon Books, 1978).

4. Walter Otto, *Dionysus: Myth and Cult* (Dallas: Spring Publications, 1981).

5. Ursula LeGuin, *The Left Hand of Darkness* (New York: Ace Books, 1969), Introduction.

Chapter 4

1. John Lilly and Joseph Hart, "The Arica Training," *Transpersonal Psychologies*, ed. Charles Tart (New York: Harper & Row, 1975), reprinted by Psychological Processes, Inc., 1983.
2. Sam Keen, "A Conversation about Ego Destruction with Oscar Ichazo," *Psychology Today* (July 1973), p. 64.
3. Claudio Naranjo, *The One Quest* (London: Wildwood House, 1974).

The Enneagram is part of an oral teaching tradition. The power of the material is best transmitted through members of each type, as they tell their stories. For information concerning video-cassette and audiocassette presentations and about intuition and Enneagram workshops that can be brought to your area, please contact

The Center for the Investigation and Training of Intuition
1442A Walnut Street
Berkeley, California 94704
(415) 843–7621

DATE DUE		
MAY 10 '89		
AUG 4 '89		
MAR 0 6 1997		
SEP 22 Ass'o		
JE 26 07		